# Understanding
# Domestic Homicide

## Neil Websdale

NORTHEASTERN UNIVERSITY PRESS

*Boston*

Northeastern University Press

*Library of Congress Cataloging-in-Publication Data*
Websdale, Neil.
   Understanding domestic homicide / Neil Websdale.
      p.  cm.—(The Northeastern series on gender, crime, and
law)
   Includes bibliographical references and index.
   ISBN 1-55553-393-0 (pbk. : alk. paper).
   —ISBN 1-55553-394-9 (cl. : alk. paper)
   1. Family violence—Florida—Statistics.  2. Homicide—
Florida—Statistics.  3. Uxoricide—Florida—Statistics.
4. Infanticide—Florida—Statistics.  5. Criminal statistics—
Florida.  I. Title.  II. Series.
   HV6626.22.F6W43   1999
   364.15′23′0975—dc21          99-18202

Designed by Joyce C. Weston

Composed in Adobe Garamond by Graphic Composition, Inc.,
Athens, Georgia. Printed and bound by Edwards Brothers, Inc.,
Lillington, North Carolina. The paper is Glatfelter Offset, an acid-
free sheet.

MANUFACTURED IN THE UNITED STATES OF AMERICA
03  02  01  00     5  4  3  2

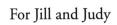
For Jill and Judy

# Contents

# List of Tables

# Acknowledgments

*Understanding Domestic Homicide* emerged out of a research project in Florida funded by Governor Lawton Chiles's Task Force on Domestic and Sexual Violence. I am grateful to a number of Task Force members for their support and encouragement. In particular, I thank Robin Hassler, Executive Director of the Task Force, for sharing with me her wealth of knowledge about domestic violence and for extending the warm hand of friendship. Thanks also to Renee Starrett, Paul Balthrop, Shelia Hankins-Jarrett, Trula Motta, Sal Lomonaco, and Kim Musgrove, each of whom helped in numerous ways. I benefited greatly from discussions with Barbara Hart and Merry Hofford about domestic homicide. I am indebted to them for their help, encouragement, and kindness. Judge Mike Town's practical need for information about the microdynamics of domestic homicide was an important driving force in the early stages of this research venture. I thank him. Likewise, Kathy Schwartz's concern with confronting domestic homicide through pragmatic, workable programs greatly contributed to my efforts in Florida. I am grateful to her. I also appreciate the expertise, support, and encouragement of Maureen Sheeran, Ruth Ann Axtell, and Billie Lee Dunford-Jackson of the Nation Council of Juvenile and Family Court Judges.

During the course of this research I talked with many police officers off the record. To these anonymous cops, a big thanks. Many others were able to speak with me on the record. I especially acknowledge the help of officers Craig Broughton, Rod Reeder, Tim Bronson, Gerry Green, Norman Gregorish, Gary Smith, Jerry Coney, Richard Scheff, Laurie Cain, Dan Grossi, George McNamara, Donna Rivera, Kevin Behan, Linda Burton, and George Marsicano. I am also indebted to various members of the Florida Coalition against Domestic Violence, including Lynn Rosenthall, Kathy Herrmann, Tiffany Carr, Beck Dunn, Rob Schroeder, and Linda Osmundson. Thanks, too, to Jenny Greenberg at the Florida Battered Women's Clemency Project. In addition, I have benefited from the perceptions of the following judges: Ron Adrine, Susan Carbon, Amy Karan, Lynn Tepper, Pete MacDonald, and Martha Glaze. A special thanks to Beckie Masaki of the Asian Women's Shelter in San Francisco for her insights into the complexities of domestic violence in Asian communities.

I talked with a large number of prosecutors and defense attorneys in the course of this research. Again, I cannot mention their names, but I greatly appreciate their ability to fill in gaps, add anomalies, and pose difficult questions. In my travels in Florida I also talked with a number of judges about domestic violence and domestic homicide, and I thank them here. Similarly, I appreciate the help of all the workers in medical examiners' offices, county courts, child protection agencies, police records divisions, and domestic violence shelters who gave me information. I also thank the staff of the newspaper library at the University of Florida in Gainesville for helping me locate and read newspaper accounts of domestic homicides.

Claire Renzetti read the first draft of the manuscript and offered a number of thoughtful suggestions. Her interest, insights, and kindness contributed greatly to the gradual emergence of the final version. I thank her. Thanks also to Bill Frohlich, Tara Mantel, and Ann Twombly at Northeastern. I am especially grateful to Frank Austin for his meticulous copyediting.

Most of this book was written in Flagstaff, Arizona. I am grateful to Alex Alvarez for his assistance with the homicide literature. Thanks as well to Jeff Ferrell for his perceptive and contagious sociological insights. The new Chair of the Department of Criminal Justice at Northern Arizona University, Marilyn McShane, has done a wonderful job of supporting my research activities. I am in her debt. My graduate assistant Christiane Schubert astutely read my preliminary drafts, and I thank her. I am also grateful to the office staff in the criminal justice department at Northern Arizona University, who helped in many ways with writing and production. Special thanks to Jan Bishop and Helena DeFina.

On my travels in Florida I was often accompanied by Byron Johnson, with whom I discussed a number of the ideas in this book. I am indebted to him for his insights into my work.

Parts of *Understanding Domestic Homicide* were written in England, and I acknowledge the help of my parents, Molly and John Websdale. The book is dedicated to my sisters, Jill Minter and Judy Flew. A special thanks to them for many kindnesses. Finally, I am grateful for the love and support of my wife, Amy, and our daughter, Mia, without whom this book could not have been written.

# 1. Researching Domestic Homicide

When I was growing up in England we talked about soccer with religious fervor, discussing the moves players made, the goals scored, different playing styles, players' speed and vision, their intentions, and, in our more reflective moments, our overenmeshment in this game of beauty, joy, and sorrow. We played soccer ourselves and of course attempted to emulate those we adored. At some level the final score or result of the competition did not matter as much as the flair, the excitement, and the departure from dull routines. Even though we scrutinized league standings and memorized such essential facts as who had scored the most goals in a season, which team had spent the most money on players, and who had won a particular trophy, these ephemera were usually a means to enter into the raw, lived experience of the art of soccer.

It was not until I came to live in the United States that I realized just how much soccer lent itself to detailed quantification. I had never heard the game discussed in percentages before. I had never seen a time clock on my television screen, marking off the minutes until the final whistle. However, I became reconciled to this cultural difference in the way soccer was appreciated and explained by telling myself that the more detailed quantification in the United States is one way fans make "everyday empirical sense" of soccer and other sports. On either side of the Atlantic, in our appreciation of soccer we employ what the sociologist C. Wright Mills once called "the everyday empiricism of common sense," which is filled with the "assumptions and stereotypes of one or another particular society; for common sense determines what is seen and how it is to be explained."[1]

Although everyday empiricism is employed to appreciate and make some sense of soccer, an "abstracted empiricism" dominates sociological and criminological understandings of homicide in the United States. Mills refers to "abstracted empiricism" as that kind of reflection which leads only to the "microscopic or subhistorical level." In his view, "What abstracted empiricists call empirical 'data' represent a very abstracted view of everyday social worlds. They normally deal, for example, with an age-level of a sex-category of an income-bracket of middle-sized cities."[2] Abstracted empiricism dominates American criminology and has limited the overall understanding of homicide in general, and of domestic homicide in particular. Amidst a plethora of causal models, regression analyses, controls for this supposedly "discrete" variable or that, criminologists lose sight of domestic homicide as a process. Rather, homicides are frozen onto the pages of a supplemental homicide report and then grafted onto some model or subjected to the latest statistical obscurity. Like packaged frozen vegetables that have long since lost touch with a field or the earth, homicide statistics and the data sets they become a part of are convenient but usually bereft of flavor. In short, the use of abstracted empiricism to understand homicide produces accounts and explanations that are about as far removed from social life and historical change as the dead bodies that generated those statistics in the first place.

Abstracted empiricism is generally ill suited to understanding the complex microprocesses and cultural dynamics of domestic homicide. Using abstracted empiricism, it is difficult to gain access to the interaction between human beings, their respective biographies, and their neighborhoods; it is also difficult to understand the broader social, economic, and political structures that affect and are in turn shaped by those microdynamics. In addition, the use of abstracted empiricism, even within the ranks of such empiricists, is fraught with difficulty if the variable "domestic homicide" is subject to multiple and conflicting social and legal definitions, at the same time as being susceptible to significant errors in reporting. The Uniform Crime Reports for 1994 informed us that there were 230 domestic homicides in Florida. Most police departments use the Florida statute on domestic violence to classify a homicide as a domestic homicide. Florida law defines "domestic violence" as "any assault, battery, sexual assault, sexual battery, or any criminal offense resulting in physical injury or death of one family or household member by another who is or was residing in the same single dwelling unit." A "family or household member" refers to "spouses, former spouses, persons related by blood or marriage, persons who are presently residing together as if a family or who have resided together in the past as if a family, and persons who have a child in common regardless of whether they have been married or have resided together at any time."[3] In classifying homicides that occurred in 1994, Florida police departments sometimes did not count child deaths stemming from abuse and neglect. Similarly, those persons who committed suicide after killing one or more family members were usually not included among the ranks of domestic-homicide victims. These omissions alone produce an underestimate of the number of domestic-violence fatalities.

Although the statutory definition of domestic violence excludes boyfriends and girlfriends who do not live together or have a child in common, these deaths (around 20 in Florida in 1994) have dynamics similar to the cases that formally meet the statutory definition. Consequently, I include such deaths as domestic homicides. Counting the boyfriend-girlfriend homicides together with all known child domestic deaths and the suicide victims gives a total of 319 domestic-homicide victims. I do not pretend that this working total is exhaustive. However, I do contend that it conveys an "everyday empirical reality" of domestic homicide that is more accurate than the official figure of 230 that became enshrined in supplementary homicide reports from Florida.

My analysis of domestic death is embedded in the constellations of daily routines and personal interactions between persons connected through networks of kinship, those who often combine their earnings, or those who survive from a common pool of resources. Although sexual intimacy is a central dynamic in many of the domestic homicides, and although it may appear that other family homicides are somehow traceable to or derivative of those sexual relationships, to focus only on sexual intimacy would be to deny the role of numerous other social forces. For example, it is difficult to explain the lethal conflicts between brothers as part of the sexual intimacy between men, or as somehow deriving from the sexual intimacy or lack thereof between their parents or caretakers.

In Chapters 2 through 6, I draw upon multiagency case files from the State of Florida to explore the microdynamics of intimate killing. Building upon an everyday empirical breakdown of who kills whom, and upon the essential demographic characteristics of perpetrators and victims, I move quickly into relationship histories, familial dynamics, neighborhood, subcultural and cultural phenomena, agency involvement, and a slew of other contextual materials. It is out of and through this pastiche of narrative resources that I build patterns, observe the subtle making and operation of social structures, and identify the intricate workings of power.

Even though I am critical of what Ann Jones once called the "bone dry" research literature on homicide, it nevertheless affords many insights into domestic homicide.[4] In what follows, I highlight the parts of this literature that are useful in understanding the character of domestic homicide. The research literature on "domestic homicide" essentially addresses murder or non-negligent manslaughter between intimate partners and family members. In most cases, "domestic" refers to those killings that occur within the confines of the family, whether the partners are married or not. The extant literature distinguishes between "intimate-partner homicide" and "family homicide." In their analysis of domestic homicides in New York City, Wilt, Illman, and Brodyfield define an "intimate partner" as one who was the victim's current or former spouse or lover.[5] A perpetrator was a "family member" and consequently committed family homicide if he or she was the victim's relative by blood or marriage. "Intimate-partner homicide" therefore specifically refers to the murder or non-negligent manslaughter of a person by her or his current or former intimate partner. For example, a husband who murders his wife commits intimate-partner homicide, as does the man who kills the woman he used to live intimately with but was not married to. The term "family homicide," on the other hand, denotes the killing of someone by a victim's relative by blood or marriage. For example, cases where a father kills his daughter, a niece murders an aunt, a grandfather murders a granddaughter, or a child murders his parents are all family homicides.

## Intimate-Partner Homicide

There is an extensive research literature on willful killings within sexual relationships. A small portion of it locates such killing within a broader framework of patriarchal relations.[6] However, the bulk of the literature documents longitudinal trends in incidence and provides detailed demographic information on perpetrators and victims. This is an important literature, as it provides insights into the social distribution of intimate killing, particularly the sex, race, and socioeconomic backgrounds of participants. It also offers statistics on age, the use of weapons, alcohol and drug use, and past histories of threatened or attempted suicides on the part of those involved. Some data sets contain a certain amount of information on indicators of a prior history of domestic violence within the family, or a record of any protective orders served on perpetrators that might suggest a history of domestic abuse. However, it is often difficult to know for sure if cases of intimate killing are preceded by domestic violence. At times police do not log their calls to domestic-violence incidents. Recent research suggests that roughly half of intimate-partner violence is reported to the police.[7]

Finally, large data sets on intimate killing also provide access to the criminal backgrounds of perpetrators and victims, enabling researchers to trace links between prior acts of criminal violence and intimate homicide. In what follows, I highlight some of the main features of the extant research on intimate-partner homicide. Much of this literature draws upon official records, police supplemental homicide reports, and Uniform Crime Report (UCR) data published by the FBI. As such, it is limited when it comes to exploring the fine details of individual cases, or some of the idiosyncrasies of relationship conflicts that do not lend themselves easily to quantification.

*Trends*  According to the Bureau of Justice Statistics (BJS), in the United States during the years from 1976 through 1996, intimate-partner murder fell from 2,959 (1976) to 1809 (1996).[8] Spousal murder, the largest subcomponent of intimate-partner murder declined 52 percent during this period. The number of U.S. women murdered by intimates fell from 1,600 in 1976 to 1,326 in 1996. Over the same years, the number of men murdered by intimates decreased from 1,357 to 516. This overall decline in intimate murder is most marked in the African-American community. The per capita rate of intimate murders among blacks was 11 times that among whites in 1976, but only 4 times the rate among whites in 1996. The sharpest decreases occurred among black male victims. The BJS report specifically notes:

> In 1976 the per capita rate of intimate murder of black men was nearly 19 times higher than that of white men. The rate among black females that year was seven times higher than the rate among white females. In 1996 the black male rate was eight times that of white males, and the black female rate was three times higher than the white female rate.[9]

The Chicago Homicide Data Set contains extensive police data from more than 22,000 homicides in the city between 1965 and 1993. The police determined that 2,556 persons were killed in intimate-partner homicides during this period.[10] Of these, 1,271 were women murdered by a male partner and 1,227 were men murdered by a female partner. Fifty-eight of the homicides occurred in domestic gay relationships.

*Age* In general, younger rather than older persons are more likely to be the victims and perpetrators of intimate homicide. In their analysis of FBI Supplemental Homicide Reports from 1976 to 1985, Mercy and Saltzman identified 16,595 spousal homicides.[11] They found that the frequency of this crime increased as the age differential between the partners increased. Daly and Wilson note that "marriages with exceptionally high age disparities . . . have homicide rates four times as high as that prevailing in marriages with the most common gap, namely those in which the husband is about 2 years older."[12] The age distribution is fractured by race or ethnicity and by gender. Block and Christakos report African-American men aged 35 to 39 are the most frequent victims of intimate-partner homicide, with a rate of 18 per 100,000 per year. Among women, African Americans aged 30 to 34 are the most victimized group, with 11 being killed by intimate partners per 100,000 per year. The risk for white and Latino women in all age ranges is much lower than for blacks.[13]

*Race and Ethnicity* African Americans are heavily overrepresented among all homicide victims. Indeed, homicide is the leading cause of death among black women under 44 and among young black men.[14] The same is true for intimate-partner homicides.[15] Block and Christakos remark that in 1990 the intimate-partner homicide rate in Chicago was 5.7 per 100,000 for African Americans, compared with rates of 1.1 for Latinos and 0.4 for whites.[16] In their longitudinal analysis of spousal homicide, Mercy and Saltzman found similar differentials by race. Among blacks, the rate of spousal homicide was 8.4 times higher than among whites.[17]

Spousal homicides among blacks decreased between 1976 and 1985.[18] However, as Stark and Flitcraft caution, this apparent decline may merely reflect the fact that black partners increasingly define themselves as unmarried. Additionally, these researchers point out that the seemingly high rates of black domestic homicide may have more to do with the lowly social class position of blacks than with race.[19] Their argument is consistent with a number of other studies that argue that socioeconomic status (SES) rather than racial differences offers a better explanation for variations in homicide rates across states and between cities.[20] For example, in his study of 222 intraracial homicides in Atlanta, Centerwall used the number of persons per room in residences as a proxy for SES. He concluded that once SES was controlled blacks were no more likely than whites to commit domestic homicide.[21] In a later study of 349 intraracial homicides in New Orleans, Centerwall found similar results. He concludes:

First in Atlanta, and now in New Orleans, six fold differences between blacks and whites in rates of intraracial domestic homicide are entirely accounted for by differences in SES between the respective black and white populations. There remain no significant residual differences in homicide rate that require recourse to cultural explanations.[22]

One of the possible mechanisms at work in producing higher rates of violent crime in the African-American community is the differential response of police and health professionals. Stark and Flitcraft suggest that police take crime less seriously in black residential areas and are more willing to tolerate and contain it until it spills over into wealthier white neighborhoods.[23] This means that intrafamilial disturbances will not be policed in the same way as they would in white communities, thereby allowing the disputes to escalate unchecked toward lethal violence. Stark observes:

> Injuries to black women from domestic assaults are dutifully treated in the emergency room, but protocols for spouse abuse are rarely introduced or followed in inner-city hospitals. Similarly, although police may be frequently called to intervene in domestic disputes among black couples, effective protection for the woman is rarely provided. . . . If inadequate police protection leads to a domestic homicide, the problem is not race, but racial bias.[24]

Recent research suggests that black women are more likely to report their intimate victimization to police than are women of other races, with two-thirds of them contacting law enforcement officers.[25] This contrasts with victimized white women, approximately half of whom notified police. Among surveyed women, 90 percent of all victims of domestic violence reported that officers responded to their call, usually arriving at the scene within 10 minutes.[26]

In her investigation of domestic homicides in six U.S. cities, Mann found that in 57 percent of the cases where women killed the deaths resulted from one pistol shot or a single stab wound.[27] She suggests that a significant number of victims might have lived had they received better medical help. Since Mann found the majority of these homicides took place in minority (particularly black) neighborhoods with histories of poor public services, she suggests the deaths may have resulted from assaults that became homicides rather than from actions designed to kill.[28]

Clearly, the disproportionately high number of intimate-partner homicides among African Americans cannot be explained by innate black tendencies toward violence or homicidal behavior.[29] If this were the case one would expect to find much higher rates of homicide in general, and domestic homicide in particular, in predominantly black cultures in Africa, and this is not so.[30] Moreover, if differential rates of domestic homicide are not attributable solely to factors such as SES, then it is likely that the legacy of slavery, oppression, and discrimination plays an important part.

*Sex*   Block and Christakos find that the risk of intimate homicide is roughly the same for men and women in Chicago over the years 1965 to 1993. Among Latinos and non-Latino whites the risk is significantly higher for women than men. For example, looking at Latino-on-Latino intimate homicides for 1965–93, they report that 82 men killed their female partners, compared with only 25 women who killed their male partners. For white-on-white killings from 1965 to 1993, 220 men killed women, compared with only 69 women killing men. However, among non-Latino African Americans the risk of being killed by an intimate was higher for men than women.[31] Specifically, among black-on-black intimate-partner homicides, 871 men killed women, compared with 1,077 women who killed men.[32]

The Chicago Homicide Data Set also reveals that the patterns of intimate-partner killing vary by the type of relationship (married, cohabiting) between the partners. This variation is also fractured by race or ethnicity and by the sex of the victim.[33] In Chicago, non-Latino whites were killed most frequently by a spouse, whereas non-Latino African Americans were killed more frequently by a girlfriend or boyfriend. Block and Christakos also found that although black male and female victims died in somewhat equal numbers, the latter were more likely to be killed by an estranged partner.[34]

In the United States between 1976 and 1985, interspousal killings accounted for an estimated 18,417 fatalities. Wives represented 10,529 victims and husbands 7,888. Using U.S. homicide data, Wilson and Daly note that "for every 100 men who killed their wives, about 75 wives killed their husbands."[35] The investigators use the term "Sex Ratio of Killing" (SROK) to refer to the "homicides perpetrated by women per 100 perpetrated by men."[36] These sex ratios are peculiar to the United States. In Australia, Canada, Denmark, England and Wales, Scotland, India, and other societies the proportion of female killers is much lower.[37] However, as Moore and Tennenbaum argue, rather than asking why the U.S. SROK of 75 is so high compared with that of other countries, a more important and central question is why the SROK is so much higher for African Americans. According to these researchers, the high black SROK drives up the total SROK for the entire country.[38] Moore and Tennenbaum note, "Excluding blacks from our analysis reduces the total SROK for the US to 48."[39] With this figure, the adjusted, non-black SROK for the United States comes much closer to that in New South Wales (31 for 1968–86), Canada (31 for 1974–83), and Scotland (40 for 1979–87).

Even though the extant research usefully documents the SROK by race and ethnicity, it offers very tentative explanations for racial and ethnic disparities. Some studies imply that cultural factors may be at least part of the explanation for race differentials in the commission of certain forms of domestic homicide. Block and Christakos suggest that the higher rates of suicide among Latino men after killing their female partners may be a manifestation of higher levels of guilt. They observe that "much research suggests that the low victimization risk for Latino women is due to a strong cultural sanction against male use of force against women. . . . Trespassing against such a sanction may result in enough guilt to produce high suicide proportions for Latino males."[40] In her analysis of 12 studies of black female homicide offenders, Coramae Mann argues that the disproportionate involvement of African-American women in homicide cannot be solely attributed "to either institutional racism or defects in the social structure."[41] In his comparison of 12 cases of homicide-suicide with 24 cases of domestic homicide in Albuquerque, New Mexico, between 1978 and 1987, Rosenbaum observes that although only 2 percent of the population was black, fully 33 percent of the perpetrators in the domestic-homicide group was black.[42] He goes on to suggest that "[p]erhaps the high number of women among the black perpetrators (five of eight) reflects the matriarchal aspect of black society, in which women are both dominant and aggressive."[43]

Other researchers, however, stop well short of describing gender relations in the African-American community as matriarchal. Wilson and Daly hypothesize that the high numbers of black women who kill their intimate partners might be attributable to the social empowerment of black women vis-à-vis black men.[44] Noting that many poorer urban black women are part of matrilineal kinship systems and that their residence patterns are often matrilocal,[45] Wilson and Daly contend that black women may be in a better position to retaliate against black men. In contrast, they point out that relatively few Latino women kill Latino men and that Latino culture is strongly patrilineal and patrilocal. Applying this logic to other countries, they indicate that in some strongly patrilineal and patrilocal East Indian and African cultures husbands are rarely killed by wives.[46] They conclude with this suggestion:

> [C]ircumstances which in effect devalue the social and economic worth of husbands provoke both male coercion and female defense, and . . . the combination of such circumstances with matrilocal residential patterns and a high incidence of step-relationships has much relevance to the high spousal SROK in Chicago and to the ethnic group differences therein.[47]

bell hooks clarifies the difference between matrilocality and matrilineality on the one hand, and matriarchy on the other.[48] Over time, she sees black women as having been a more acutely oppressed group than black men. Citing historical evidence, hooks argues that the stereotype of the African-American matriarch arose during slavery and has endured to this day. However, the imagery is misleading precisely because it ignores the double oppression of race and gender. Notions of a black matriarchy confuse the centrality of black women in families and their important role in raising children with power and domination. As hooks sees it, "[T]he independent role black women were obliged to play both in the labor force and in the family was automatically perceived as unladylike."[49] This led many whites to think "black women were masculinized, castrating, ball-busters."[50] With this stereotype of African-American women in mind, it might be tempting for some criminologists to explain higher rates of black female intimate-partner homicide through black women's aggressiveness rather than the differential oppression they have endured. Indeed, one might make sense of African-American women's differentially high reports of interpersonal victimization[51] as being but one more aspect of their historical oppression as women.

Between 1976 and 1996, 20,311 men were victims of intimate murder (62 percent killed by wives, 4 percent by former wives, and 34 percent by nonmarital partners such as girlfriends). In the same period, 31,260 women died at the hands of intimates (approximately 64 percent killed by husbands, 5 percent by former husbands, and 32 percent by nonmarital partners such as boyfriends). While the overall rate of intimate-partner murder has declined the SROK has also declined, meaning that women are increasingly more likely than men to be the victims of intimate murder.[52]

*Dynamics*  Marvin Wolfgang's classic study of 588 homicides in Philadelphia reveals that in the case of intimate-partner homicide the killing of men differs substantially from the killing of women.[53] In the 47 cases in which wives killed husbands, Wolfgang concludes that 28 of the men had precipitated their own deaths by striking the woman or showing and using a deadly weapon. This compares with only nine of a hundred wife killings that Wolfgang deems "victim precipitated." Overall, in 38 of the 47 cases where wives killed husbands Wolfgang finds the men had "strongly provoked" the act.

Barnard and his colleagues interviewed 34 persons (11 women and 23 men) accused of intimate-partner homicide and awaiting trial in the courts of north central Florida between 1970 and 1980.[54] They prepared in-depth case studies of the context of the killings to render a psychiatric assessment of the ability of the offenders to stand trial. Eight of the 11 women reported having been battered by the spouse-victim they later killed. In contrast, only 5 of the 23 men reported being the victims of violence perpetrated by the wives they later killed.[55] In the killings done by men, Barnard and his associates found that "sex role threat" was the most important reason given for committing homicide. Whereas women feared men's potential to use violence against them, men did not feel that their lives were in immediate danger. Rather, they reported being upset by the victim's threat to leave the relationship, or by a demand by the victims that they perceived as transcending the parameters of assigned female sex roles.[56]

*Killing the Competition*  As intimate relationships change, new partners can arrive on the scene. Sometimes they compete with old partners for the affections of their newfound lovers. At times these competitions, nearly always between men, end in lethal violence. As such, these so called love-triangle killings between competitors for the same person can be seen as deriving from the conflict between sexual intimates, and particularly from the tension surrounding women leaving one partner and developing a love interest elsewhere. In some of these cases the term *love triangle* can be misleading and inaccurate since it implies that women are still in love with former batterers, when in fact they have new lovers. Wilson and Daly's analysis of social conflict homicides among unrelated persons in Detroit reveals that conflicts involving sexual jealousy figure prominently.[57] Among such killings by men, these "jealousy conflicts" (20 cases) rank behind only "retaliation for previous verbal or physical abuse" (26 cases) and "escalated showing off disputes" (75 cases).[58] In their classic and often-cited study, *Homicide,* Wilson and Daly remark that "[s]exual jealousy and rivalry have been prominent in virtually every study of homicide motives."[59] Indeed, these authors coined the phrase "killing the competition" to refer to how men eliminate each other because of their common interests in women,[60] a violent phenomenon that appears to be universal.

Kenneth Polk's research into patterns of male killing in Australia identifies 12 cases, out of a sample of 102 involving sexual bonds, in which "the violence of the male reached out to the sexual rival of the male."[61] In discussing a typical case of sexual jealousy and the killing of a love triangle antagonist, Polk points out that "there are often clear warnings of the lethal violence to come. The woman, his possession, was not just slipping out from under his control, but even worse she was taking up with a new sexual partner."[62] Even though Polk emphasizes that the most frequent target of the abusive man's rage is his estranged lover, he also comments, "In a common variant of this scenario of jealousy, the action shifts to encompass the male competition in the sexual triangle."[63]

## Family Homicide

*Parricide*   The killing of parents by their children is a form of domestic homicide that has received scant attention in the extant literature.[64] Kathleen Heide identifies three types of persons who kill their parents: severely abused children, severely mentally ill children, and dangerously antisocial children. The "severely abused child" is most frequently encountered among the ranks of those who commit parricide;[65] according to Mones, more than 90 percent of youths who commit parricide have been abused by their parents.[66] Such killers typically endure one or more forms of physical, sexual, or emotional abuse, or they witness some combination of these abusive episodes within their families.[67] Much less often, individuals who kill parent(s) are mentally ill to the point that they qualify as psychotic. Heide describes these persons as follows: "Psychotic individuals have lost contact with reality. Their personalities are typically severely disorganized, their perceptions are distorted, and their communications are often disjointed. Their behavior may be inappropriate to the setting and characterized by repetitive, purposeless actions. . . . They may experience hallucinations . . . and bizarre delusions."[68] Finally, Heide mentions the dangerously antisocial child, nowadays referred to as someone with a conduct disorder or antisocial personality disorder. These individuals do not suffer from delusions and hallucinations. Among the ranks of such offenders we may see those who kill their parents for personal gain.

*Fratricide and Sororicide*   Ewing finds that sibling killings are about as common as parricides.[69] Most are committed by males, and over 80 percent of the victims and perpetrators are adults. These forms of family homicide, like intimate-partner killings, are often preceded by a long history of domestic rivalry and unresolved conflicts. As in other kinds of domestic homicide, the precipitating event takes place in a context of long-standing antagonism that is often exacerbated before the killing by a change in one of the sibling's circumstances. Ewing puts it as follows:

> In many adult sibling homicides, perpetrators are dealing not only with unresolved childhood conflicts and the stress of living with a brother or sister but often trying to cope with a variety of other problems in living. Indeed, in many cases, these other stressors—such as unemployment, divorce, substance abuse, and illness—have forced the perpetrator into a situation of being financially dependent on parents and/or the sibling who is eventually killed.[70]

*The Domestic Killing of Children*   Martin and Besharov observe that the number of child abuse deaths nationally fell from about 3,000 in 1975 to about 1,200 in 1988.[71] Using death certificate data, McClain and colleagues estimate the annual number of child deaths from abuse and neglect between 1979 and 1988 to range from 949 to 2,022 for ages up to 17 years.[72] According to Ewing, in 1995 there were 1,215 documented child fatalities in the United States caused by child abuse, neglect, or both.[73] However, these estimates typically do not include those girls and boys killed in homicide-suicides and familicides that are not counted as abuse fatalities.

*Perpetrators of Child Homicide*   Ann Goetting reports that the typical person arrested for the domestic killing of children is a locally born, Protestant black man or woman in his or her middle twenties who is married and residing with the family. "He or she is undereducated, unemployed, and has an arrest record. The parent-child relationship is severed in a rage of impatience and anger at a private residence as a result of beating or shaking."[74] As members of a racial minority, these perpetrators tend to be marginalized and deeply disadvantaged. Although they possessed highly developed "street smarts," these men and women lacked knowledge of the rudiments of successful parenting.

In their study of 14 cases of fatal child abuse and neglect, Hicks and Gaughan identify fathers as perpetrators in 4 cases and mothers' boyfriends in another 4.[75] Using a much larger sample of 104 cases, Schloesser, Pierpont, and Poertner identify 34 male perpetrators (56.7 percent of known perpetrators) of child fatalities, most of whom were fathers, stepfathers, or boyfriends, and 22 mothers (36.7 percent of known perpetrators) who killed their children.[76] The researchers were not able to identify a perpetrator in 44 of the 104 cases.

*Age*   In their description of the interagency review of 637 deaths of children aged 12 or under in Orange County, California, between 1989 and 1991, Gellert and his collaborators report that 72 percent of the boys and girls who died unattended or in questionable circumstances were less than 2 years of age.[77] Of those deaths definitely attributed to homicide, 72 percent involved children under the age of 4. Indeed, in a majority of the homicides the victims were less than 2 years old. In Copeland's study of 62 child abuse fatalities investigated by medical examiners in Dade County, Florida, between 1956 and 1982, 45.6 percent of the victims were under the age of 1, 33.8 percent were aged 1 to 2 years, and 11.8 percent were from 2 to 3 years old.[78] These findings are consistent with other research showing that younger abused children are at greater risk of severe injury and homicide.[79]

Gellert and his colleagues found that, in their sample, the majority of the children killed were boys.[80] Their proportion for all age categories was 58 percent, with the ratio varying little by age (53 percent to 59 percent). However, when these researchers examined child homicides and child abuse deaths there was no significant difference in the sex ratios of decedents. Such a finding of sex symmetry echoes a number of other studies.[81]

*Race and Ethnicity*   A number of investigations show that some racial and ethnic groups exhibit higher rates of child abuse and neglect deaths than others. In their study of 437 deaths of children younger than 15 in Cook County, Illinois, between 1977 and 1982 that resulted from either homicide or unexplained causes, Christoffel, Anzinger, and Merrill showed that violent death rates for black children far outstripped those for whites. They comment, "[T]he ratio of black to white homicide rates ranged from a low of 1.0 (for 10 and 11 year old boys in Chicago) to a high of 10.4 (for 3 and 4 year old girls in Chicago), with values between 2 and 5.5 for most subgroups."[82] Since parents were responsible for the majority of deaths among children under 5 years old, the investigation by Christoffel and her associates points to a disproportionate number of domestic child homicides in the black community. A number of other studies reach similar conclusions.[83]

Ann Goetting points out that although African Americans made up 63 percent of Detroit's population in 1980, they constituted 90.5 percent of child homicide victims in 1982 and 67 percent in 1983.[84] Abel's findings regarding 62 child homicides in Erie County, New York, between 1972 and 1984 are similar to those of Christoffel, Anzinger, and Merrill and of Goetting in highlighting the disproportionately high rates of child homicide among African Americans. Specifically, Abel comments, "For black children 4 years of age and younger, the homicide rate was especially high (17.9 per 100,000) compared with white children (1.63 per 100,000)."[85] Sorenson, Richardson, and Peterson studied the cases of 246 children (newborn to 14 years old) who were murdered in Los Angeles between 1980 and 1989. They conclude that non-Hispanic white children are at the lowest risk of death due to homicide, followed by Hispanic and then black youngsters: "Black children (both those 4 years and younger and those aged 5 to 14 years) are at an extremely high risk of homicide. Black male and female children are at 13.75- and 5.42-fold greater risk of homicide, respectively, than their non-Hispanic white peers."[86]

In their study of 267 child abuse or neglect deaths in Texas over the years 1975 to 1977, Anderson and her collaborators not only found an overrepresentation of black homicide victims, but also noted that Mexican-American children were significantly more likely than Anglo and black children to die from medical neglect.[87] Indeed, 46.5 percent of Mexican-American child homicide deaths stemmed from medical neglect, compared to only 18.5 percent and 21.1 percent for Anglos and blacks, respectively.

Even though these various studies document the disproportionate domestic killing of minority (particularly African-American) children, very few actually explain racial or ethnic differentials in child homicide. A number of researchers have pointed to the folly of drawing conclusions from the high rates of African-American child homicides without controlling for factors such as social class or socioeconomic status. For example, Kunz and Bahr note that "African-American children were 39% of the victims of child homicide, even though African Americans comprised only 12% of the population."[88] However, the authors also remark that "comparisons by race do not mean much without controlling for socioeconomic status."[89] Using Ohio Vital Statistics records and U.S. Census data to analyze 574 childhood homicides in that state between 1974 and 1984, Muscat concludes that, although child homicide rates are significantly higher in the black community, the differentials "tend to fade when SES is taken into consideration."[90]

## Multiple Domestic Killings

Household homicides in which more than one person dies involve various permutations and combinations of victims, among them intimate partners, competitors or love triangle antagonists, family members (including children), and the perpetrators themselves. As such, these killings combine many of the features of intimate-partner, love triangle, and family homicides. However, multiple domestic killings also have a number of unique characteristics that warrant mention.

*Homicide-Suicide*   This form of domestic killing involves the death of one or more persons followed soon after by the suicide of the perpetrator. It is usually men who kill their wives and former wives, lovers and former lovers. In their study of homicide-suicide in North Carolina over the years 1972 through 1977, Palmer and Humphrey found few women among the perpetrators. Out of 90 homicide-suicides during this period, only 6 percent were committed by women.[91] Wolfgang's Philadelphia study found that out of 24 cases of homicide-suicide, only 8 percent were committed by women.[92] It should be borne in mind that woman battering is a significant antecedent to homicide-suicide committed by men. For example, Marzuk, Tardiff, and Hirsch note that "[w]hile some murder-suicides occur shortly after the onset of 'malignant jealousy,' more often there has been a chronically chaotic relationship fraught with jealous suspicions, verbal abuse, and sub-lethal violence."[93]

Sherry Currens and her associates examined homicide-suicide occurring in Kentucky from 1985 to 1990.[94] These researchers defined a homicide-suicide cluster as one or more willful killings with the subsequent suicide of the perpetrator. The 67 homicide-suicide clusters accounted for 6 percent of all homicides during the period studied. Perhaps most significantly, 65 of the 67 perpetrators (97 percent) were men, and 58 of the 80 homicide victims (73 percent) were women. In 64 homicide-suicide clusters (96 percent of the total), the homicide victim and perpetrator knew each other. Again very significantly, in 47 of the 67 clusters (70 percent) the perpetrator was either a current husband (37 clusters), boyfriend (7 clusters), or a former husband (3 clusters) of the victim. Currens and her fellow researchers found that many homicide-suicides are preceded by a history of woman abuse. They observe that "the typical perpetrator is a man married [to] or living with a woman in a relationship marked by physical abuse."[95]

Steven Stack reports that the odds of a suicide following a homicide rise significantly if the victim is or was in an intimate relationship with the perpetrator.[96] Analyzing 16,245 homicides (including 265 homicide-suicides) in Chicago, and controlling for sociodemographic variables, Stack concludes that if the victim is the former spouse or lover of the perpetrator, then the risk of suicide is 12.68 times higher than it is for nonintimate homicides.[97] Suicide risk is also higher if perpetrators kill their own child (10.28), their current spouse (8.0), their current girlfriend or boyfriend (6.11), or a friend (1.88). The risk of suicide declines as the socially prescribed intensity of the bond between the perpetrator and victim diminishes. Drawing upon the work of qualitative researchers, Stack identifies the relationship between perpetrators and victims as "frustrated, chaotic," and "marked by jealousy and ambivalence." Also present is a feeling on the part of the perpetrator

> that one cannot live with the other person but cannot live without them either. A separation or threatened separation arouses anger and depression at the same time. The act of homicide overcomes a sense of helplessness. However, the associated depression and guilt over the loss of one's love object result in suicide.[98]

Numerous other studies examine the role of psychological factors as precursors to homicide-suicide.[99] Although these studies were conducted at different times and used different data sources, often in different countries, there seems to be some agreement as to the importance of such factors as depression, manic depression, and morbid jealousy as antecedents of these fatalities.

*Suicide Pacts and Mercy Killing*    A number of authors allude to the role of the serious and usually chronic illness of the victim, perpetrator, or both as a motive in these forms of domestic homicide.[100] Usually the elderly male partner, who may himself be in ill health, kills the ailing woman with a gun and then commits suicide. The motive for the homicide is allegedly to end her suffering. The killer's suicide is attributed to the loss of his love object, the prospect of impending helplessness, and, more rarely, guilt. Cavan points out that the impending loss of one of the partners in an intimate relationship can be too much for the remaining partner to contemplate—"[T]he loss of the relationship wrecks so large a part of the life-organization of each that an adjustment seems impossible."[101] This is one reason suicide pacts are found almost exclusively among those in intimate relationships. However, these pacts and so-called mercy killings are not as simple as they might at first appear. In Chapter 2, I introduce information that suggests a more cautious interpretation. Rather than accepting that one partner kills the other out of kindness, I explore the possibility that some of these acts constitute murder and may have been preceded by abuse.

*Familicide*   Daniel Cohen's richly textured historical analysis of family killing in the early American Republic identifies acute psychosis, depression, and delusional jealousy as being at the heart of the contemporary psychiatric explanations of these relatively rare atrocities.[102] However, Cohen is careful to indicate that although many persons must have suffered from these emotional problems few took the lives of their entire families. He argues for an examination of familicide not only through the emotional constitution of the perpetrator, but by reference to the shifting social and cultural milieu within which he or she acted. Cohen notes the significance during the early Republic of geographical mobility, economic opportunity, the "revolution against patriarchal authority," and the role of changing religious beliefs as cultural frames of reference against which to make sense of the behavior of those who killed their families.[103]

Analyses of modern-day familicides emphasize the manner in which socio-economic pressures and perpetrators' concerns about their social standing compound or supersede psychiatric problems as the primary cause of these tragedies. Charles Ewing observes that it is almost always men who kill their entire families. He suggests that they do so not just as the culmination of increasing attempts to control their female partners. Rather, Ewing notes, "[T]he typical family killer is more likely to have been concerned about losing control over more than just his wife or family. His concern is more often with losing control over all aspects of his life, or at least those that he most values. He is a man who, in his own eyes, is, or is about to become, a failure."[104]

### Interrelated Antecedents to Intimate-Partner Homicide

The research literature on domestic killings identifies a number of interconnected precursors to lethal violence. These antecedents include escalating domestic violence and the increasing entrapment of battered women;[105] the separation, estrangement, or divorce of the parties;[106] obsessive possessiveness or morbid jealousy shown by the abusive partner;[107] threats to commit intimate-partner homicide, suicide, or both;[108] prior agency involvement, particularly with the police;[109] the issuance of protective or restraining orders against one of the parties, nearly always the man; depression on the part of the abuser;[110] and a prior criminal history of violent behavior on the part of the abusive man.[111]

Dobash and her colleagues nicely summarize these antecedents:

Men often kill wives after lengthy periods of prolonged physical violence accompanied by other forms of abuse and coercion; the roles in such cases are seldom if ever reversed. Men perpetrate familicidal massacres, killing spouse and children together; women do not. Men commonly hunt down and kill wives who have left them; women hardly ever behave similarly. Men kill wives as part of planned murder-suicides; analogous acts by women are almost unheard of. Men kill in response to revelations of wifely infidelity; women almost never respond similarly, though their mates are more often adulterous. The evidence is overwhelming that a large proportion of the spouse-killing perpetrated by wives, but almost none of those perpetrated by husbands, are acts of self-defense.[112]

*Prior History of Domestic Violence*   The role of some antecedents has been documented more substantially than others. An escalating history of domestic violence seems to be widely recognized as the most important of these, although its greater prevalence has not been clearly spelled out empirically. Stark and Flitcraft argue that most spousal, intersexual, and child homicides have at their root a history of woman battering.[113] Partner abuse usually escalates before the fatal incident, and the degree of "entrapment" rises. Increasing entrapment is usually evidenced by physical and sexual abuse alongside rigid control of women's movements, sociability, money, food, working life, and sexual activities.[114] According to Stark and Flitcraft, it is this rising level of entrapment that is the most significant risk factor for gendered homicide.

In Goetting's analysis of 84 men and women arrested for killing their spouses in Detroit, she stresses that

the marital homicide experience differs significantly by gender: For the homicidal husband the act is nearly always offensive; for the wife it is usually defensive. This supports the popular contention that marital homicide, regardless of who inflicts the fatal blow, typically is a reflection of wife abuse.[115]

Research on women who kill their intimate partners demonstrates how the majority are driven to such violence as a final act of self-preservation.[116] Like that of a number of previous investigators, Ann Goetting's research (on intimate-partner homicide in Detroit) captures the qualitative differences between male- and female-perpetrated intimate killing. In discussing the 46 men arrested for killing their mates in Detroit during 1982 and 1983, she observes that the typical perpetrator

is an undereducated, unemployed father with an arrest record, whose final act in a series of heated arguments or confrontations with his slightly younger current or former wife or girlfriend culminated in an offensive gunshot.[117]

Women, for their part, do not always kill men in self-defense. In examining instances where women killed their male partners, Polk and Ransom note that

in 6 of the 7 cases . . . the woman was protecting herself from the violence of the male. That violence in all cases was extensive, and had continued for some time. . . . The one case where a woman killed for reasons other than responding to her partner's violence involved a woman who used homicide as the method for discarding her current partner in order to take up a relationship with another male.[118]

*Obsessive Possessiveness and Morbid Jealousy*    In their cross-cultural analysis of homicide, Daly and Wilson attribute marital violence in general to men's attempts to regulate women, especially their reproductive capacities.[119] Citing Manfred Guttmacher's 1955 analysis of 31 persons (24 men and 7 women) in Baltimore who had killed their spouses, they conclude that "81 percent of the 31 spousal homicides were motivated by sexual proprietariness."[120] According to Daly and Wilson, spousal murder, whether committed by men or women, is steeped in "male sexual proprietariness."[121] The role of this factor has been identified in diverse cultural settings, including India, Uganda, the former Belgian Congo, and Samoa.[122] Easteal specifically identifies what she calls "obsessive" or "pathological" jealousy, in which the perpetrator sees his partner as an integral part of himself. Consequently, any actual or threatened separation of the woman is a threat to the abuser's identity. Easteal traces this characteristic of some intimate relationships to "a society where women have been long regarded as the property or possessions of men."[123] Some studies attach more importance to excessive jealousy than do others.[124] Stack highlights the paranoid beliefs of perpetrators that their partners are being unfaithful to them. He describes "morbid jealousy" as a "delusion," or a mistaken belief, that one's sexual partner has been sexually unfaithful.[125]

*Escaping: Separation, Estrangement, Divorce*   The extant research literature shows that women experience an increased risk of lethal violence when they leave intimate relationships with men.[126] Wilson and Daly's analysis of interspousal homicide from summary data in Canada (1974–90), New South Wales (1968–86), and Chicago (1965–90) reveals that wives experienced a "substantially elevated" risk of lethal victimization when estranged from and no longer living with their husbands.[127] These researchers comment that among married, cohabiting Canadian spouses between 1974 and 1983 "a man was almost four times as likely to kill his wife as to be killed by her; among estranged couples, he was more than *nine* times as likely to kill her as she him."[128] According to Wilson and Daly the significantly increased risk was not due to an escalation of the violence that was already present in these marital relationships. Rather, they point out that batterers warned their wives that if they left they would be killed; they then followed through on those threats.[129]

Easteal also reports that the suicide of the perpetrator of intimate-partner homicide is more likely if the parties were separated before the killing, although she contends that the length of the separation does not seem to be important.[130] For Easteal, in cases of homicide-suicide it is the inability of the offender to conceive of himself as an entity separate from his partner that propels him toward killing.

*Prior Threats to Kill*   As mentioned above, Wilson and Daly emphasize that batterers tell their partners they will kill them if they attempt to leave the relationship. However, threats to kill are integral parts of many abusive relationships, most of which do not end in homicide. According to the BJS, 7 of 10 women who reported being the victims of intimate violence stated that they were physically attacked; for the others, the attack was attempted or threatened. Among this remaining group, 31 percent reported that the offenders threatened to kill them.[131] Other researchers anecdotally report that abusive men threaten the lives of the women they end up killing.[132]

*Prior Agency Contacts*   State offices such as social services and the police have often had dealings with one or more family members before a household killing. Citing research in Detroit and Kansas City, Angela Browne observes that in 85 to 90 percent of domestic homicides "police had been called to the home at least once during the two years before the incident, and in half (54 percent) of the cases, they had been called five or more times."[133] Referencing research conducted on women incarcerated for killing their abusers, Browne notes that "all the women who had killed abusive mates reported that they called for police help at least five times before taking the life of the man."[134] For Stark and Flitcraft, the health, justice, and social service response to battering often ends up reinforcing women's entrapment, thereby increasing the chances of a fatality.[135]

For many studies of domestic homicide, the data on the prior role of police and the courts are sketchy. Part of the reason is that official reports of homicide do not always include information on prior criminal justice interventions. In addition, even if police agencies do come to the scene of domestic disturbances before a homicide, officers do not always enter the call into the official record. Easteal, for example, found formal evidence of earlier police calls to a residence, existing restraining orders, or a pending assault charge in only 18.2 percent of 110 cases.[136]

*Prior Criminal Histories*   Research reveals that many men who use sublethal and lethal violence against women have prior arrests and convictions for violent offenses. One might expect that perpetrators of intimate-partner homicide, like perpetrators of domestic violence in general, have records of committing violent acts against others, and not just their partners. Fagan, Stewart, and Hansen, using a national sample of battered women, show that more than half of the batterers had a history of nondomestic violence.[137] Of these men, more than 80 percent had been arrested at least once for such assaults. Investigating the backgrounds of 644 male batterers arrested in Quincy, Massachusetts,

Klein reports that 43 percent had criminal histories. Among those arrested batterers, he notes that nearly two-thirds had committed crimes against males as well as females and that, on average, they had committed 4.5 prior crimes against persons.[138]

Block and Christakos find that male perpetrators of intimate-partner homicide are more likely than their female counterparts to have arrest histories. In the Chicago data set they observe that 40 percent of male perpetrators had previous arrests for a violent offense, compared with only 18 percent of female perpetrators.[139] The BJS report on intimate violence reaches similar conclusions. It records that among those jailed for intimate violence fully 78 percent had a conviction history, although not necessarily for acts of domestic violence. Of those jailed for intimate violence, 40 percent were then under the supervision of the criminal justice system, with roughly 20 percent on probation, 9 percent governed by the terms of an active restraining order, and just under 10 percent on either parole, pretrial release, or some other condition.[140]

*Alcohol, Drugs, or Both*    The use of alcohol correlates highly with the commission of sublethal domestic violence. The BJS report points out that more than half of both prison and jail inmates incarcerated for intimate violence admitted to using alcohol, drugs, or both when they committed their offenses.[141] However, correlation is not proof of causation, and researchers have not identified the precise role of alcohol, drug use, or both in either sublethal or lethal violence involving intimate partners. Most studies of intimate-partner homicide report alcohol use before or at the time of the fatality to be a much more significant correlate than drug use.[142] Easteal notes that over 50 percent of those who killed intimate partners in the Australian states of New South Wales and Victoria between 1988 and 1990 used alcohol during the fatal episode.[143] Block and Christakos report that alcohol was more likely to be involved in the Chicago intimate-partner homicides in which women killed men, an effect especially pronounced among Latinos.[144] Easteal also points out that the effects of alcohol differ by race. She found that Aboriginal offenders were more likely to have been drinking at the time they killed their intimate partners.[145]

## Interrelated Antecedents to Child Homicide

There is a dearth of information about the interrelated antecedents to the killing of girls and boys in the home. Apart from the demographic characteristics of the key social actors involved in child homicides, the three antecedents that emerge from the literature are a history of child abuse, prior agency involvement with the family, and a history of adult domestic violence in the family.

*Prior History of Child Abuse*    Sabotta and Davis estimate that boys and girls reported to the child abuse registry in Washington State during the years 1973 to 1986 were almost 20 times more likely than those not reported to die from homicide.[146] Wilczynski analyzed 48 child homicides brought to the attention of the director of public prosecutions in England and Wales in 1984. The children were killed by parents or parent substitutes. In half of the 48 cases the perpetrator had previously used violence against the child. Two-thirds of male perpetrators had previously used violence, as against only one-third of females.[147] The severity of prior violence also differed by the sex of the offender. It was nearly always men who committed the "severe" acts, with only one woman engaging in such violence before killing her child.

*Prior Agency Contact*    Research shows that child protection agencies have had prior involvement with a quarter to a half of children who die from abuse and neglect.[148] Wilczynski found that two-thirds of the 48 perpetrators of child homicide in England and Wales had previous dealings with various agencies; the level of contact was similar for men and women. Not surprisingly, perhaps, perpetrators of neonaticide who killed their children within 24 hours after birth had the lowest levels of contact with agencies.[149]

*The Role of Parental or Caretaker Domestic Violence*    A number of studies point to the connection between adult domestic violence and child abuse.[150] The research of Bowker, Arbitell, and McFerron indicates that "[c]hildren of battered wives are very likely to be battered by their fathers. The severity of the wife beating is predictive of the severity of child abuse. Husband-dominance is also a predictor of child abuse."[151] These authors also suggest that paternal and maternal child abuse are "cut from a rather different cloth."[152] Likewise, Stark and Flitcraft's research found that, of the 116 mothers of children referred to the Yale–New Haven Hospital for suspicion of abuse, neglect, or both from July 1977 to June 1978, "[f]ifty-two (45 percent) had a history that put them at risk for battering and another six (5 percent) had a history of marital conflict, though it was impossible to tell from their trauma history or other medical information whether they had been abused."[153]

From their own investigations and the work of others, Stark and Flitcraft conclude that "woman battering . . . is a major context for child abuse" and that "child abuse in these relationships represents the extension of ongoing violence and is an intermediary point in an unfolding history of battering." Both studies caution readers that it is difficult to know precisely the nature and extent either of woman battering or of child abuse or neglect. In addition, Stark and Flitcraft point to one of the methodological problems with exploring the connection between woman battering and child abuse: "Like the child abuse literature in general, the files of the hospital . . . were silent about domestic violence and the children's records rarely mentioned the man's violence. Instead, emphasis was placed on the mother's failure to fulfill her feminine role."[154]

There is practically nothing written on the connection between adult domestic violence and child homicide. Although the literature on both topics is substantial, there is a dire need to explore the connections between the two at both empirical and theoretical levels. Some studies hint at a link, but the connections are implicit and remain largely undeveloped. For example, the important research by Southall and his colleagues on 39 cases of apparently life-threatening events in children's lives identifies 17 cases where boys and girls were either physically or sexually abused by fathers or male relatives and 5 clear-cut cases of mothers reporting prior domestic violence at the hands of husbands. These "abuse antecedents" are neither discussed in the article nor proposed as one possible context for exploring apparently life-threatening events.[155]

## Conclusion

I have highlighted some of the themes in the extant research on domestic homicide. The evidence shows that intimate-partner homicide is a profoundly gendered affair. Not only do men commit the bulk of these offenses, they do so for different reasons than women who kill their intimate partners. Men typically kill as part of an ongoing pattern of abuse directed at women; women nearly always kill in self-defense. The gendering of domestic homicide forms one of the principal organizational axes for Chapters 2 through 6. Indeed, one of the contributions of *Understanding Domestic Homicide* is its use of rich multiagency archival material to explore the microdynamics of this gendered killing.

It is also apparent from the literature that intimate-partner killing differs according to race and ethnicity. African Americans commit a disproportionately high number of such homicides, although the precise reasons for this remain somewhat obscure. Black women are much more likely to kill black male intimate partners than white or Latino women are to kill their partners. Although it might be tempting to explain this by the presence of a matriarchy in the African-American community, a more accurate understanding is likely to lie in the higher levels of entrapment found among black women as compared to white and Latino women. I return to this central issue in the case study narratives and in closing Chapter 7.

Family homicides involve persons related by blood or marriage. They take a number of different forms, including parricide, fratricide, sororicide, and the killing of children. In all these forms, men constitute the majority of the perpetrators. As with homicide in general, family homicides are more likely among racial minorities and the poor. According to the research, it also appears that they are preceded by an ongoing dispute between the parties or by a somewhat stressful change in living arrangements. However, the dynamics of family homicides differ from those of intimate-partner killings insofar as it is not the norm that one family member feels he or she has proprietary rights over the other in the way that a typically male partner may feel he exerts control over his female intimate partner.

In multiple domestic killings such as homicide-suicides, "mercy killings" and suicide pacts, and familicides, the offender typically assumes the roles of perpetrator and, later, victim. Usually the male perpetrator kills his partner, or his children, or both, and then takes his own life. Sometimes he takes the life of male sexual competitors as well. These killings share a number of themes with the killing of individual partners, or children, or both. However, multiple domestic killings are sufficiently distinctive to warrant separate archival analysis (see Chapters 2 and 3).

Since intimate-partner homicides constitute such an important component of adult domestic killings, I have briefly reviewed the research into the interrelated antecedents to such deaths. These precursors include a history of domestic violence, which often results in the increasing entrapment of women; the separation, estrangement, or divorce of the parties; obsessive possessiveness and morbid jealousy by the abusive partner; threats to commit intimate-partner homicide; prior agency involvement, including police and courts; depression; the criminal history of perpetrators; and the use of alcohol, or drugs, or both. I have noted that the extant research delves into such interrelated precursors to differing degrees. I explore these antecedents at length in subsequent chapters. The literature on the factors leading up to child fatalities is scanty and requires urgent attention. I have noted research into the role of prior child abuse, prior agency contact, and parental or caretaker domestic violence. These observations provide a useful entree into my multiagency analysis of the 83 child homicides in Florida in 1994.

# 2. Men as Perpetrators of Multiple Killings

I have noted the gendered nature of multiple homicide. The term "gendered" captures two qualities of such killing between intimates, family members, boyfriends and girlfriends, and male sexual competitors. First, men commit nearly all multiple homicides in families. Second, in concert with the pattern in single domestic homicides, men typically kill as the final act of aggressive or offensive violence in intimate relationships in which they have been the abusers. In contrast, on those rare occasions when women kill their intimate partners or their children and then themselves, the dynamics are different and do not signify the high-water mark in a tide of violence directed against their victims.

The findings from the case studies in Florida are entirely consistent with these general statistical trends. Multiple killings constitute a significant portion of domestic homicides in general. Thirty-seven percent (117 of 319) of the domestic fatalities in Florida in 1994 resulted from such killings. Men perpetrated 47 of the 53 multiple homicides, whereas women committed 6. Among the 117 victims in multiple domestic killings, men killed 104 persons and women killed 13.[1]

The 47 male-perpetrated multiple killings took four distinct forms: familicides, homicide-suicides, parricides, and "others." By familicide, I refer to the killing of the entire family living at the residence. In Florida in 1994 there were six such cases. Men committed four of the familicides and women two. Nearly always, the killing of an entire family is followed by the suicide of the perpetrator,[2] although in one of the four male-perpetrated Florida familicides the killer fled, being apprehended much later.

In the typical case of homicide-suicide the perpetrator kills his intimate partner and then himself. Less often, he kills another person, such as his partner's or former partner's new boyfriend, before taking his own life. Like familicide, homicide-suicide is largely a male affair. Men committed 36 homicide-

TABLE 2.1

Types of male-perpetrated multiple domestic homicides

| Form of multiple killing | Familicide | Homicide-suicide | Parricide | Other | Totals |
|---|---|---|---|---|---|
| Number of cases | 4 | 36 | 2 | 5 | 47 |
| Male victim | 7 | 42 | 2 | 6 | 57 |
| Female victim | 7 | 34 | 2 | 4 | 47 |
| Totals | 14 | 76 | 4 | 10 | 104 |

suicides in Florida in 1994. In four of these cases another person was killed in addition to the intimate partner and the perpetrator. Two of the four deaths involved love triangles in which the perpetrator killed the female partner's new boyfriend. In the third case the perpetrator killed his son as well as his intimate partner. In the fourth instance a friend who was living in the residence at the time of the killing also lost her life.

There were only two parricides in the sample of multiple killings. One middle-aged man killed both his elderly parents, and another son killed his father and his grandmother.

Five male-perpetrated multiple domestic killings fall into the "other" category. These cases had the following dynamics: a boyfriend killed his onetime girlfriend, only to be shot dead by her brother in a gun battle at the scene; a father killed his son and his son's friend during an argument; an uncle killed his two nieces, one of whom was an 11-year-old he was infatuated with; a displaced gay lover killed his former boyfriend, as well as a new lodger who just happened to have moved into the apartment; finally, a spurned boyfriend killed his erstwhile girlfriend and her father.

Table 2.1 reveals that the bulk of male-perpetrated multiple killings take the form of homicide-suicides. Out of the 104 fatalities in such killings, 76 involved homicide-suicides and 14 involved familicides.

Crime statistics in Florida typically do not include suicides among the ranks of those deemed officially to have perished in domestic fatalities. This is misleading. As the case studies will show, those men who kill themselves have typically been the aggressors in turbulent domestic relationships that usually culminate in the death of their female intimate partners and the subsequent taking of their own lives. Regardless of whether a perpetrator's demise is self-inflicted, his death warrants inclusion among the ranks of domestic fatalities because the etiology of the death is profoundly domestic in character. Table 2.2

| TABLE 2.2 | |
|---|---|
| Victims of male perpetrators of multiple homicides | |
| Victims | Male perpetrators (sex of victims) |
| Intimate partners | 37 (35 female, 2 gay male) |
| Family members | 19 (10 female, 9 male) |
| Love triangle antagonists | 6 (all male) |
| Suicide (i.e., perpetrators kill themselves) | 39 (all male: 18 white, 8 black, and 13 Latino) |
| Friends/bystanders | 3 (2 female, 1 male) |
| Total victims | 104 (47 female, 57 male) |

indicates that a significant majority of the men who perish in multiple domestic killings take their own lives.

As shown in Table 2.3, most multiple domestic killings by men were intraracial or intra-ethnic. Of the 104 victims, 48 were killed by white men. These figures include 18 white men who took their own lives. Latino men accounted for 34 victims, among them the 13 Latino men who committed suicide. Black men took 22 lives, including the 8 black male suicides. Overall, whites perpetrate nearly half of all multiple killings (46.2 percent), Latinos nearly one-third (32.7 percent), and blacks roughly one-fifth (21.2 percent).

These ratios of killing do not reflect the racial or ethnic composition of Florida's population. Based upon the evidence to be presented in Chapters 2 through 6, I contend that the racial or ethnic background of perpetrators should not be considered apart from social class and gender. Indeed, the intersection of class, gender, and race or ethnicity lies at the heart of making sense of domestic killing in all its guises. It also makes it necessary to consider the delivery of various social, medical, and criminal justice services before reaching even tentative conclusions about the differential distribution of domestic fatalities by race or ethnicity.

In addition to the racial or ethnic background of perpetrators and victims in multiple domestic killings, the research literature also addresses the marital status of those involved in intimate-partner homicides. Table 2.4 displays the marital status of white, black, and Latino intimate partners. Taken as a whole, slightly more partners were married than not (21 to 16). This finding is consistent with Stack's general observation that suicide is more likely to follow homi-

### TABLE 2.3
Racial/ethnic background of the male perpetrator–victim dyad

| Race/ethnicity of perpetrator | Race/ethnicity of victim | Totals |
|---|---|---|
| WM | WM | 22 |
| WM | WF | 20 |
| WM | AF | 1 |
| WM | WA F | 1 |
| WM | WA M | 1 |
| WM | LF | 1 |
| WM | LM | 2 |
| BM | BM | 11 |
| BM | BF | 11 |
| LM | LM | 20 |
| LM | BL M | 1 |
| LM | LF | 13 |
| Total | | 104 |

Code: W= White; B = Black; L = Latino; A = Asian; M = Male; F = Female

### TABLE 2.4
Breakdown of intimate-partner homicides in multiple killings

| Race/ethnicity of perpetrator | Race/ethnicity of victim | Partners married | Partners unmarried | Totals |
|---|---|---|---|---|
| WM | WF | 9 | 7 | 16 |
| BM | BF | 6 | 3 | 9 |
| LM | LF | 4 | 4 | 8 |
| WM | LM | 0 | 1 | 1 |
| WM | LF | 1 | 0 | 1 |
| LM | BL M | 0 | 1 | 1 |
| WM | AF | 1 | 0 | 1 |
| Totals | | 21 | 16 | 37 |

Code: W= White; B = Black; L = Latino; A = Asian; M = Male; F = Female cide if the parties are closely related.[3] Among African Americans, twice as many were married as unmarried (6 to 3). Four Latino couples were married and four (excluding a gay couple) were unmarried. These are important observations because, as I will point out later, the marital status of the parties changes markedly for single as opposed to multiple domestic killings.

Having laid out some of the basic demographic statistics on the 104 multiple domestic killings carried out by men, I now turn to case studies. Exploring the interpersonal dynamics between parties, their lifestyles, jobs, neighborhoods, families, and kinship systems, these records present a culturally nuanced analysis of the killings. I rely in this effort upon an approach that Clifford Geertz calls "thick description."[4] For example, I introduce the diversity of familial and kinship relationships, taking care to place my observations in the context of the work of other researchers. Although the nature of patriarchy varies in different racial and ethnic groups, all kinship systems tend to be patriarchal. For example, African-American kinship arrangements tend to be more matrilocal, whereas Latino systems tend to be more patrilocal. Even this effect differs by social class. Although it may be accurate to say that race trumps social class as the master status of black Americans, it is important to scrutinize black kinship systems and intimate homicide against the backdrop of social class. As Chapters 2 through 6 unfold, the story on race, ethnicity, social class, and domestic homicide emerges.

In Florida, as a general rule, men who commit multiple domestic homicides tend to have more economic resources than those who commit single domestic homicides. Additionally, it is clear that compared with men who commit single intimate-partner homicides, far fewer male multiple killers have criminal records. For the most part, they did not have criminal histories as murderers, armed robbers, burglars, thieves, or drug dealers. Indeed, only 3 had criminal histories apart from domestic-violence offenses. One man was a convicted murderer, another had one arrest and conviction for theft, and the third had a history of drug offenses. Seven others had criminal histories involving domestic violence, making a total of 10 out of the 47 perpetrators (21.3 percent) with prior criminal records. West notes the same phenomenon in his study of 148 perpetrators of homicide-suicide, where only 17 men and 2 women (13 percent of the total) had earlier criminal convictions.[5] A number of men in the Florida sample had histories of domestic violence, but these are usually categorized as misdemeanor offenses. One man had committed homicide, and another was well known as a drug trafficker and had served time for drug pos-

TABLE 2.5

Characteristics of the 47 relationships ending in multiple domestic killings

| Characteristic | No. cases | % of 47 |
|---|---|---|
| Prior history of domestic violence (classic woman battering, except in one of parricide cases) | 34 | 72.3 |
| Parties estranged, separated, or in process of separating | 33 | 70.2 |
| Male perpetrator displays obsessive possessiveness or morbid jealousy about victim | 22 | 46.8 |
| Prior police contact with parties regarding domestic violence | 15 | 31.9 |
| Male perpetrator makes threats to kill victim prior to doing so | 14 | 29.8 |
| Drug and/or alcohol consumption by perpetrator preceding fatality | 12 | 25.5 |
| Victim obtained restraining order(s) against male perpetrator at some point prior to killing | 11 | 23.4 |
| Perpetrator had prior criminal history | 10 | 21.3 |

session and distribution. However, they were the exceptions rather than the rule.

Table 2.5 summarizes the themes present in each of the 47 cases of male-perpetrated multiple domestic killing.[6] From the available information, two themes stand out. First, there was a significant history of domestic violence, which in all but one case meant woman battering. Second, there was estrangement or the beginnings of a separation between the parties, which almost always meant the woman leaving or preparing to leave her male partner.

### Interrelated Antecedents to Familicide and Homicide-Suicide

Although there were only four cases of family killing by men, these resulted in the loss of 14 lives. Three of the four familicides involved Latino families. Nearly all of the male-perpetrated multiple domestic killings show a history of woman battering, some other kind of acute conflict between the partners, or major stressors in the families.

With regard to familicides and homicide-suicides, I highlight and explore overlapping and interrelated themes common to the killings. Since most of the multiple killings took the form of homicide-suicides, my observations largely apply to them. Clearly, a "prior history of woman battering" may include events such as "prior threats to kill." However, such themes are potent subcomponents of an escalating pattern of domestic violence, and they warrant close attention in their own right.

*Woman Battering*   Any analysis of the Florida case files will produce an underestimate of the proportion of relationships in which domestic violence was present. In spite of this likelihood of miscalculating the presence of prior domestic violence, it is clear from the files that such a history is the most common element of these relationships. I will now narrate three multiple domestic homicides with female victims of white, black, and Asian origin in order to explore the potential role of woman battering prior to the killing.

An apartment complex employee entered the residence of Albert Kaplan and Susan Bryant after coworkers telephoned saying that Kaplan had not been in to work for two days (these are not their real names; pseudonyms have been used throughout). The employee found the dead bodies of Albert (an immigrant from Israel) and Susan (Caucasian) lying on the couch in their apartment. Blood was still seeping from Albert's head. He had apparently shot Susan in the neck and then shot himself in the mouth. The apartment complex is situated in a beautiful area of Miami Beach overlooking the ocean and is patrolled by 24-hour security. Albert held the one-year lease and paid over $700 per month in rent. Susan Bryant worked as a dancer in an adult entertainment club in Miami. Albert, the daytime manager there, drew an annual salary of around $30,000. He had been dating Susan for four months before the homicide-suicide. The club's owner, Rob Rendell, had served with Albert in the Israeli military between the mid-1970s and 1985. He told police that Kaplan had dated a number of the dancers at the club, although none of them "seriously."

Some of these dancers reluctantly talked to the police. One refused to reveal her telephone number, and others stated they knew little of Albert's relationship with Susan. Two dancers did tell police that Albert beat Susan. Belinda Dorval reported that Susan told her that Albert became violent when he was drunk and that Susan sported black eyes and bleeding lips on a number of occasions. She also said that Susan was trying to leave Albert, but that he owed her around $1,500. According to Dorval, Albert was very controlling and seemed "real insecure" about Susan having friends outside of his intimate relationship with her. When Susan visited Belinda, Albert would wait for her in his car outside Belinda's apartment. Numerous witnesses confirmed that Albert carried a gun as part of his job at the club. Rob Rendell told police that Albert had been warned about drinking at work. According to one witness, he "nearly always drank to intoxication." Rendell reported that although he did not consider Albert to be suicidal, when drinking "he had a very violent nature."

In the Florida fatalities as a whole, it is evident that some abusive men move from one victim to the next. It is also clear that some women have been abused by more than one male partner. Susan Bryant was such a victim. This is not to say that she, or women like her, purposely seek out such men or are responsible for the violence they experience. Rather, it is to point out that some women, through multiple factors in their lives, are exposed to or vulnerable to disproportionate amounts of male violence. One such group of women is prostitutes, who suffer very high levels of male violence.[7] One might speculate that Susan Bryant, a nude dancer, was exposed to similar victimizing forces.

According to several witnesses, Susan had previously lived with Ron Marley, a black Jamaican man. Jayne Wynette, who had known her for over four years, reported that she and Susan first met when they were working at an auto parts store in northeast Miami. At that time, Susan was living in a battered women's shelter. It is not clear from the investigative reports who was battering her at the time. Gloria Stern, who also danced at the club, reported Susan told her that her previous boyfriend, Ron Marley, had beaten her continuously and had held a gun to her head and threatened to kill her on several occasions. Police confirmed these facts, noting that Marley had been arrested for domestic violence in February 1994. Apparently Susan left Marley while he was in jail for this offense.

A number of questions emerge from the deaths of Susan Bryant and Albert Kaplan. Was he suicidal? Did Kaplan plan to murder Bryant? Or was the homicide an event that took place in the heat of the moment? Even if it was planned, one cannot assume that Kaplan intended to take his own life. It could be that he killed Susan, was then overcome by guilt, remorse, and a number of other suicidal emotions, and as a result killed himself as well. The record shows that Albert was controlling and resented Susan having other friends. Was it also the case that he suffered from the kind of "ambivalence" reported in the qualitative research literature that led him to feel he could neither live with Susan nor live without her?[8] There is some evidence that Albert was jealous of Susan's friends. There is no evidence, however, that he suffered from the kind of severe depression researchers have linked to suicidal behavior.[9]

The case of Shawna and Keithan Reed serves as an example of a homicide-suicide in the African-American community. The autopsy revealed that Keithan had shot Shawna in the face and then had shot himself in the head. At the time of her death Shawna worked as a travel agent. Keithan was employed as a bus driver; he had no regular route, apparently filling in for drivers who were absent. His supervisor at the Metropolitan Transit Authority told police that Keithan's employment was unremarkable except for his absenteeism. However, he did take an unusual amount of sick leave, and in the weeks leading up to the killing Keithan had complained of fatigue, chest pains, headaches, and an inability to sleep. Three weeks before his death he was referred to the Employee Assistance Program.

After being held hostage at gunpoint all weekend by Keithan, Shawna called her sister, Tamiel Johnson, who lived in New Jersey. She asked if Tamiel could pick her up at Newark International Airport. Apparently Shawna reported that she was ready to leave Keithan. While she was on the phone to her sister, Keithan grabbed the receiver and told Tamiel not to worry and that he and Shawna were just having a lovers' spat. He went on to try to assure Tamiel that he was "making up" with her sister. Keithan's reassurances did nothing to convince Tamiel, who quickly called police in Miami. She knew from Shawna that Keithan had battered her throughout their marriage. The police quickly arrived at the scene, but both Shawna and Keithan were already dead. In one of the bedrooms they found two suitcases packed with women's clothing, indicating Shawna was preparing to leave the relationship immediately and perhaps carry out her stated intention to fly to Newark.

Tamiel Johnson later told police that Keithan had a "stalking" personality. He would not let Shawna have friends of her own and would often check on her at work. On occasion, he created disturbances in Shawna's workplaces, forcing her to move from one job to the next. Tamiel also reported that Keithan kept the ringer to their telephone turned off to stop Shawna's receiving calls. These abusive tactics were no surprise to police, who had come to the residence at least twice in the preceding two years and filed domestic-violence reports on both occasions.

The Reed case also gives evidence of the active involvement of the mothers of Keithan and Shawna. Mrs. Reed visited the apartment just hours before the shooting. Apparently her mortgage had been foreclosed and she intended to live with her son. Keithan turned his mother away. Shawna's mother told police of a recent conversation with Keithan in which he told her that Shawna had asked him for a divorce, saying she did not love him any more. Such involvement of female members of African-American families in domestic disturbances may be more common than it is in Caucasian families because of the more matrilocal and matrifocal nature of black kinship systems. Here one observes these sorts of ties between the mothers and the sisters; one also sees the poverty of Mrs. Reed, who was clearly in financial distress. However, Shawna and Keithan were both employed and were not living below the poverty line. Shawna, for example, seems to have had the financial resources to purchase a plane ticket to Newark.

Although the domestic violence in the Kaplan-Bryant and the Reed homicide-suicides is easy to identify, in the familicide committed by Lech Sikorski such prior violence is difficult to discern. Here, Sikorski killed his wife, Kunja, and their two children, Emily, aged five, and George, aged seven, and then fled. This case, as I will point out, may illustrate Ewing's observation, mentioned in Chapter 1, that men who commit familicide do so because of generalized loss of control and a sense of impending "failure," rather than because of a more specific need to control or get back at their female partners. Kunja had asked Lech for a divorce and had also stated a desire to return to her native Korea. This familicide might therefore also be understood as a violent expression of male proprietariness. The latter viewpoint is aptly articulated by Daly and Wilson, who note: "The prospect of losing his family through death apparently strikes the desperate familicidal father as no more disastrous than the prospect of losing them through desertion! Better, perhaps, since at least he has called the shots and exerted his authority."[10]

There may be cultural reasons why information about a history of woman battering in this case did not filter through to the investigative files and the press. Lech Sikorski, a Caucasian male, was a technical sergeant in the air force. Kunja Sikorski was a native of Korea. The interracial nature of the relationship marks this case as rare among the Florida domestic-homicide files. Indeed, in their analysis of supplemental homicide reports from 1976 to 1985, Mercy and Saltzman estimate that spousal homicide incidence rates are "7.7 times higher in interracial marriages, relative to intraracial marriages."[11]

Kunja Sikorski told a friend just weeks before the familicide that she had cut her waist-length hair in order to use the time spent in looking after it for fixing up their newly acquired family home. The wife of the pastor at the local church reported that buying the new home had put an immense strain on the family. The pastor of the Korean community church that Kunja attended reported that she had injured her arm while working on the house. Kunja also told the pastor and his wife that she was thinking of taking a job to help make the payments. A friend told police that Kunja said she had recently argued with her husband. Put simply, here is probable earlier domestic conflict, combined with the acknowledged "strain" of settling in to a new house, to form the background precipitants of familicide.

The bodies of Kunja, Emily, and George were found hacked to death in the bathroom of their new house on a Monday afternoon by local police. On the Friday before the killing Lech withdrew $5,400 from their savings and disappeared. Autopsy results put the time of death at Friday night or early Saturday morning. When Lech failed to turn up for work on Monday the police were notified. Apparently he absconded to Hawaii with the money and lived on the remote island of Molokai for several months before turning himself in after seeing his picture on the television show *Unsolved Mysteries*. He was charged with murder.

The Sikorski case is a perplexing one for researchers. Doris, who works in the domestic-violence shelter that serves the area where the Sikorskis lived, recalled the family. She told me that Lech wanted a subservient wife, so he chose Kunja, who was a native of Korea. According to Doris, this stereotypical belief in the subservience of Asian women is particularly pronounced among military men, especially those who come from rural regions of the United States and have had little exposure to Asians. When those men go overseas on a tour of duty, such beliefs may be reinforced by the huge sex industry present in cities like Seoul, Bangkok, and Manila. However, as Karin Wang points out, it is important to remember that the cultural background of Asian-American women may make it more difficult for them to make use of the support services offered by a predominantly white-run movement against domestic violence.[12] In addressing this issue, Wang argues that battered Asian-American women have not been well understood by the domestic-violence movement. These women differ from their white counterparts in at least three ways. First, Wang observes that the majority of Asian women are immigrants and therefore experience numerous language problems. These make it difficult for them to obtain help from police, social services, or immigration services. For example, if police officers called to domestic disputes at Asian homes can understand the man and not the woman, it is likely that without special translator services her story will be marginalized or go unheard. Second, the Asian cultural emphasis on saving face and valuing the family above the individual makes Asian women more hesitant about breaking up the family. Such a pronounced belief in the sanctity of the family, even in the face of violent victimization, combined with a cultural antipathy toward divorce, may make it more difficult for white shelter workers and advocates to offer support and understanding to groups like Korean women. Third, the traditional Asian gender roles of male provider and female homemaker are often disrupted by an American economy that requires both partners to work outside the home. This may be seen as liberating by Asian women, but, as Wang points out, it may be very threatening to their partners.[13]

Additionally, there is the myth that women from Asia are "exotic sex objects imbued with an innate understanding of how to please, serve, and titillate men. Rooted historically in the belief that all Chinese and Japanese immigrant women were prostitutes, Asian women have yet to escape the 'ultra-femininity myth' which portrays [them] as sensual yet submissive."[14] Did Kunja Sikorski somehow begin to fail to live up to these ideals that her tech sergeant husband may have had of Asian women? Here one enters the domain of cultural representation and its meaning to social audiences, of which Lech Sikorski was but a single member. Wang is right to comment that these stereotypes make it difficult for Asian women to receive the support of the largely white-operated shelter movement. For her part, bell hooks observes that these stereotypes of Asian women also function to separate them from other female groups. She recalls becoming "fascinated by how a lot of the stereotypes for Asian women ('passive,' 'non assertive,' 'quiet') are just the opposite of the stereotypes that plague black women ('aggressive,' 'loud,' 'mean'). It's like we exist in two radically different poles in the economy of racism. And it's those positionings that make it hard for Asian women and black women to come together."[15]

Weighing all the evidence in the Sikorski case leads me to believe there was prior woman battering in this relationship. For cultural reasons, it is perhaps true that few persons were told about the violence and no agencies were contacted for support. It is nonetheless hard to believe that the level of rage expressed in the familicide was not preceded by some form of woman battering. On the other hand, it is also important to recognize that the family was under immense stress and that Lech Sikorski may have deeply internalized his failure to "make it" in the way American providers should.

*Obsessive Possessiveness and Morbid Jealousy*   Some abusers will do practically anything not to lose their partners. Wilson and Daly cite one case in which an Illinois man said to his wife, "I swear if you ever leave me, I'll follow you to the ends of the earth and kill you."[16] Other authors point to the role of obsessiveness about one's partner as an important factor propelling an abuser toward the use of lethal violence. Barbara Hart notes that if an abuser has threatened homicide or suicide, and has fantasized about killing his partner, then obsessiveness could be a major predictor of lethality. In her view, "A batterer who is obsessive about his battered partner—who either idolizes her and feels he cannot live without her or believes he somehow owns her because she is his wife— is likely to act more dangerously to keep his partner."[17]

As Table 2.5 indicates, almost half of the male perpetrators of multiple killings displayed obsessive-possessive beliefs about their partners or former partners, or a morbid jealousy about those women's association or perceived association with new men. The obsessive possessiveness and morbid jealousy appear to transcend racial, ethnic, and class boundaries, although as one of the root precipitants of homicide the phenomena are almost exclusively associated with men. In what follows, I introduce two cases in which extreme jealousy and possessiveness seem to have played a pivotal role in the commission of multiple homicides.

Late one evening, a pilot was talking on the phone with a friend when he heard two loud bangs, like gun shots. The pilot left his residence in Tampa and walked a short way to an intersection. He told police that he observed a man kneeling on the ground holding a rifle. The man turned out to be Don Hartmann, who was apparently aiming the rifle across the street. The pilot told police he called out, "What's going on?" Hartmann yelled, "Get back, get away!" The pilot repeated his question. This time Hartmann pointed the rifle in the pilot's direction. At this point he shouted to Hartmann, "I'm going to call the police." Hartmann replied, "Call whoever you want, it won't matter in a while." In total, the pilot reported that he heard two shots while he was on the phone to his friend, one or two more as he was walking toward the intersection, and five to seven shots after his brief exchange with Hartmann. Three persons died as a result of the shooting. Another witness, who had been watching television when the incident began, told police that Hartmann was "very intense" around the crime scene. As the autopsy later revealed, he shot his former girlfriend Tasha Wojeck three times. She bled to death after one of the bullets struck her femoral artery. During the shooting Hartmann also killed her new boyfriend, Steve Billings. At the time of the killing Hartmann paced around Tasha and at one point was heard to yell at her, "I told you I was gonna fuckin' do it!" At another moment during the shooting he walked in between two cars to try to light a cigarette. Passing drivers were apparently slowing down to see what was happening, because they could see Tasha lying on the ground. Hartmann yelled at them, "Mind your own fuckin' business!" As police arrived at the scene, one of the officers witnessed Hartmann lie on the ground behind Tasha and "cuddle up to her." He shot her again, this time with a handgun. He then turned the weapon toward his head and shot himself. At the same time police shot 8 to 10 times into Hartmann's body.

Tasha Wojeck and Don Hartmann had a two-year intimate relationship, which Tasha broke off in December 1993. She eventually began dating Steve Billings, of whom Hartmann was extremely jealous. He told his mother how upset he was that Tasha "flaunted other men in his face." Julie Sims, a friend of Tasha's, told police after the killing that Tasha was "scared to death of Hartmann" and that he "was verbally, physically, and mentally abusive to Tasha." Tasha had purchased a handgun to protect herself against him. The acuteness of Hartmann's jealousy and possessiveness was combined with a numbing clinical depression. Tasha's mother told police that he was "very depressed and was under psychiatric care for it." She also told them that he had been prescribed Prozac to help alleviate the depression.

The multiple killing perpetrated by Don Hartmann illustrates a number of themes reported in the research literature. His jealousy was extreme and he had the sense that he could not live without Tasha. He died curled beside her, as if to make the two of them one. Although his depression was acute, it does not appear to have been related to financial problems. Hartmann was unemployed at the time of the killings, but his mother told police he had recently received $35,000 in a workmen's compensation payout.[18] His hopelessness and despair at losing his "love object" are reflected in his abject disregard for all others at the scene, an attitude revealed perhaps most sharply in his killing of Steve Billings, Tasha's new lover. Hartmann's morbid possessiveness is consistent with the attitudes displayed by other intimate killers who have lost their "love objects."[19]

Some researchers have identified "guilt" as an emotion that contributes to the subsequent suicide in homicide-suicides.[20] This is difficult to discern in the Hartmann case. He seems to have known he was going to die in the near future. At the time of his breakup with Tasha, Hartmann had talked with his brother about killing himself; about then, he had also made out a will on his computer. Furthermore, he had surreptitiously acquired the rifle used in the killings from his father and secreted it away until the fateful evening. Taken as a whole, the evidence suggests Hartmann planned the double homicide and his own suicide and that he was motivated by jealousy, possessiveness, and the ensuing dilemma of how to live on without his lost object of love.

Don Hartmann thought that Tasha flaunted other men in front of him, and a number of other multiple killings reveal like sentiments among the perpetrators. Take, for example, the case of Jose Camacho, a Latino male aged 49, who murdered his wife, Carmen, aged 43, and their adopted daughter, Linda, aged 9. (Linda was actually Carmen's granddaughter.) Jose shot Carmen in the back of the head and used a pillow to muffle the sound as he shot Linda in the head, presumably as she lay sleeping. Linda's biological mother, Serena Serano, aged 28, also lived in the house. It was Serena who found the dead bodies of her mother and daughter. Jose, who was Serena's stepfather, apparently parked his car about a mile from the crime scene and committed suicide in his vehicle by shooting himself in the chest. He left a handwritten confession note close to his wife's corpse. Unlike the Hartmann case, it is easy to identify a sense of remorse and guilt in Jose's note, which reads:

> To all. I am so sorry for what I have done. I wish I could bring her back. But it's too late. . . . My nerves got to a point that I exploded. Again please forgive me. To my mom and dad, please try to understand what happened. I love you all always. Love, Jose.

At the time of the killings Jose was living with his parents because he and Carmen were having what Serena called "marital problems." They had been separated for several days. According to Serena, Jose was "extremely distraught" over the separation and had been acting "extremely strange lately." Apparently he wanted to get back together with Carmen. A neighbor, who lived three doors down from the Camacho residence, told police that Jose thought his wife was having an affair. Jose, a long-distance truck driver, felt his wife was seeing someone else when he was away. Carmen had a job delivering medical records. The neighbor also told police that six months before the shootings Jose confided to her that he was going to kill Carmen, Linda, and himself. He apparently repeated these threats about a week before the homicides, telling his neighbor he could not live there any more with the thought of his wife being unfaithful to him. When the neighbor asked why Jose would kill nine-year-old

Linda, Jose replied that he loved the little girl and could not stand the thought of leaving Linda with her biological mother, his stepdaughter.

There is some evidence to suggest that Jose abused Carmen. Neighbors told police and newspaper reporters that she was known around the neighborhood for taking in stray animals and looking after them. She also helped other families adopt pets. Serena Serano told police that a few months before the homicides Jose shot and killed one of Carmen's dogs because it was barking loudly and bothering him.[21] There is no evidence that Carmen was having an affair. Indeed, Jose may have been close to the kind of offender West identifies as being dangerously delusional about his female partner's perceived infidelity.[22] The small amount of evidence available on why Jose killed Linda suggests a motive approximating that found when women kill their children. A number of neighbors in this apparently tight-knit Latino community in Hollywood attested to Jose's love for his adopted daughter. Jose's statement that he could not face leaving Linda with her biological mother is akin to the ideas expressed by some mothers who kill their children. These women, often in desperate emotional and financial turmoil, say they could not see killing themselves and merely leaving their very dependent children in the care of someone else.[23]

*Perceptions of Betrayal*  Some perpetrators felt they had been deceived or abandoned by their partners. This should come as no surprise, since many men who beat their intimate female partners report feeling betrayed by them. In the instances of homicide, as perhaps in cases of nonlethal battering, the feeling of having been duped is associated with much more than obsessive possessiveness toward the love object. Doubtless, when victims of battering call the police some men interpret the call as a form of betrayal. However, my use of the term embodies much more than a sense of being profoundly wronged in one incident. When women moved beyond existing sex role prescriptions men articulated a deep sense of abandonment. Abusers who reported being betrayed often relied excessively on the victim for their "being in the social world" and had pinned their future on the partner. As an antecedent, "betrayal" also permeates a number of the other situations I refer to. Men who exhibited obsessive possessiveness, men whose love objects had left them, and men who perceived their female partners to be having affairs were among those more likely to voice a sense of betrayal. Although men reported betrayal with limited frequency in the archival data (it was not mentioned enough to warrant inclusion in Table 2.5), I suspect it is much more common than the files show. And when a deep sense of betrayal did surface in the case files, it appeared to be a galvanizing emotion and a spark for violent retribution. Discernible feelings of betrayal in the case files were almost exclusively the preserve of men. Two cases illustrate these feelings and highlight the kinds of situational details around which such intense feelings crystallize.

On July 15, 1994, Tosca Perez shot and killed his daughter, Felicia Perez, aged 14, and then himself as they sat in his car parked outside the new home of his estranged wife and his daughter. There was a long history of domestic violence in this case. Police responded to incidents at their residence in October and December 1992. Tosca Perez was arrested on a domestic-violence charge stemming from an assault against Judith Perez, his wife, in summer 1993. As Tosca was led away in handcuffs by police, a neighbor reported his daughter screaming at him, "Why did you hit her?" On May 27, 1994, Judith moved out of their home, taking Felicia with her, and moved in with Judith's mother. The violence and controlling behavior then seemed to escalate. Tosca assaulted her once in public at a Dairy Queen just days before the killings. Apparently, he had also been stalking his wife at the apartment complex where she worked. In the months leading up to the killings Judith had been seeing another man, and she was planning to file for divorce. His wife obtained a restraining order against Tosca on July 12, 1994, which was served on July 13, 1994.

Tosca was deeply disturbed at what he saw as his wife's betrayal of him. According to witnesses, on Wednesday evening, July 13, Tosca said, "I'm going to get the motherfuckers for what they did to me." The term "motherfuckers" reportedly referred to his wife, Judith, his daughter, Felicia, and his stepsister. Witnesses remarked that Tosca's behavior had changed markedly in the days prior to the killings. His nephew, who had moved in with him, told police that Tosca slept little the week before the homicide-suicide. Tosca would pace the apartment, leave and walk around the complex, come back in, and go out again. In addition to his obsessiveness, Tosca also told his nephew he had been spying on Judith. Some witnesses attributed part of his behavioral changes to a minor stroke he suffered a year or so before. After the stroke Tosca apparently lost his memory for a short period. A family member told police that it seemed as though his tolerance for the general stresses of life went down and he became angry and aggressive far more easily.

Tosca may have made up his mind to kill himself, other family members, or both earlier on during that week. He had purchased a firearm on July 8,

1994, and picked it up the day after the injunction was issued, two days before the homicide-suicide. His nephew, Juan Perez, told police that on July 10 or 11 Tosca handed him a large envelope and told him that if anything happened to him to open it. A note inside read:

Dear Juan
I'm sorry it had to be like this. . . I am leaving you $2,000 and I hope you can both get good jobs and enjoy this place. People here are all very friendly. Give a great kiss to my mother when she gets here and tell her that I will always love her and the same for my brothers and sisters. I love you all. Thanks. Tosca.

Tosca's sense of being betrayed did not preclude extreme jealousy. Joe Valdez, one of his coworkers and a friend of about a decade, told police that Tosca said to him that he was extremely upset and jealous that his wife was seeing another man. Tosca apparently told his friend he was still in love with Judith. Joe was concerned for Tosca's well-being and invited him to stay at his apartment for a while "until his mind cleared." On the Friday afternoon of the killing, Joe learned that Tosca had left a box for him at Tosca's house along with a little red book. The leaving of the red book alarmed Joe, because it was the one issued to marines to record their personal experiences. He later told investigators that the book is not usually given away. Indeed, when Joe finally obtained it a note was attached to the book from Tosca saying, "Make sure no one else gets this." In a personal note left to Joe he wrote, "I would like to be buried next to Judith so we can both go to hell together."

All witnesses interviewed attested to Tosca's love for his daughter. Indeed, after the killings Judith found a note from him to Felicia saying that he was leaving a couple of photographs so she could "remember me this way." Tosca went on to say that "I love you very much and I wish you a happy birthday and many, many more." It appears from this evidence that Tosca may have been contemplating suicide rather than homicide-suicide or familicide. However, in a later note to his friend Joe, dated July 15, Tosca explains why, in his mind, he had to kill his daughter. The note reads:

Damn, Joe, I have been trying like crazy to get this woman, but it seems like she's got everybody looking around for me. So I can't get on her property, but today is going to be a different day because today I am taking what belongs to me and she can go fuck in hell afterwards. Yes, I am picking up Felicia after school today for lunch because that's what it has come to. I am going to take her life so that she won't be brought up like myself this clown in my house. Then I am going to Judith's property to do myself in. If I can take out somebody else, it's going to be a pleasure.

It seems from the note that Tosca wanted to kill his wife and himself but could not get near her. It is significant here that the protection order took effect on July 13 and, together with Judith's support from family and friends, seems to have frustrated Tosca's efforts to kill her. He then decided to take his daughter's life as a way of getting back at his wife. Tosca states that part of the reason for killing Felicia was that he did not want her to become a "clown in my house" like himself. On July 15, 1994, Tosca called Judith and asked if she could have lunch with Felicia and him. At this point it is fairly certain that he had planned to kill both his daughter and himself. From the note to Joe, one may infer that Tosca would have killed Judith as well if he had got the opportunity. Judith told Tosca that she could not join them for lunch because the protective order was active. However, she said that he was welcome to pick up Felicia from where Judith was working so the two of them could get together.

In the Perez case the numerous elements that contributed to Tosca's perception that he had been betrayed are clearly evident. Given that many men who use interpersonal violence against their female partners report feeling betrayed, it is likely that many perpetrators of homicide-suicide shared this view. My limited reporting of such perceptions of betrayal reflects one of the limitations of the archival approach. Researchers cannot always gain access to the lived feelings of participants, unless those participants have shared their feelings with others and unless agencies have both become aware of those feelings and recorded them.

One case where perceptions of betrayal are likely, but not certain, involved the Gouldners. In this homicide-suicide, Ray Gouldner, a 49-year-old white man, shot and killed his estranged wife, Samantha Gouldner, a white woman aged 45, before taking his own life. The Gouldners' daughter-in-law found the bodies in a utility shed on Wednesday, March 23, 1994, at roughly 1:45 P.M. When police arrived and examined Ray they found soot on his tongue, a telltale sign that he had shot himself in the mouth with the shotgun found at the scene. Samantha had powder burns on her cheek, indicating she had been shot at close range. The corpses exhibited a number of the characteristics of other homicide-suicides. The police homicide narrative describes the scene as follows. Note how Ray's corpse, even in death, is nestled up to Samantha's.

> Laying next to the female was a male subject laying on his back that had an apparent exit wound to the left side of his head. There was what appeared to be a shotgun laying across his stomach. . . . Further examination of the room showed blood and what appeared to be blood matter on the wall above the male subject's head. There was also blood and brain matter on the south, west and north wall. There was a human ear laying near a pillow on the bed in the room. The male subject had [a] very large pool of blood near his head. . . . His right leg was laying on top of the female's left leg.

Ray Gouldner was disabled by an automobile accident in 1991. His injuries left him in pain, and his inability to work left him depressed; at the time of his death he was taking both antipain and antidepressant medications. According to the couple's son, Samantha had grown increasingly unhappy with her relationship with Ray. The two of them used to go dancing and bowling, activities that she greatly enjoyed. However, Ray's injuries ended his participation. From the police file it is impossible to tell if there was any history of domestic violence. Unlike the Perez case, there had been no police calls to the residence and there was no history of restraining orders. In February 1994, Samantha began seeing another man. On March 15 she moved out with the couple's children and told Ray she was dissolving their 32-year marriage. The next day she informed him that she had begun sleeping with the new man in her life.

Ray expressed suicidal thoughts a number of times prior to the homicide-suicide. He told his son just before the killings, "One of these days I won't be here, one of these days I'll kill myself" and "I should put a bullet through my head." Again, these statements remind one that a person who is suicidal should also be considered potentially homicidal. Ray's act of homicide-suicide seems to have been instigated by his wife's stated aim to end their marriage. Whether he saw Samantha's behavior as "betrayal" is open to conjecture. She told their daughter-in-law that Ray took the news of her impending departure well and seemed to accept her decision. It could be that Ray was hiding his jealousy about Samantha's newfound love. However, it seems more likely that he killed out of an overall perception of having been betrayed by his wife of 32 years. This view had probably been growing since his accident and coexisted with his worsening depression.

*Prior Threats to Kill*   The multiagency archival data reveal that in almost one-third of multiple homicides men threatened to kill their intimate female partners at some point before the fatality. At times these threats were issued to the woman herself, who later reported them to others. On other occasions the man communicated these threats to neighbors, friends, or relatives.

Jose Camacho told a neighbor that he was going to kill his wife and their adopted daughter, Linda. It does not seem as if many other persons knew of his intentions. There were no documented police calls to the residence during which officers recorded such intentions. Nor were there any documented restraining orders containing information on threats against the lives of any of the Camacho family. In some cases, however, prior threats to kill stand out in the vocabularies of abuse heaped on women by men. Of course, very few of these threats are actually carried out, although an apparent failure to follow through should not mean underestimating the importance of these threats against life in general. Like a history of woman battering and extreme jealousy, prior threats to kill punctuate many of the abusive scenarios and vocabularies of motive that escalate to lethal violence. As always, researchers are remarkably dependent upon the archival data from agencies such as law enforcement and the courts to document the presence of earlier threats to kill. However, one cannot assume that the absence of such threats in these documents means that no such threats were made. I now turn to a case in which the threats to kill were broadly publicized and duly noted by both the criminal justice system and family members close to the decedents. By doing so, I do not mean to suggest that well-known threats are better predictors of lethal violence than those uttered more discreetly.

Hours after being served with divorce papers, Bob Jordan lay in wait for his estranged wife, Sheila Jordan, at their home in Tampa. He shot her in the chest, killing her, and then shot himself in the head. The incident occurred in the presence of their 15-year-old daughter. During their 14 years of marriage, the black couple had six children; they also adopted a niece when her mother was shot to death in front of a liquor store in 1992. The Jordans had been separated for a couple of months before the killing. Apparently, Bob told a number of family members he was going to kill his wife if she did not take him back. Sheila herself described these threats in two separate petitions for orders of protection. In the one dated May 1994, she told the judge that Bob had threatened to kill her if she did not see him. On one occasion she was forced to have sex with him. In the process of fighting him off she received a bruised lip. Sheila reported that Bob then threatened to kill her and himself. A later order issued just days before her death records Sheila telling the court that Bob kept calling her at work and asking if she was seeing someone else. At one point she reported that Bob said "he had a big gun and he knew where I lived. He said he would use the gun on me if he had to."

Sharing threats to kill with family members and the victim herself (and, indirectly, with the criminal justice system) represents a highly visible and menacing level of intimidation. According to family members, the Jordans' marriage started to come apart after Bob became addicted to crack cocaine several years before the homicide-suicide. An additional strain was that Sheila had just received a promotion at the telephone company where she worked and her life was beginning to move in a direction that did not include her estranged husband. Note also the typical obsessive possessiveness that I described earlier. As Bob's brother Brad Jordan commented, "He wanted her and no one else was going to have her if he didn't. He wanted her, but she didn't want him."

*Prior Police Involvement*   It is clear from the cases I have already introduced that the police sometimes had previous contact with the parties to multiple killings. Taking the male-perpetrated multiple homicides as a whole, the files reveal earlier police contact with the parties in domestic disputes in almost one-third of cases.

Pamela Ruby was in the process of leaving Warren Ruby, her third husband, and suing for divorce. Warren terrified Pamela so much that she bought a gun to protect herself. Purchasing it was no light decision for her. Pamela knew that Warren, a survivalist, was well versed in the use of firearms.

Warren killed Pamela by shooting her three times and then killed himself. Police were summoned to the residence by neighbors. They found a survivor hidden under a bed, a four-year-old girl who Pamela was baby-sitting at the time. Police found Pamela's corpse in a position that suggested she had been trying to get under another bed to escape gunfire. A telephone was observed next to her right hand, indicating she had been on the phone at the time she died. Officers interviewed Ron Gatty, Pamela's first husband and the father of her two children. He reported receiving a call from her the day of the killings. Pamela told Gatty that she was having domestic problems with Warren and asked if he would take their two children for a while. Because she and

Gatty had fought a long custody battle, this request implied to him that she feared for her life. She then told him that Warren had held her and a friend at gun point the day before. Gatty also reported to police that Pamela said Warren had threatened to kill her on a number of occasions. She was acutely cognizant of Warren's facility with guns and told Gatty that he had automatic weapons. Apparently a sheriff's deputy came to the scene after Warren held the two women at gun point and recommended that Pamela leave the area. Her older daughter confirmed this incident and also told officers that her mother went to the local sheriff's office to obtain protection. A sergeant there requested that Pamela sign a complaint affidavit then and there so that officers might arrest Warren for aggravated assault. The sergeant also gave her information on the local spouse abuse shelter and a number of pamphlets itemizing local support services for battered women. Pamela stated that she did not wish to go to the shelter at that time. She also told the sergeant that she did not want to sign an affidavit attesting to Warren's violence. By his account, the sergeant offered to sign the affidavit for Pamela. She declined. Finally, he recommended that Pamela go home and discuss the issue with other family members. Since she believed that Warren was staying out of town that evening, Pamela felt she could better make out the complaint at home. The three-page document that she filled in after this visit to the sheriff's office was found near her corpse. In the complaint, Pamela stated that Warren had assaulted her earlier that day and threatened her with a gun.

In the interviews after the killings, Ron Gatty put Pamela's fear in context and asked local sheriffs investigators why they had not done more to protect her. The conversation went as follows:

> *Gatty*  Here's a woman who would fight, tooth and nail . . . to keep those kids. This woman wouldn't give those kids over to me unless she was terrified. She said, "Ron, you don't know what he's capable of." She said that Warren's father had come to her place yesterday and begged her to go to marriage counseling with Warren. She said she told his dad, "I won't go, because that'll give him some glimmer of hope of us getting back together." She said his dad told her that Warren had already killed one person. [The reference probably is to Pamela's second husband, who police knew disappeared under mysterious circumstances.] And if she told all this to police, why weren't they with her yesterday? Why weren't they with her today? Why wasn't somebody there keepin' an eye on her?

These kids lost their stepdaddy two years ago and now they gotta lose their mama?

*Investigator*   Like I said, I'm not aware of that. I don't know what happened. This is the first time we got called on this.

*Protection Orders*   Just as police have prior involvement in domestic cases that culminate in multiple killings, so do the courts. According to the BJS, about half of those offenders incarcerated for violence directed at intimates had earlier restraining orders against them for similar offenses.[24] As Table 2.5 shows, in roughly a quarter of those cases in which men committed multiple domestic homicide they had earlier been the subjects of restraining orders. I have already mentioned how the issuance of two such orders in the Jordan case did nothing to protect Sheila Jordan. For another example, consider the case of Tony Jones, who, while under the restraint of a protection order, killed two persons, one of whom was his estranged wife, Marianna Jones.

At the time of the killings on May 7, 1994, Marianna was living at the family home of her new boyfriend, Antonio Alvarez. Antonio's parents, a Latino couple, knew that she was having problems with Tony. As a result, they offered Marianna a place in their home while she made the transition out of her relationship with Tony and established herself in the new relationship with Antonio. Consistent with patterns in other cases, Tony's abusiveness escalated as Marianna made moves toward separating from him. Tony raped her at knife point in March 1994. On March 28, 1994, Marianna obtained an injunction against him. A divorce hearing was set for May, 18, 1994. Tony said to Marianna that he would kill her and her mother if she did not return to him. After the homicides, one witness told police that Tony had remarked that "he could not live without her," a statement heard so often in multiple killings. During the week preceding the double murder, Tony stalked Marianna, learning where she lived. At around 11:30 P.M. on May 7 Antonio and Marianna returned to the Alvarez residence. Shortly before midnight, Tony Jones walked in the unlocked front door and shot and killed Antonio's father, Alonso Alvarez, and Marianna.

Antonio intervened after the double shooting, wrestling the gun from Jones and dragging him out of the house. He gradually dragged Jones down the street toward the house of his aunt, who had a telephone. Neighbors who knew Alvarez asked him what the matter was. One neighbor, Vincente Saldivar, helped pin Jones to the ground. Once Jones was restrained, Antonio ran back to his own residence to check on the condition of his father and girlfriend.

*Escaping: Separation, Estrangement, Divorce*   The extant research literature clearly shows that women's attempts to end conflictual relationships by resorting to separation, estrangement, or divorce can engender rage in abusers. Attempts to leave violent men are one of the most significant correlates with domestic death. The Florida sample is no exception. As noted in Table 2.5, in 70.2 percent of the multiple domestic homicides women had either separated from the perpetrator or were in the process of doing so at the time of the killing. This finding is consistent with the qualitative studies of homicide-suicide, which clearly reveal that one of the key provocations is the woman's decision to leave the relationship, her act of departure, or both. For example, Buteau, Lesage, and Kiely found a history of recent separation in 59 percent of the homicide-suicides they studied.[25]

As I have pointed out, multiple intimate killings take place at various stages in conflictual relationships. Some happen while the partners are still residing together, others occur after women leave men and establish new intimate relationships, and still others take place after women serve notice that they want a divorce. Such notice may be accompanied by the securing of a protection order or by some kind of police involvement. Women may try to leave violent men on a number of occasions, only to be killed during their final attempt. One such woman, Clara Vasquez, left her abusive partner, Manuel Cacho, several times before being killed by him in a homicide-suicide.

Metro–Dade police were summoned to the Vasquez-Cacho apartment by neighbors who reported hearing a woman screaming. As police arrived, neighbors heard two gun shots. After knocking on the apartment door and receiving no response, they entered the bedroom. There they discovered Cacho in a fetal position on top of Clara Vasquez, who was lying supine on the bed. Although she was still breathing when police arrived, Vasquez died of a gunshot wound to her head on the way to the hospital. One of the patrol officers at the scene told investigators that he had arrested Cacho for aggravated assault and battery against Vasquez just a week before the homicide-suicide. During that incident Cacho had apparently grabbed Vasquez in a headlock and put a butcher knife to her throat, threatening to kill her if she called the police. (Neighbors made the call.)

Clara Vasquez had tried to leave the relationship before. The manager of their apartment complex reported the couple had separated three times in the preceding three months. Apparently they had moved to Miami from New York in 1992. Since being there, Clara had found and then lost a job as a secretary.

Although Manuel worked in a leather factory, the two were experiencing acute financial problems just prior to the homicide-suicide. According to Clara's second cousin Eva Sanchez, they had indebted themselves heavily by purchasing furniture and other items for their house on credit. Unable to make the payments, they were constantly being harassed by debt collectors. The disputes between Clara and Manuel increased as their financial situation worsened.

Two days before the killing Clara approached the co-owner of the apartment house, Mrs. Hernandez, with roses and asked her to write a reference for her so that she could get a new apartment. Mr. Hernandez, the other co-owner, reported that she was "a lovely person." Clara did not tell him the reason she was moving out, but he sensed it was because of the problems she was having with Manuel. On the night of the killings, both Clara and Manuel talked with Eva Sanchez on the phone. Eva said to police that Clara told her she was staying one last night in the apartment with Manuel and then moving out the next morning. Eva also reported that Manuel was extremely depressed over Clara moving out and severing their relationship. Manuel seems to have told Eva that he was also distraught over being arrested for aggravated assault and battery and was terrified of the possibility of going to jail. In fact, he told Eva he would do "anything to avoid going to jail." That Manuel felt hopeless and depressed was also conveyed to Clara's mother, Patricia Vasquez, in yet another phone call just hours before the killing. He apologized to Mrs. Vasquez for what she perceived to be the dissolution of his nine-year relationship with Clara. Patricia Vasquez told police she felt his apology was very "strange."

The Cacho-Vasquez homicide-suicide was characterized by more than a history of woman battering, prior police calls to the residence, and acute depression on the part of the perpetrator. It is also clear that Clara had tried to leave on several occasions but was unsuccessful. On the night of the killing her second cousin asked her about the gun that Manuel owned and whether she felt safe. Clara reassured Eva Sanchez that she had hidden the gun outside their apartment and that she did not fear for her life. Although she cannot be blamed, Clara obviously misread the situation and Manuel's potential for lethal violence. One must also note Clara's unemployment, her debts, and her attempts to secure a reference from her landlord so that she might move out as evidence that economic factors profoundly impact women's ability to leave dangerous and violent relationships cleanly.

In one of the two multiple killings involving homosexuals, one of the victims was trying to terminate the gay relationship.[26] Carlos Juantorena, a 24-

year-old white Cuban, and Manuel Castro, a 49-year-old black Cuban, lived together as lovers. After an interval of one month, during which time Castro had asked Juantorena to move out of the older man's apartment, Juantorena shot and killed both Castro and Jorges Cervantes, a 29-year-old Latino male. He had arrived in Miami just one week before on a raft from Cuba and was apparently simply living in the apartment. Juantorena himself had come to the United States on a raft from Cuba in 1992. One witness, Georgio Quintana, who traveled to the United States with him, told police that Juantorena first moved to California. After a month, he moved back to Miami to live with Castro. It seems that the older man was something of a bridge for men who entered the United States from Cuba. The two quickly became lovers. Apparently, Castro had been contacted by Juantorena's father, who still lived in Cuba. He had asked Castro to take his son in and look out for him.

One month before killing Manuel Castro and Jorges Cervantes, Carlos Juantorena was arrested for grand larceny at his place of employment, where he worked as a janitor. Although Castro bailed him out of jail after his arrest, he told Juantorena that he had to leave the apartment. One witness described Juantorena as emaciated and told police he looked like he was suffering from AIDS.[27] The records do not reveal what role, if any, the possible HIV infection played in the killings. Apparently, Juantorena moved out temporarily to live with Georgio Quintana and his family for a few weeks after Castro asked him to leave. On the morning of the killings Juantorena returned to his old apartment and argued with Castro. Cervantes tried to intervene and was shot and killed along with Castro. There is no evidence in the investigative files that Castro and Cervantes were lovers, or that Castro was somehow replacing Juantorena with Cervantes. The possibility of a gay lovers' triangle cannot be ruled out, however.

Like many of the multiple killings among heterosexuals, this case involves the termination of an intimate relationship. However, there was no history of domestic violence between the partners, no documented earlier threats to kill, no history of either morbid jealousy or protective orders, and no prior police calls to the residence. This absence of factors typically associated with multiple killings might reflect the fact that Castro lived in an apartment complex heavily populated by Latinos with strong ties to Cuba. Not only was he known to help Cuban nationals who had illegally entered the United States, but he was also homosexual. For both reasons, with the former probably being more important, Castro may have kept his lifestyle very much to himself. This seems likely, because police interviewed a large number of residents in the apartment complex after the killings and only one person reported knowing anything of Castro's way of living.

*Alcohol, Drugs, or Both*    There has always been a high correlation between drug and alcohol use and domestic violence.[28] This does not mean that the use of intoxicants causes the violence. Nor does it mean that the majority of persons who use drugs and alcohol engage in violence; clearly, they do not. Rather, these substances are best seen as accompaniments, the chronic use of which coincides with a number of symptoms such as depressive behavior and suicidal ideations. According to the archival data, drug and alcohol use is present during or immediately prior to one-quarter of the male-perpetrated multiple homicides. However, to argue that this is anything more than an associative factor is not supported by the evidence from the case studies.

The homicide-suicide perpetrated by John Rushton is a case in point. Rushton shot and killed his common-law wife, Celia Capston, and then killed himself a day or two later. Excessive drug and alcohol use featured prominently in this case, but as an explanation for the homicide-suicide other factors eclipse it.

News reports focused on the fact that Rushton was one of a group of convicted murderers mistakenly released from Florida prisons between 1988 and 1992. Rushton seems to have been released seven years early from the West Palm Beach Community Correctional Center in November 1992. He had been in prison for fewer than seven years for the fatal stabbing of a man during a cocaine deal. Rushton, whose propensity for violence was well known, stabbed him 41 times. His master status as a violent career criminal was intimately associated with his drug use and drug dealing. It was his drug use that took center stage after police found the bodies.

Detectives entered the apartment he and Capston shared after receiving a phone call from Celia's sister saying she was concerned for Celia's safety. The sister told police Rushton had battered Celia before, on one occasion breaking her jaw. When detectives opened the front door the odor of decaying bodies was very strong. After murdering Celia, Rushton had remained in the apartment for one to two days using cocaine, marijuana, and alcohol. It was only after this binge that Rushton took his own life. The autopsy report describes how he sat at the foot of the bed, looking down at Celia's body, and killed himself with a revolver. Police found several grams of powder cocaine on a small plate, along with a three-inch straw. A half-empty quart bottle of Absolut vodka sat on a kitchen counter. In a storage compartment in the sofa detectives came upon a large stash of marijuana in a plastic bag. Another bag, containing 50.5 grams of marijuana, was discovered wrapped in aluminum foil inside the refrigerator. When interviewed by detectives, Celia's mother reported that her daughter abused drugs and alcohol. An autopsy, though, revealed no drug or alcohol use before her demise.

Other evidence points to the associative rather than causal role of drugs and alcohol in this case. As noted, Rushton had beaten Celia Capston before, breaking her jaw, an injury that required it to be wired in the hospital. Detectives found a suitcase partially packed with Capston's clothes, suggesting she was about to leave the apartment and the relationship. They also discovered other marks on her body, suggesting that Celia was beaten once more before she was killed. Other witnesses suggested that she was planning to end the relationship. The assistant manager of the apartment complex where the couple lived as husband and wife told police that Rushton approached her about three weeks before the homicide-suicide. He wanted to know how to take Celia's name off the lease and still remain in the apartment himself. The assistant manager told Rushton that Celia would have to sign off the contract. When the three got together to alter the lease agreement, Celia told the assistant manager that her jaw had been broken in a traffic accident. When Rushton left the room, Celia confided that he had broken her jaw.

Putting all these facts together, the Rushton-Capston homicide-suicide looks very much like the others, insofar as there is a history of woman battering and an attempt by the victim to get out of the relationship. It is difficult to know whether Rushton's suicide was prompted by his guilt over killing Capston or was inspired by a constellation of factors that made life not worth living. Rushton's autopsy revealed a plethora of tattoos, so commonly associated with ex-cons. One of them was a profile of a smiling panther, over the slogan Never Say Die.

*Depression and Other Psychiatric Disorders*    West's classic study of 78 English cases of murder followed by suicide showed that depression was the most prevalent psychiatric condition among the perpetrators.[29] Unlike some American studies,[30] West's investigation showed that 45 of the 78 offenders exhibited some kind of "mental abnormality": 28 endured depressive illness, 7 suffered from "severe neurotic instability," 4 had schizophrenia, 2 displayed "morbid jealousy," and another 4 were deemed to be "aggressive psychopaths." The American studies seem to reveal lower levels of so-called mental illness. Wolfgang reported only 3 out of 24 perpetrators of homicide-suicide to be "insane."[31] Ruth Cavan's classic study of suicide in Cook County, Illinois, identified only 1 perpetrator out of 18 who committed homicide-suicide to have been "insane." However, it is difficult to compare studies that use different sources of data and different operational definitions. West's "mental abnormality" is not only applied to a different culture at a different time than Cavan's, but it also appears inherently broader than her notion of insanity, which she defines as "a more or less permanent disorganized state of emotions and usually of reasoning ability."[32]

West acquired his information on mental illness from police and coroners files and took additional data from doctors, social workers, and hospitals. However, he stopped short of interviewing the family members of perpetrators and victims to become more familiar with their mental health status. In contrast, Rosenbaum spoke with family members, relatives, and friends of the deceased to learn more about their psychological state prior to the fatalities. He found marked differences in depression rates between the perpetrators of homicide-suicide and domestic homicide.[33] He observes, "In the murder-suicide group, the large majority of perpetrators . . . suffered from depression. . . . [N]one of the perpetrators in the homicide group suffered from depression."[34] In their study using coroners' files of 121 cases of homicide, Polk and Ransom find that men who committed homicide-suicide tended to be older and depressed. Those who killed women but did not subsequently take their own lives appeared to be less often depressed and, rather, consisted of jealous and violent batterers.[35]

It is not certain whether the archival sources I used—such as homicide files, autopsy reports, court documents like protection orders, newspaper accounts, and data from domestic-violence centers—would contain comprehensive information on the mental health of perpetrators and victims in cases of multiple killing. Taken as a whole, the Florida archival materials suggest that male perpetrators are not mentally deranged or suffering from some kind of verifiable mental illness or "disorganized" personality. On the contrary, they frequently plan these killings and are often quite secretive about how they manipulate their victims into compromising and unsafe situations. In some cases men are also very guarded about disclosing their feelings of rage to their lost love objects. Again, this implies that they selectively express their feelings, retaining some element of control. The simplistic notion that men who commit multiple domestic homicides "just snap" does not mesh with the fact patterns of the cases.

Among the 47 male perpetrators who killed their intimate female partners (and perhaps their children, themselves, or both), only 7 had documented emotional problems. Most of these men suffered from deep depression, all but 1 were on medications such as lithium (for manic depression) or Prozac (for depression) immediately prior to the lethal episodes, and several had received some kind of counseling or psychiatric care in the recent past. This is consistent with Rosenbaum's finding that, "[i]n cases of murder followed by suicide, the mental illness is usually depression."[36] Likewise, he found that "three of the 12 instigators of murder-suicide were in treatment (counseling) at the time of the tragedy."[37]

A Florida case in which the mental illness of the perpetrator was steeped in a more generalized depression about perceived lost love involved the murder of Francesca and Irena Spitz by their 19-year-old unemployed uncle, Robert Clinton. Clinton was infatuated with and obsessed by 11-year-old Irena, who, together with her 13-year-old sister, Francesca, lived with their grandmother, Helen Clinton, who was Robert's mother. He shot both girls to death as they played on a bed. Robert seemed clinically depressed, and he told police after the shooting, "[L]ife ain't worth living." His history of mental problems stretched back into his childhood. The family was known well among its Tampa neighbors, one of whom reported that Helen Clinton dearly loved her two granddaughters and kept a close eye on them. A second neighbor, aged 13, recalled, "Those girls were nicer than nice, just like the grandmother." On the other hand, persons in the area were also aware of Robert's mental problems. Unlike the six other male perpetrators of multiple intimate killings who had a documented history of mostly depressive disorders, Robert's mental problems were publicly visible in a variety of ways. One neighbor said he was known for his "odd behavior." Another mentioned that Robert would "mumble incoherently and at other times dance wildly in the parking lot." Apparently, he was on medication and had spent his earlier life in and out of youth homes.

*Suicide Pacts and Mercy Killing*   There is documented research on the resemblance between offenders who commit homicide-suicide and elderly white men who take their own lives out of loneliness, widowerhood, depression, poor health, or despair.[38] Researchers have often assumed that suicide pacts indicate intimacy and therefore preclude a history of woman battering, morbid jealousy, threats to kill someone maliciously, and a history of agency intervention involving such things as visits to the residence by law enforcement officers or protection orders filed on behalf of women.[39] However, the hallmark of gender role prescriptions is still evident in these "suicide pact killings." Both of the alleged mercy killings in the Florida sample of cases were committed by men. The parties appear to have signed a letter to their children indicating they had jointly planned the killing. None of the multiagency archival materials suggest any history of domestic violence.[40] However, one cannot be too careful in assessing the etiology of these cases. As Cupitt notes, elder abuse is one of the last forms of family violence to reach the public eye.[41] This being the case, a history of domestic violence between partners who eventually die through a suicide pact might be difficult to identify. Indeed, the gerontologist Donna Cohen finds that homicide-suicides involving elderly women in west central Florida doubled between 1988 and 1994. In all, such killings made up 20 percent of the total homicides of persons older than 55.[42] Cohen also observes that although the health of half of the women had deteriorated, two-thirds had expressed "no desire to die."[43] Evidence that women communicated a desire not to die is somewhat inconsistent with an interpretation that they freely entered into suicide pacts. If they did not enter freely into such pacts then it is possible, if not likely, that they were murdered. Given that most murder-suicides are preceded by woman battering, it is not unreasonable to infer that these murdered women were battered at some point before their deaths.

The homicide-suicide involving Rex and Celia Williams is typical of "clear-cut" cases of mercy killing, where there is little doubt as to the motives behind the homicide. Celia Williams, a white woman aged 84, lived in a Tampa nursing home. She was suffering from Alzheimer's disease. Her husband, Rex Williams, who visited her every day, took her for an outing in her wheelchair. He stopped off at his vehicle, took out his rifle, and shot her dead before killing himself. Relatives, friends, neighbors, and staff members at the nursing home described them as a loving couple. One witness characterized their relationship as "excellent." The suicide note left behind was addressed to their son. It said, among other things:

> You know we are to be cremated. . . . I hope you now have the freedom you always wanted and you will not be tied here because of us. Love, Mom and Dad.

Vivian Marshal of the Alzheimer's Association reported: "Women caregivers tend to call us early on to find out what kind of services we offer. We generally hear from men when it reaches a crisis point."[44] It is likely, too, that elderly men who become caregivers of partners who have Alzheimer's experience considerable depression. One might speculate that this was the case with Rex Williams. However, even if the file revealed his state of mind (which it does not), Rex's own health was also failing in a number of ways. Consequently, it would be impossible to know whether to attribute his depression to Celia's loss of vigor, his own deterioration, his growing sense that he could no longer care for her, or some combination of these possibilities.

Suicide pacts between two persons involve one of them, usually the man, killing the other and then himself. When such an arrangement goes awry, it may be because the male perpetrator has been victimizing his deceased partner and in fact intended to kill only her. Al Ferrell, a white man aged 74, shot his wife, Helena Ferrell, a white woman aged 65, killing her. Apparently he tried to shoot himself, but, as he told detectives later, the gun jammed. According to Al Ferrell, he and his wife had made a suicide pact. Al himself was dying of cancer. Although on the surface this case looked like a classic instance of a suicide arrangement that failed, when detectives began to question family members they uncovered a different story. According to Helena Ferrell's son Randolph, his mother was in good health and would never have agreed to a suicide pact. Although detectives found no history of domestic violence, they concluded that this was a case of murder, not a suicide pact. Before they could arrest Al Ferrell, however, he was hospitalized with complications associated with his cancer. He died several days later of a gastrointestinal hemorrhage.

*Parricide*   In the Florida domestic-homicide cases in 1994, two children killed both of their parents. Heide identifies three types of persons who kill their mothers, fathers, or both: severely abused children, severely mentally ill children, and dangerously antisocial children.[45] Of the three, it is the "severely abused child" that is most frequently encountered among those who commit parricide. According to Mones, more than 90 percent of youths who kill their parents have been abused by them.[46] Severely abused children typically endure one or more forms of physical, sexual, or emotional abuse, or else they witness some combination of these kinds of abuse within their families. Much less often, children who kill parent(s) are suffering from mental illness to the point that they qualify as psychotic. Finally, Heide notes that the dangerously antisocial child is nowadays referred to as someone with a "conduct disorder or anti-social personality disorder." These individuals do not suffer from delusions and hallucinations. Those who kill their parents for personal gain are among the ranks of such offenders.

Both of the Florida cases of parricide involve white adults. In the one I shall discuss here, Phil Gerard, aged 29, repeatedly stabbed three of his family members with a butcher knife, killing two of them. He killed his father, Matt Gerard, aged 59, by stabbing him five times, producing wounds up to seven inches deep. He killed his grandmother, Janice Green, aged 83, by stabbing her in the back and puncturing her lung. His mother, Anne Gerard, aged 64, was also stabbed as she tried to intervene, but she survived the knife attack. Police responded to the residence after neighbors reported a violent domestic dispute in progress. When the officers arrived they saw Phil attempting to pull his mother, who was covered in blood, back into the house. She had apparently run outside screaming and had alerted the neighbors. Phil jumped into his pickup, put it in reverse, and tried to run over his mother. A neighbor inter-vened and dragged her to safety. The police chased Phil; after crashing, he emerged from the truck with a bottle of whiskey in hand. His blood alcohol level was three times the legal limit for intoxication. He had also smoked crack cocaine the night before and that morning.

A month prior to the killings, Phil had been jailed on a battery charge for fighting with his father. He was released on $500 bail. The investigation also revealed that Gerard had a long history of violent behavior, suicide threats, drug and alcohol abuse, and psychiatric hospitalization. When Phil finally gave his statement to police, he alternated between denying knowledge of the inci-dent, expressing remorse, laughing, and crying before eventually confessing.

## Conclusion

Male perpetrators of multiple domestic homicides in Florida killed 47 females and 57 males. Roughly three-quarters of the victims died in homicide-suicides. Although white men figure prominently among the ranks of perpetrators, they are underrepresented compared to their presence in the population. Put differ-ently, blacks and Latinos are somewhat overrepresented among the ranks of perpetrators and victims of multiple domestic fatalities. The reason for the overrepresentation of persons from minority groups is not clear. However, I return to this issue in subsequent chapters, and I explore possible explanations in Chapter 7.

Compared with the Florida homicide statistics in general, and the single domestic homicides in the Florida sample in particular, perpetrators of homicide-suicide tended to be more secure economically. Most perpetrators of homicide-suicide came from families where one or both partners earned reasonable incomes. Unlike male perpetrators of single domestic homicides, multiple offenders tended not to have criminal histories, although a number had prior misdemeanor domestic-violence offenses on their records.

It is clear from the tables and the case study illustrations that the majority of multiple domestic homicides, and any accompanying suicides, occur in profoundly conflictual relationships. In some cases, particularly the familicides, there seem to have been additional stressors in the family so great that perpetrators may have perceived their whole world as caving in around them. A history of male violence directed at women underpins the majority of these cases and is the single most salient theme in the etiologies. The parties were often estranged, going through a separation, or considering a separation at the time of the killings. Women typically initiated the separations. Many men exhibited signs of "obsessive possessiveness" that seemed to transcend the usual possessiveness that pervades most heterosexual relationships, especially concerning the issue of perceived sexual and emotional "loyalty." Although the archival material is somewhat limited in this regard, a number of case files reveal that men threatened to kill women and others during the more intense moments prior to the fatalities.

Given that some police officers do not log their calls to domestic disputes, it is not possible to obtain a precise measure of just how many of the multiple killings were preceded by earlier police contact. As I mentioned in Chapter 1, Angela Browne cites research showing that in 85 to 90 percent of intimate-partner homicides in Detroit and Kansas City police had been called to the residence at least once during the two years before the lethal incident. The available records indicate that it is unlikely police were previously called to such a high proportion of the residences before the Florida multiple domestic fatalities. From the available information in the multiagency case files, it also does not appear that police tardiness or lack of response, or a delay or absence of emergency medical services, contributed directly to the majority of these homicides. Finally, less than a quarter of women held restraining orders against their abusers when they were killed.

# 3. Women as Perpetrators of Multiple Killings

Criminal behavior among women has always been much less common than among men, and typically less violent. Numerous studies document the close connections between female crime and the patriarchally compromised position of women in general. Chesney-Lind notes that, from 1787 to 1852, 24,960 women from Britain and Ireland were transported to Australia for such trivial offenses as petty theft and prostitution.[1] Like many other researchers, she points to the close connections between women's subordinate and disadvantaged position in a patriarchal society and offenses such as prostitution.[2] Chesney-Lind also points out that among the rigors of penal transportation were systematic rape and sexual assault by ships' officers and sailors. Her observations about transportation (which was also designed to increase the number of women in Australia) resemble those of bell hooks in her account of how female slaves experienced atrocities on their forced journeys to the New World.[3]

A number of authors have also explored more serious offenses, including those in which women kill. Citing the work of Ann Jones, Chesney-Lind observes that many of America's early female murderers were deeply compromised and oppressed indentured servants. She describes one form of killing: "Raped by calculating masters who understood that giving birth to a 'bastard' would add 1 to 2 years to a woman's term of service, these desperate women hid their pregnancies and then committed infanticide."[4] Chesney-Lind also notes that a handful also killed intimate male partners who brutalized them. Historically, women who committed infanticide and intimate-partner homicide constituted the principal group of "serious" female offenders. Such is still the case. This chapter tells the story of that small number of women in the Florida sample who decided to take the lives of their children or their intimate partners before killing themselves. Their motives, like those of their predeces-

**TABLE 3.1**

Types of female-perpetrated multiple domestic homicides

| Form of multiple killing | Familicide (attenuated) | Homicide-suicide | Other[a] | Totals |
|---|---|---|---|---|
| Number of cases | 2 | 3 | 1 | 6 |
| Male victim | 2 | 2 | 0 | 4 |
| Female victim | 4 | 4 | 1 | 9 |
| Totals | 6 | 6 | 1 | 13 |

[a]Involves the case of a woman who shot two children, one her daughter and the other her daughter's friend. Her daughter remains in a vegetative state; the daughter's friend died.

**TABLE 3.2**

Victims of female perpetrators of multiple homicides

| Victims | Female perpetrators (sex of victims) |
|---|---|
| Intimate partners | 2 (both male) |
| Family members | 5 (3 female, 2 male) |
| Love triangle antagonists | 0 |
| Suicide (i.e., perpetrators kill themselves) | 5 (all female) |
| Friends/bystanders | 1 (female) |
| Total victims | 13 (9 female, 4 male) |

sors, typically stemmed from their compromised positions as mothers and lovers in a patriarchal social order.

There are many differences between male and female perpetrators. From the absence of female-committed parricide and female-orchestrated suicide pacts, it appears that women are much less likely than men to offend in these ways. Additionally, there were no homicide-suicides involving lesbian couples, and, among the 117 victims of multiple domestic homicide, only 2 men were killed by women who then killed themselves. Table 3.1 classifies female-perpetrated familicides and homicide-suicides.

Whereas 104 victims were killed by men in multiple domestic homicides, only 13 persons lost their lives in such killings perpetrated by women, as is shown in Table 3.2. Again, it bears repeating that no woman committed familicide in the sense that she killed all of her family members, including her intimate partner or former partner, and then herself. These kinds of killings by women were, in this sense, "attenuated" familicides. It is also notable that

TABLE 3.3

Victims of male and female perpetrators of multiple homicides

| Victims | Male perpetrators (sex of victims) | Female perpetrators (sex of victims) | Totals |
|---|---|---|---|
| Intimate partners | 37 (35 female, 2 gay male) | 2 (both male)[a] | 39 |
| Family members | 19 (10 female, 9 male) | 5 (3 female, 2 male) | 24 |
| Love triangle antagonists | 6 (all male) | 0 | 6 |
| Suicide (i.e., perpetrators kill themselves) | 39 (all male) | 5 (all female) | 44 |
| Friends/bystanders | 3 (2 female, 1 male) | 1 (female) | 4 |
| Total victims | 104 (47 female, 57 male) | 13 (9 female, 4 male) | 117 |

[a]One female perpetrator was married to the intimate male partner she killed; the other woman was not married. Both female perpetrators of intimate-partner homicide were white.

women were not involved in female love triangle disputes during the commission of a multiple homicide. Moreover, they killed only 2 intimate partners during the multiple killings, significantly fewer than the 35 intimate female partners killed by men.

Table 3.3 combines the findings presented in Tables 2.2 and 3.2, allowing a comparison of the forms and numbers of male- and female-perpetrated multiple domestic killings in Florida in 1994. Taking these homicides as a whole, 39 persons died at the hands of intimate partners. Thirty-five men killed women, two gay men killed their lover or former lover, and two women killed men. Dividing the number of women killing men by the number of men killing women, in this case 2 by 35, yield a "Sex Ratio of Killing" (SROK) of 5.7 per 100 for intimate-partner homicides in multiple domestic killings. This is an extremely low figure compared with that reported in later chapters for single domestic killings; it is also extremely low compared with SROKs reported in the research literature mentioned in Chapter 1. The SROK of 5.7 indicates that multiple domestic killings in Florida in 1994 overwhelmingly have at their heart the tendency of men to kill women. Table 3.3 also reveals 19 of the 24 family members who died in multiple homicides were killed by men, and all 6 men who lost their lives during love triangle disputes were murdered by other men. Finally, and still typical of their overrepresentation, 39 men, as compared with only 5 women, committed suicide.

Table 3.4 identifies the racial or ethnic background of female perpetrators

### TABLE 3.4
Racial/ethnic background of the female perpetrator–victim dyad

| Race/ethnicity of perpetrator | Race/ethnicity of victim | Totals |
| --- | --- | --- |
| WF | WF | 5 |
| WF | WM | 3 |
| BF | BF | 1 |
| AF | WA F | 1 |
| BF | BM | 1 |
| LF | LF | 2 |
| Total | | 13 |

Code: W = White; B = Black; L = Latino; A = Asian; M = Male; F = Female

of multiple domestic homicides and their victims. Notably, 9 of the 13 victims were white. Table 3.5 combines findings from Tables 2.3 and 3.4 to show the racial or ethnic background of male and female perpetrators of multiple domestic killings.

In spite of the low numbers of deaths attributable to women, it is important to investigate the etiologies of these fatalities. Accordingly, I discuss all of the cases where women committed multiple domestic homicide.

### Homicide-Suicide: Women Killing Intimate Partners and Themselves

In Chapter 4, I examine those cases where women kill their intimate partners without taking their own lives. As I have noted, homicide-suicide differs from intimate-partner homicide insofar as in the former the killer takes on the dual role of perpetrator and victim. Homicide-suicide carried out by men usually occurs after years of abuse, normally committed by the man. Similarly, when women commit intimate-partner homicide-suicide it is usually after years of abuse at the hands of their male partner. This is accompanied by the kind of gut-wrenching depression, hopelessness, and desperation also seen in those few women who kill their children and then themselves.

Beth and Roger Colthurst moved to Florida from North Carolina just three months before she shot and killed her husband and then turned the gun on herself, taking her own life. Roger's mother, Norma Magson, informed police that Beth had been suffering from emotional and mental problems for

| TABLE 3.5 | | |
|---|---|---|
| Racial/ethnic background of the perpetrator-victim dyad in both male- and female-perpetrated multiple killings | | |
| Race/ethnicity of perpetrator | Race/ethnicity of victim | Totals |
| WM | WM | 22 |
| WM | WF | 20 |
| WM | AF | 1 |
| WM | WA F | 1 |
| WM | WA M | 1 |
| WM | LF | 1 |
| WM | LM | 2 |
| BM | BM | 11 |
| BM | BF | 11 |
| LM | LM | 20 |
| LM | BL M | 1 |
| LM | LF | 13 |
| WF | WF | 5 |
| WF | WM | 3 |
| AF | WA F | 1 |
| BF | BF | 1 |
| BF | BM | 1 |
| LF | LF | 2 |
| Total | | 117 |

Code: W = White; B = Black; L = Latino; A = Asian; M = Male; F = Female

quite some time and had been treated for them in North Carolina. Another witness, Jose Morales, who worked with Roger Colthurst, told police that he last spoke with him two days before the homicide-suicide and that "there had been no domestic quarrels between the two parties that he was aware of." As I have remarked, it is difficult to establish clearly the existence, nature, and extent of domestic violence once the perpetrator, and particularly the victim, is deceased. However, police found telltale signs at the crime scene indicating woman battering occurred just before the killings. In noting the condition of Beth's body, the detective's narrative reads, "On turning her over, it appeared that she had either been struck in her left eye or that she had sustained some type of injury to her facial area."

When investigators contacted the medical doctor who had treated Beth in North Carolina he provided them with the all-too-familiar details, including a history of woman battering (which local police were aware of) and a history of suicide attempts. Beth's sister and mother both informed police that the Colthursts had been married for 11 to 12 years and that Beth had a 16-year-old daughter by a previous marriage who now lived with Beth's sister. The two women confirmed the reports of the physician that there was an extensive history of Beth being battered by her husband. They stated that religious differences were often at the center of their disputes, as Roger was Jewish and Beth was Christian. They described him as being "very domineering and physically abusive as well as verbally and emotionally abusive toward Beth during the time they had been married." At one point she felt so threatened by her husband that she obtained a restraining order against him in North Carolina. The local police there also told investigators that they knew of the Colthursts' case and that they had responded to domestic calls at the residence on numerous occasions. On one of these, they arrested Roger for domestic assault. It was after this arrest that Beth obtained the restraining order against him in March 1994, just six months before the killings in October 1994.

Investigators also talked with Beth's psychologist, who told them she had been treated for depression and suicide attempts in the past. On one occasion, in November 1993, Beth complained to her psychologist that Roger had hit her in the face in the presence of his mother, Norma Magson. She told the psychologist that Norma had subsequently denied the assault ever took place.

The story of the Colthursts presents an etiology somewhat different from that of the cases in which women kill intimate male partners but do not commit suicide. As I will point out in Chapter 5, Beth's case resembles the female-perpetrated homicide insofar as she had long been subject to abuse. However, unlike many women in this situation, she committed suicide after she had killed her abuser. This raises the question of why someone like Beth, in her circumstances, would elect to take her own life, whereas so many other women do not. Her depression seemed fairly acute, and this perhaps contributed to her past suicide attempts and to her suicidal state. However, her level of abuse is also well documented and seems particularly high, proceeding up to the period immediately before the killings. Perhaps Beth was so deeply depressed by her oppressive circumstances that suicide seemed the only way out. Perhaps she felt the kind of entrapment that Stark and Flitcraft identify at the heart of much female suicidality. They note specifically that "in most cases we believe battered women are provoked to attempt suicide by the extent of control exercised over their lives."[5]

As noted, police officers found that Beth had been assaulted by Roger just prior to the homicide-suicide. According to Stark and Flitcraft, this proximity between woman battering and women's suicide attempts, in general, strongly suggests that battering may be one of the principal causes of the suicide attempts. It could be that acute or deep depression is the manifested response to battering that somehow translated, in Beth's case among others, into suicidal behavior. Stark and Flitcraft point out that a number of studies show abuse as a factor in as much as 44 percent of all female suicide attempts.[6] However, researchers have tended to focus on the general psychological characteristics of women that seem to predispose them to commit suicide. Stark and Flitcraft comment, "Rather than explore the role this fear, 'friction,' and 'acute conflict' might have played in suicidality, however, researchers traced these complaints to personality problems such as 'general hostility,' 'depression,' or 'rigid personality.'"[7]

For these two investigators,[8] it is very telling that over a third of the battered women in their sample "visited the hospital with an abuse-related injury or complaint on the same day as their suicide attempt."[9] Indeed, they go on to point out that Durkheim identified "fatalistic suicide" that arises from "excessive regulation" where futures were "pitilessly blocked," passions "violently choked," and "physical and moral despotism" held sway.[10] Stark and Flitcraft liken fatalistic suicide to the self-killing found in relationships where battered women experience "entrapment."

Alternatively, there could have been things in Beth's life besides her abusive past that contributed to her suicidal thinking and eventual final act. Whatever the reasons for her taking her own life, one can situate Beth among a minority of female perpetrators of domestic homicide, and indeed intimate killers in general, who end up killing themselves.

Penny Piper, a 37-year-old white woman, shot her boyfriend, Nathan Richie, a 27-year-old white man, in the back of the head, killing him, before committing suicide by shooting herself in the mouth. As a result of the autopsy findings, investigators deduced that Penny shot Nathan as he was getting out of a truck they owned jointly; about 10 seconds later, she shot herself. Penny used her own gun for both shootings. According to her parents, she had owned the weapon for a long time. A coworker at the Waffle House restaurant where Penny had been employed up until three weeks before her death told police that she "kept the gun hidden from Nathan because he went to bars a lot and got into fights, and she didn't want him to have the gun because of that." The coworker did not say that Penny feared Nathan might use the gun against her. It seems from the record that both of them were alcoholics. When police went to Penny's trailer after her autopsy they found the garbage can in the yard full of empty beer cans. They also found marijuana on a tray inside the trailer. One of Nathan's friends told police, "He was just a good dude who liked to drink beer and play pool on his off days." Nathan's own brother and stepbrother told police the couple were alcoholics and always had "domestic problems." On the night before the homicide-suicide Nathan was out drinking until 2:30 A.M. Rather than return home to the trailer he shared with Penny, Nathan spent the night at a friend's house.

There is little information on the precise details of the domestic turmoil between Penny and Nathan. It is known, however, that they split up approximately three weeks before the shooting, after having been together for about a year. They got back together again after a few days. According to witnesses, the couple argued two nights before the shooting and Nathan slept on the couch at the trailer. Janis Kipling, another coworker at the Waffle House, told police that Nathan called her about a month before the homicide-suicide and asked her to check on Penny at the trailer because she was suicidal. Apparently, he also called the manager of the trailer park at the same time for the same reason. Janis Kipling went out to the trailer and knocked for roughly 20 minutes, eventually rousing Penny. Janis told police that when she came to the door Penny was "very depressed." Janis asked if she was contemplating suicide and Penny replied that she was not. At that time she also reported Penny telling her that she really loved Nathan. When asked whether Penny confided in her that he had been battering her, Janis replied no. Claudette Parker, a third Waffle House employee, told police that Penny had been planning to kill Nathan for six months. They could not confirm this allegation with any other witness.

Police interviews with Penny's parents reveal that her two sons left her to live with their grandparents "years ago because Penny's boyfriends always came first." This may have been a euphemism indicating that Penny was a prostitute. She had been arrested during the early 1980s for prostitution, loitering, commercial sex, and grand larceny. Nathan's niece told police that Penny was obsessed with Nathan. She commented, "He [Nathan] told me she [Penny] kept calling his ex-wife . . . making sure he wasn't over there."

It is always difficult to know for certain whether woman battering occurred in cases such as the homicide-suicide involving Penny Piper and Nathan Richie. Penny had lived a hard life. She was alcoholic, separated from her children, and it seems likely that she was a prostitute, at least for a while. Penny was also sufficiently aware of Nathan's violent tendencies to conceal from him the fact that she owned a gun. One coworker said, "All we know is she worked with us and was a very nice person." Research on women who live at society's margins, as Penny seems to have done, suggests they endure enormous amounts of brutalization at the hands of men.[11] She appears to have escaped at least some of these hardships, but was nevertheless left an alcoholic. Given that many women are driven to prostitution to escape violence and abuse in their lives, one might expect Penny's past to have borne the hallmarks of men's violence. None of these possibilities are inconsistent with the fact that she may have had an all-encompassing desire to hold on to Nathan, that she may have planned to kill him with her own gun, and that indeed she was obsessed with him in a manner that resembles the way many men who commit multiple intimate-partner homicides are obsessed with the women they kill. All of these possibilities provide a context for understanding her crime. When men commit intimate-partner homicide-suicide, it is usually after they have abused the women they kill for a long time. There is no evidence that Penny abused Nathan in such a manner.

## Attenuated Familicides

Three women took the lives of five children in homicide-suicides, and one woman killed one of her children's friends before trying to commit suicide. Each case warrants attention. The following narration helps to unravel some of these difficulties in the lives of these women.

In October 1994, Maria Stone, a 35-year-old white Latino mother, shot her 12-year-old daughter, Emily Stone, in the head, killing her. She then shot herself dead. Maria, her 14-year-old son, Mario, and Emily lived in the Little Havana district of Miami. They shared a two-bedroom apartment with another family. The Stones slept in one bedroom and the second family slept in the other. Members of this family were in the apartment at the time of the killing. According to the police report, Emily was in their bedroom and found a gun in a gun box under the bed. She called her aunt, who lived nearby, so that they could question Maria about who owned the gun. According to the aunt, Maria asked Emily to give her a hug. The aunt then left the room to call for help. She heard the gunshots at that moment.

The Stones' neighborhood consists of low-income multifamily buildings, mostly housing Latinos from Central and South America. Spanish is the dominant language, and the residents live in very close proximity to each other. Maria and her husband, Alberto, divorced in 1990. He lived about a block away, also in Little Havana.

Maria was suffering from clinically diagnosed depression before the homicide-suicide. She had become disabled and lost her job as a result of being rear-ended in a motor vehicle accident. According to witnesses, including her former husband, she was very depressed about the breakup of her marriage and the ensuing divorce. On the day of the killings Alberto was due to pick up their two children to take them to Nicaragua for roughly three months. According to witnesses, the pending trip was also depressing Maria. She had threatened suicide on a number of occasions, and one of her relatives took her to a mental health facility for treatment. There she was prescribed an antidepressant, Zolof, in combination with tranquilizers to help her sleep. Just after the homicide-suicide, investigators found medications belonging to Maria, including Zolof, Prozac, Benadryl, and Trazodone. Without full access to her medical history, little can be known of the way in which she followed her treatment regimen. However, the files do reveal that she stopped attending outpatient counseling and failed to attend treatment scheduled in August 1994.

The day before the homicide-suicide, Maria invited her former husband over to stay the night. When police interviewed Alberto he told them Maria was "desperately trying to convince him to spend the night." According to the police file, "It appears the offender may have been attempting to kill the ex-husband and children before taking her own life." Had this been Maria's intention, it would have been rather unusual. As Daly and Wilson note, "[W]omen who resolve to die and to take their loved ones with them seem never to include their husbands in their 'rescue fantasies.' The husbands are more likely to be part of the problem that the women are trying to rescue themselves and their children from."[12]

The nature of the relationship between Maria and Alberto is uncertain. Clearly, they lived near each other, and both had contact with the children.

She was known to be depressed about the divorce, although it is not clear what aspect of the relationship or the divorce concerned her. There are indications from Maria's autopsy report that she suffered a number of injuries either during or a while before the homicide-suicide. The report reads, in part: "Lateral to the left nipple are irregular punctuate abrasions surrounded by a bruise. Medial to the left nipple are irregular stippled abrasions surrounded by a bruise. On the left upper chest above the left breast is an irregular bruise. On the posterior aspect of her left forearm is a 2.2 × 1 centimeter abrasion surrounded by a bruise. On the left elbow are two irregular abrasions." It is impossible to tell how she got these injuries. However, it cannot be ruled out that Maria may have been subjected to some form of violence, possibly by her former husband.

The research on mothers who kill their children and then themselves is instructive here. In Cavan's analysis of 39 women who committed these acts, she observes that they killed the children out of "perceived altruism." In discussing cases that are very similar to those of Maria Stone and the other Florida women who killed multiple younger children, Cavan remarks, "These mothers apparently did not as yet regard their infant children as separate personalities with an independent right to life, but really as part of themselves, sharing their troubles and to be taken on with them into death."[13] West's study also throws light upon the Stone homicide-suicide.[14] In his view, mothers who killed their children and then themselves had their own suicide uppermost in their minds. Most of the women in West's sample did not maltreat their children or act in a hostile or aggressive manner toward them. Rather, the mother sought to rescue the children from being raised by someone else after her suicide.

The simultaneity of the killing of the mother and the child perhaps reflects the coalescence, in the mother's mind, of their two personalities. That Maria Stone killed Emily and then immediately shot herself suggests that guilt had little time to accumulate and that the double killing is more akin, putting it rather crudely, to an extension of the mother's suicide.

There is a similar set of circumstances in the two other Florida homicide-suicides in which mothers kill children and then themselves. Susie Rock, a 27-year-old Caucasian, shot all three of her children in the head as they slept in their bedrooms in the family home. Like Maria Stone, Susie Rock was a clinically depressed single parent; she had threatened to kill herself and her children several times before doing so. Susie had attempted suicide three years earlier, and as a teenager she had taken an overdose of pills when her parents divorced. Her brother informed police that her depression had worsened because of a recent weight gain, attributed to medication for chronic depression. In another Catch-22, Susie's depression grew deeper after family members said they would seek custody of her children because of her threats to kill them. As in the case of Maria Stone, witnesses reported that Susie loved her children. They attended the school at All Souls Catholic Church. The principal there, Amelia Mindham, was quoted as saying, "Susie loved her children and would have done anything for them." She speculated, "Susie believed in an afterlife and . . . perhaps she believed sending them to God was best for them."

Among the Florida multiple killings, there was only one African-American woman out of the six female perpetrators. Jackie Favor, aged 33, shot and killed her 10-year-old son, John Favor, while he slept in bed. She then shot herself in the head. Jackie lived in a house owned by her mother, Myra Hinckley, 53, who also lived there. As the literature reveals, this kind of living arrangement is not uncommon in the black community, with mothers and other female relatives offering a support network for their daughters and grandchildren. Jackie had a number of health problems stemming from an operation she had in 1989 to remove a brain tumor. At that time she received radiation treatment, and her physician later told police that the tumor was completely removed. The autopsy report confirmed the physician's interpretation. However, Jackie still suffered motor problems and at times lost her balance. She also reported experiencing tremendous physical pain in the years following the surgery. On many occasions she told her mother that she wanted to take her own life. Indeed, the night of the killing she and her mother sat up until 1:00 A.M. talking about her desire to commit suicide. Myra told police that Jackie said if she did commit suicide she would "take John with her" so that her mother would not have to take care of him. Whether this was because Jackie felt her mother could not cope with John remains unclear. The files do show that paramedics came to the residence in 1991 after Jackie called them saying her mother had passed out and was unresponsive. She was concerned then that her mother had taken some kind of medication, and she told the paramedics that her mother had "family troubles."

Jackie's act of homicide-suicide fits the classic pattern for women. The only characteristic that distinguishes it from the Stone and Rock cases is that Jackie Favor was living with her mother. None of the three women abused their children prior to the killing, and their reasons for shooting them are, arguably, altruistic. West recognizes the altruistic elements in the killing of children by their mothers, although he sees them as part of delusional thought processes:

"[In] the majority of the killings by melancholics, and especially in the cases of sacrifices of children by depressed mothers, manifestly hostile motives towards the victims were conspicuously absent, and the incidents conformed more or less closely to the pattern of deluded altruism."[15]

The last case relevant to this discussion is that of Nancy James, an Asian mother, aged 39, who almost killed her 5-year-old daughter, Amy James, and did kill one of Amy's friends, 8-year-old Justine Portal. She then attempted suicide, failing because her husband wrestled the gun away from her. Although strictly speaking not a multiple homicide, this case fits closely enough into the pattern of the others to warrant inclusion. One of the investigating detectives commented that if Nancy's husband had not intervened she would have killed three people, if not four.[16] Reports of the incident reveal that Nancy shot Justine as she slept with Nancy's own two children on a waterbed. Statements she made at the time told witnesses that Nancy believed she had shot her own children, not Justine Portal. Her older daughter, Rene James, aged 8, awoke to find her sister and her friend covered in blood. Rene called out for her father, Ron James, who entered the room and wrestled the rifle away from his wife. He later told police that Nancy kept saying to him "just shoot me, just shoot me."

As in the Stone, Rock, and Favor cases, all of which involved mothers killing their daughters or sons and then themselves, Nancy James was clinically depressed. Apparently she had also been suffering from anxiety and a sleep disorder. Two different doctors had prescribed her Zolof (an antidepressant), Navane (a major tranquilizer, generic name thiothixene), Amoxil, and Trazodone (another antidepressant). Just 10 days before the shooting, Nancy James had been discharged from a mental health facility. Ron James had taken her there after she had repeatedly said she wanted to commit suicide.

Her next-door neighbor Mrs. Reeves reported that Nancy was from the Philippines and that she would cook Philippine dishes and share them with her and with other neighbors. Mrs. Reeves added that she thought Nancy was a good mother and that her children "were extremely well mannered and always well kept." Apparently Mrs. Reeves's children played with Amy and Rene James all the time and Mrs. Reeves was never concerned for her own children's safety. Her son, Billy, aged 11, had known Nancy James all his life and concurred with his mother's impressions. However, he did say that in the 10 days since her release from the mental health facility Nancy had been shouting at the children. He also reported that she offered to teach him how to shoot a rifle, before quickly withdrawing the offer. Billy said that this behavior seemed unusual, given that Nancy had never shown any interest in the firearm. She had also told Billy that she had suffered from a constant headache for the year preceding the attenuated familicide and that she had a hard time sleeping.

Nancy was also worried because her husband, Ron, had recently lost his job. One of her friends, Zoe Black, reported that her physical appearance had deteriorated in the six weeks or so leading up to the killing. Apparently Zoe and her husband were going to attend an Amway seminar along with Ron and Nancy, and the two couples were working together to get tickets. The Blacks later told police that the Jameses did not attend the seminar. Zoe Black revealed to investigators that in the month preceding the killing Nancy had wrecked the family car. As a result, Ron apparently "got mad at her and she emotionally fell apart." On the Friday night after Nancy came out of the mental health facility, the Blacks had the Jameses over to their house. Nancy still looked wiped out. Zoe told police that when it came time for Nancy to leave, she "clung on to [me] and cried like a baby."

Given that it is difficult for many women to reveal that they have been abused, and given that this may especially be the case for Asian women, nonetheless there is again trace evidence that Ron James may have been at least emotionally abusive to his wife of 10 years. It could have been that their family situation worsened because he lost his job. Informants at the police department and the prosecutors office that I spoke with about this case told me that they thought Ron James's unemployment was a very significant stressor. These comments are again in tune with Ewing's observations that familicides usually involve more than the endpoint explosion in an increasingly abusive relationship, if indeed systematic abuse is present in the relationship at all.

## Conclusion

The low number of cases in which women committed multiple domestic homicides makes it difficult to draw firm conclusions. However, it is the low number of such offenses that is perhaps most striking. The SROK for intimate-partner killings during multiple domestic homicides was a very low 5.7, further evidence of the underrepresentation of women among the ranks of perpetrators of these crimes. Only five women committed multiple domestic homicide, with one attempting to kill what she perceived to be her children but killing one of their friends instead. Another glaring point of difference from the same crime as committed by men is motive. In Florida in 1994, women who killed children all appeared to exhibit great love and concern for them prior to the lethal episode. In this sense, one might even use the term "mercy killing." Murdering their own sons and daughters and then taking, or attempting to take, their own lives was not the endpoint in a series of abusive episodes in which these women directed violence at their loved ones. Unlike their male counterparts, female perpetrators did not use violence as a final expression of power and control. The more psychiatrically oriented literature might describe the behavior of these women as a kind of "delusional altruism." It might be more appropriate, however, to talk of the real choices available to profoundly depressed mothers in a patriarchal society that prescribes and demands certain levels of feminine caring and nurturing, but provides little material support to assist in their day-to-day delivery.

Looked at in this way, women who killed their children during attenuated familicides may be seen as engaging in perfectly rational behavior, given their perceptions of their social calling in a patriarchal society. Too distraught, depressed, and impoverished to meet the demands of "caring sufficiently," a small number of women take what seems to them the only rational way out. Rather than labeling the homicidal behavior of such women as "delusional," society would do well to explore how women who kill their children perceive their plight and their options, duties, and responsibilities. Only by socially situating women's choices and horizons will it begin to be understood how a small number come to see killing their children as the only recourse.

# 4. The Death of Women in Single Killings

Earlier chapters have shown how the etiology of male-perpetrated domestic homicide differs from that of such crimes when perpetrated by women. Not only do men from all racial and ethnic groups kill their intimate partners and family members more often than do women, but they also kill for different reasons. In this chapter I explore the deaths of 78 Florida women in single incidents of intimate-partner homicide and family homicide.[1] As Table 4.1 reveals, 67 women died at the hands of an intimate male partner and 11 were killed by a family member. Only 2 women were killed by other women, and in each instance these deaths stemmed from family disputes: in one case a daughter killed her mother; in the other a woman was murdered by her sister, with whom she had a long-standing dispute. No woman was killed by a female love triangle antagonist, there were no intimate-partner homicides among lesbian couples, and no women died during domestic stand-offs with police. Additionally, not one woman precipitated her own demise at the hands of a man through her own use of aggressive violence.[2]

Of the 67 women killed by intimate partners, 30 were married to the perpetrators at the time of their demise, although they were not necessarily living with them. The remaining 37 women were killed by men they were not married to. Table 4.2 examines the marital status and racial or ethnic background of the women killed by their intimate partners. Like most such homicides, the killings within families were intraracial or intra-ethnic events. Among the family homicides, four whites killed other family members, as did three African Americans and three Latinos (see Table 4.4). In the remaining family homicide the racial or ethnic background of the parties is unknown.

Slightly more male-perpetrated intimate-partner homicides involved unmarried as opposed to married couples. However, as Table 4.2 shows, this effect differs by race or ethnicity. More white perpetrator-victim dyads were married than unmarried (15 to 12). For Latinos the numbers are similar (5 mar-

## TABLE 4.1

Breakdown of women killed

| Adult female victim's relationship to perpetrator | Male perpetrator | Female perpetrator | Totals |
| --- | --- | --- | --- |
| Intimate partner | 67 | 0 | 67 |
| Family member | 9 | 2 | 11 |
| Love triangle antagonist | 0 | 0 | 0 |
| Police domestic shooting | 0 | 0 | 0 |
| Friend/bystander | 0 | 0 | 0 |
| Total adult female victims | 76 | 2 | 78 |

## TABLE 4.2

Breakdown of intimate-partner killing with one female victim

| Race/ethnicity of perpetrator | Race/ethnicity of victim | Partners married | Partners unmarried | Totals |
| --- | --- | --- | --- | --- |
| WM | WF | 15 | 12 | 27 |
| BM | BF | 9 | 18 | 27 |
| BL M | LF | 0 | 1 | 1 |
| LM | LF | 5 | 3 | 8 |
| LM | WF | 0 | 2 | 2 |
| Un | Un | 1 | 1 | 2 |
| Totals | | 30 | 37 | 67 |

Code: W = White; B = Black; L = Latino; M = Male; F = Female; Un = unknown

ried, 4 unmarried). However, for blacks only one-third of the partners were married (9 out of 27).

## The Microdynamics of Men Killing Their Intimate Female Partners

When men kill their wives or female lovers they usually do so in a very stylized manner. The killing is often the terminal event in a battering relationship of variable duration. In many ways men's lethal violence is the final assertion of their power and control over women and, paradoxically, an acknowledgment of their loss of control. The 67 Florida women who died in 1994 in individual intimate-partner homicides usually experienced increasingly violent victimization. At the same time, such escalating abuse seems to have changed the way these women devised strategies for coping, heightened their sensitivity to violence, and led them to engage in new acts of resistance. A high proportion of the perpetrators exhibited an obsessive possessiveness and morbid jealousy about the ways in which their partners were moving away from them. Some men, many more than will ever be known from archival research, explicitly threatened to kill their partners. Often they communicated these threats to family members, friends, neighbors, and others. In several cases, police had extensive prior contact with the intimate partners, often responding to domestic violence calls, sometimes making arrests. As active agents in their own lives, women adopted new strategies of resistance and turned again to old ones. Some moved their social lives in a different direction, seeking out new friends, and sometimes finding new partners. Others sought any combination of new work, new residences, protective orders, further education, and help from agencies such as domestic-violence shelters to protect themselves, their children, or both from increasing danger. Just as in the cases where men killed women in familicides and homicide-suicides, they sometimes were acutely threatened by women's new maneuvers. Some men perceived women's adjustments to violence as flagrant forms of betrayal. Such perceived betrayal stirred deep emotions in batterers, who reacted by further escalating their violent tactics. Among all these socially situated themes one finds the presence of drugs and alcohol as an important correlate of lethal violence. There is also the factor of easy access to and facility with weaponry, especially firearms, an observation not unrelated to the fact that over two-fifths of perpetrators had criminal histories.

Although remaining cognizant of the essential connectedness of the themes evident in case files, in what follows I tease them apart and bring them to life through case histories. As I mentioned in Chapter 2, such a breakdown may make these themes seem something less than integral parts of what is essentially an abusive relationship. This is not my intent. Rather, I hope to show through the cases that the themes cannot be studied in isolation. Some cases illustrate some themes better than others. For various reasons, some files contain records about the jealous tendencies of abusers whereas others do not. Some police agencies and individual officers record more of the dynamics of battering relationships than do others. Some agencies focus on the minutiae of the killing—describing where the victim's body was found, the room it was found in, the overall scene, the chain of custody of the evidence, and so on—without commenting very much on the difficulties in the relationship or noting what neighbors might have said about patterns of abuse or earlier threats to kill. The essential point is that most killings shared at least some of the

## TABLE 4.3

Characteristics of the 67 relationships ending in the killing of intimate female partners

| Characteristic | No. Cases | % of 67 |
|---|---|---|
| Prior history of woman battering | 58 | 86.6 |
| Parties estranged, separated, or in process of separating | 39 | 58.2 |
| Male perpetrator displays obsessive possessiveness or morbid jealousy about victim | 34 | 50.7 |
| Prior police contact with parties regarding domestic violence | 34 | 50.7 |
| Male perpetrator makes threats to kill victim prior to doing so | 32 | 47.8 |
| Perpetrator has prior criminal history[a] | 29 | 43.3 |
| Drug and/or alcohol consumption by perpetrator preceding fatality | 28 | 41.8 |
| Victim obtained restraining order(s) against male perpetrator at some point prior to killing | 19 | 28.4 |

[a]Wolfgang (1958a: 177) finds that roughly 70 percent of U.S. homicide offenders had been arrested in the past. The finding of 43 percent in the Florida sample is consistent with studies of U.S. homicide offenders that show about half of them to have prior convictions for criminal offenses (see Kleck and Bordua, 1983: 293).

themes that the following subheadings address. In some cases the files are able to inform us accurately whether the perpetrator had a prior criminal history or whether the victim had at some time possessed a protective order. However, the presence of other themes is more elusive. Some files contain no evidence of a history of woman battering, but it would be foolhardy to conclude that no such violence took place. Likewise, other case files may not be able to tell us whether the perpetrator threatened the victim's life prior to the fatality. Again, it would be wrong to conclude that such threats were absent if they are not discernible in the case files. Rather, one is left with the possibility that the perpetrator still knows whether such threats were made, and that the victim may have taken this and other information to her grave. Table 4.3 summarizes, as far as is possible, the presence of these leading themes in the killings of the 67 women in Florida.

*Woman Battering* As Table 4.3 indicates, 86.6 percent of women killed by their intimate male partners experienced violent victimization at the hands of those men before their deaths. This is an underestimate of the extent of prior violent victimization because not all the archival files address whether earlier battering occurred. These findings make a history of woman battering the most significant correlate of intimate-partner homicide.

Using multiple archival sources provides a series of snapshots of prior domestic violence. It is not always possible to discern from these serial snapshots an escalating pattern of battering that culminates in death. Insofar as all the sublethal violence ended in lethal violence, one might say that the victimization "progressed" toward death. However, given the archival material available, it is not appropriate to argue that the sublethal violence, in and of itself, "progresses" or "escalates." Although this kind of movement seems logical, it is often a stretch of the archival materials to interpret them as providing evidence of such a progression or culmination. It may be tempting to impute escalation and read the files and incidents of abuse as increasingly threatening, violent, and controlling. However, such a reading is teleological and clearly influenced by the fact that a particular series of abusive incidents or episodes ended in death. Without detailed observations from entrapped women about how they perceived and responded to the controlling maneuvers of their abusers, all that is left is a piecemeal reconstruction of the deaths. Notwithstanding the usefulness and power of such reconstructions, they nevertheless signal the epistemological limitations of the archival material. The work of other researchers is helpful here in alluding to the other characteristics of intimate-partner homicides that present a more subjective sense of entrapment. Stark and Flitcraft perceptively note that,

> [d]espite the dramatic nature of physical assault, the single most important risk factor for gendered homicide is the level of entrapment established when physical domination through beatings and sexual assault (rape) is supported by intimidation, isolation, and control over money, food, sex, work, and access to family and friends.[3]

The following case illustrates the role of prior woman battering as an antecedent to domestic homicide. Alfredo Sanchez had just begun working as a driver for his brother Hector's medical transportation business. Alfredo and his wife, Daria, both from the Dominican Republic, had lived in Miami for four years. Hector told police that Alfredo called him, saying, "I just killed my wife." He asked his brother if he was joking. "I am serious," Alfredo replied, and then went on to tell him, "My son is your son. Keep working hard like you have."

Hector left immediately and took eight or nine minutes to reach the trailer park where his brother lived with Daria. Several neighbors, most of them Cuban males whom Hector recognized, had gathered around the trailer. Alfredo apparently allowed one of these men, Pascual Lima, inside and said to him, "Come into the bathroom and look; I killed her. Don't touch her." As Hector arrived he saw his brother leave in his car. He entered the trailer and found Daria's body partially in the bathtub. At that time fire-rescue personnel arrived and took her to the hospital.

Pascual Lima told investigators that he had heard several domestic disturbances at the trailer. Daria had apparently remarked to Pascual that her husband abused her. Alfredo told police that he removed their two-year-old son from the trailer before killing his wife because "he knew what he was going to do." According to Alfredo, she had been "emotionally cold" toward him for a long time; when he would come home from work and sit down in a chair, Daria would make sure she sat down in a different location. He also told officers that "it got to the point where we would only have sexual relations once a month." On the day of the killing, Alfredo said to investigators, he returned home around 7:00 P.M. and asked Daria if they could work out their problems. She apparently laughed at him and told him no. It was then that he removed his son from the trailer. He returned to kill his wife by drowning her in a bathtub full of water. During their struggle the only words Alfredo remembered Daria saying were "think of the kid." Apparently, he had already "thought of the kid," as demonstrated by his later-stated wish that his brother assume guardianship. According to Alfredo, he was so furious with Daria that he could not speak to her while killing her.

As police began to interview female witnesses, stories of an escalating and more menacing form of domestic tyranny began to emerge. Matilde Romero told investigators she had lived across the street from the Sanchez residence for nearly a year and had become friends with Daria. She confided in Matilde that she and Alfredo had ongoing marital problems. The police had been called to their trailer once before for what Daria described as a battering incident. Matilde told officers that within the last two months the disputes had become increasingly violent. The day before the killing, Daria told Matilde that Alfredo had raped her. Additionally, she confided in Matilde her fear that Alfredo "would one day kill her." According to Matilde's statement, Alfredo had forbidden Daria to have any friends of her own. Toward the end, she talked to Matilde every day to share just how vulnerable she was becoming.

The patrilocal pattern of her family network, a common characteristic of Latino cultures, made it more difficult for Daria to break away entirely from Alfredo. She told Matilde that his mother was "very angry with her for having called the police on her son." Apparently her mother-in-law came to Daria's trailer and threatened her because she had called the police. Matilde also told officers that she herself had been threatened by Alfredo's mother because she had "interfered with Daria's marital problems." Matilde remarked to investigators that Daria was planning to leave Alfredo within the next couple of days and intended to take their son with her. Apparently Daria was deciding on a way to seek refuge at a shelter for battered women. Matilde also informed officers that she saw Alfredo's grandfather leave Daria's trailer about 50 minutes before the police arrived. Matilde accurately described this man and said he was carrying a brown briefcase out of the trailer. She believed it to be the one Daria had shown her three months before the killings. Daria had said the briefcase contained important documents, including birth certificates, passports, marriage papers, and others related to property and ownership. Matilde told investigators the grandfather returned to the trailer carrying the briefcase. When confronted with these allegations by police the grandfather denied them. However, Matilde was adamant that when the grandfather left Daria and Alfredo's residence the trailer was dark and that Daria had not yet returned home. Her observations, if accurate, point to the possibility that Alfredo's parents and grandfather had somehow conspired to make it more difficult for Daria to get out of the relationship.

*Obsessive Possessiveness and Morbid Jealousy*  From the available evidence, just over half of the men who killed their present or former intimate female partners were obsessively possessive toward them. Such a finding is entirely consistent with the research literature. Indeed, Daly and Wilson cite "male sexual proprietariness" as being at the root of most spousal homicides.[4] This factor was present in the Sanchez case, although I made no more than passing reference to it. Many witnesses, both male and female, spoke of how Alfredo was overly possessive of Daria. However, the centrality of this theme in intimate-partner killing is best seen through two other Florida cases. As I will point out, the case files tend to present this obsessive possessiveness in different ways. Sometimes extreme jealousy seems to emerge spontaneously and explosively out of an ostensibly innocuous incident, the end result being homicide. In other cases, the jealousy appears to build gradually and find expression in what seems to be a less volatile manner. The morbid jealousy is often focused on one particular act that the perpetrator perceives as a pivotally important signifier of rejection. At other times, the obsessive possessiveness looks to be more generalized and diffuse and is directed at an overall pattern of behavior by women that men see as threatening. However, these apparent differences in how jealousy is expressed are as likely to stem from the way the case files document behavior as they are from the actual differential expression of jealousy among abusers. It is likely that the case files, comprehensive as they are, do not capture the entire range of jealous episodes and eruptions. It is also clear, though, that men differ in the intensity of their jealous rage and in how they deal with feelings of deep envy and perceived threats to their emotional security and social status.

Oscar Tejeda, a black Cuban man in his mid-forties, shot and killed Clarinda Garcia, a white Latino woman in her early thirties, in a fit of jealous rage. Oscar had come to the United States in 1980 during the Mariel Boatlift.[5] The fatality occurred in the Miami Motel. The doctor who was called to the scene noted that Clarinda had bruises around both eyes, three bite marks on her upper torso, a large amount of blood under her head, and blood trickling from her left ear. He concluded she had been shot in the head. There were numerous cigarette butts around the room. The motel clerk remembered selling Oscar Tejeda a pack of Marlboros before the killing. The two men conversed in Spanish, and Oscar told him he would be leaving the motel in 15 or 20 minutes. A maid overheard the conversation between Oscar and Clarinda in the minutes before the killing. Clarinda, speaking in Spanish, was apparently crying. The maid reported that she said, "Papi, I swear to you that it was not me, ask Anton that it was not me. I was not there."

Clarinda's sister identified Oscar from photographs police showed her. She told them that he was the man who hit her sister over the head with a gun a couple of weeks earlier. Clarinda's former boyfriend of five years, Anton Torres, informed officers he last saw her two days before the murder. He said that the two of them had talked of getting back together. Oscar, having fled the crime scene, was nowhere to be found. Detectives checked bars and other known haunts but came up empty. One of Anton's neighbors mentioned to him that Oscar had been peering through Anton's apartment window in the early morning hours two days after the killing and that Oscar was carrying a handgun. One detective contacted a female informant who said that Davide Eusebio perhaps could tell police where Oscar had fled to. Eusebio called the detective and suggested he might be able to help locate Oscar. He told him that after the killing Oscar was holed-up in a bar called La Hacienda and that he was given some money by a friend, Frank Camacho, so he could leave Miami. Eusebio offered to help police, but only if they could do something about his outstanding arrest warrant for possession of narcotics. The detective reportedly told Eusebio he would see what he could do but that Eusebio would have to deal with the state's attorney's office and a judge to get the narcotics violation "resolved." Another informant let detectives know that Frank Camacho, the man who had apparently supplied Oscar with money to aid his getaway, was playing dominoes at La Hacienda. Detectives interviewed Camacho, who reported that Oscar had confessed to killing Clarinda. After giving him money to escape, Camacho drove Oscar to the Greyhound station in Hollywood, Florida. Through the informant grapevine, investigators learned Oscar had traveled by bus to New York City. Given Camacho's statement and a latent fingerprint of Oscar's that they lifted from a beer bottle at the crime scene, the assistant state's attorney told police they had probable cause to obtain a warrant for Oscar's arrest.

The NYPD picked up Oscar and Miami detectives flew to New York and interviewed him. He confessed to killing Clarinda and supplied a number of missing details. Oscar said he and Clarinda had been dating for several months. They did not live together. Oscar lived on his own and Clarinda lived with her sister. Two days before the killing, he and Clarinda met at La Hacienda. He said that he told her they had not had sex for over a week and that he wanted to have sex with her. Consequently, he invited her to the Miami Motel. There, he noticed a bruise on one of Clarinda's thighs. This upset him and made him extremely jealous. His mood worsened when Clarinda refused to tell him how she suffered the bruise. Oscar went on to say that the two argued and he hit her. By his account, "they made up and had sex"; he then left to use the restroom. When he came back a few minutes later, Clarinda hurriedly and nervously put down the telephone receiver after she saw him. This again enraged Oscar, and when he challenged her about who she was talking with she replied "nobody." According to Oscar, the couple "made up" once more. They snorted some cocaine, had sex again, and then went to sleep. On the following morning, the day before the killing, Oscar said he was "beeped" early and had to go to work. When detectives asked him what kind of work, he replied he "had to make a drug run." He told the investigators he returned to the room without notice, about 30 minutes after leaving, to bring Clarinda breakfast since she had nothing to eat. There he found a Latino man sitting on the bed next to her. The man knew Oscar and told him "he did not want any trouble." The man apparently left. Oscar then told police he beat Clarinda. She tried to be "sweet to him" and "had him almost convinced" that there was nothing to the man's visit. However, Oscar could not get the other man out of his mind. Again, he beat Clarinda. Oscar remarked to one of the detectives, "You know how women are, they try to brainwash you." After the last beating Clarinda apparently pulled a gun that she kept in her purse and pointed it at Oscar. He told her to "go ahead and shoot me." She did not. Oscar then left the room to make the drug run that he originally set out to make. When he returned Clarinda reportedly told him, "You see how I love you. I could have left when you were not here." He apparently replied threateningly, "You could not have hidden from me because I would have found you anywhere and I would have run over you with my car." That night, the night before the murder, they slept together but did not have sex. On the morning of the murder, they got up, took separate showers, and then snorted some cocaine. Oscar told detectives that as he was snorting Clarinda warned him, "Keep snorting cocaine and this will soon come to an end." Her statement further enraged him, since he continued to carry the image of the other man sitting beside Clarinda on the bed. Oscar beat her again. She drew the gun on him but he took it away from her this time. Clarinda began to hug and kiss him. As he was kissing her Oscar shot her in the head.

Obsessive possessiveness also played a role in the murder of Trish Temple, a 19-year-old white woman. Trish was found dead on a Tampa sidewalk lying in a pool of blood. She was shot dead by her former boyfriend, Rod Clements, a 22-year-old white man, as she was walking home with a girlfriend from a concert. Clements then attempted suicide by shooting himself in the head. Trish had recently ended her cohabiting relationship with Clements, with whom she had an infant son.

The two met in high school in 1988 in West Virginia and dated from around 1991. They had been in Tampa for about a year. Trish herself had never become accustomed to the large city after spending most of her life in a small mountain town. Indeed, Rod kept her mostly confined to the apartment, forbidding her to go out. The relationship was violent, with ongoing battering. A police report made on March 4, 1993, regarding a battery charge against Rod contained the following comment made by Trish:

> My boyfriend and I live together at a friend's apartment. The argument has been endless for 2 days because Rod is not taking any responsibility

for his son. He can go out and party but my son has no diapers. . . . Then he approached me choking me to the point I'm unable to gasp for any air. He let go once but did it again. When I got up to move he threw me into the wicker chair. . . . He punched me in the chest and I lost it. I hit him back several times, yelling, "I'm tired of being beat!" He got worse, pulling my hair extremely hard, beating my chest and face and head. He grabbed my breasts, squeezing them and hurting them. I ran out of the house, [and] he was behind me ripping my clothes. I got in the car and went to the Women's Center and called the police.[6]

Rod was charged with battery for this violence, but the judge dismissed the case after Trish refused to testify. She told a victims advocate that she was moving back to West Virginia and was too scared to testify. Eventually she returned to Tampa. Rod beat Trish again on January 9, 1994; as a result, she moved out of her apartment to stay with Melissa Tonnies, her girlfriend. From January 28 to February 8, 1994, Rod threatened Trish over the telephone on a number of occasions, leading Melissa to file a complaint with the Tampa police. Rod's friends told police that he could not get Trish out of his mind. One of them commented to officers that Rod, on one occasion after talking with Trish, was so angry that he fired his gun into a dresser at his father's residence. Rod's messages on her answering machine attest to his obsession. A week before the killing, one of his friends told police, Rod called Trish saying something like, "I can't believe what you've done to me. I'm going to kill you." The day before the murder he said, "I love you no matter what happens, you're always gonna be mine, no matter what happens." A message Rod left on the day of the shooting, "[W]ait till you see what I've got for you tonight," implied he had already decided to kill her. He used words similar to these just before the killing. On the night of her death, when Trish was walking home from the concert she had attended, one of the friends walking with her recalled Rod approaching Trish and saying, "I have something for you, just wait." Apparently she replied, "No man, just get away from me." About six hours before the shooting he left another message: "Babe, I love you. We're gonna be together forever. I promise you. It'll be a good life." It seems that not being with Trish ate away at Rod. One friend of hers met Rod outside the concert, where he apparently said, "I saw Trish. I can't stand it." Still other witnesses attested to Rod's obsession with his former girlfriend, the mother of his son.

When asked by police what his attitude was on the day of the shooting, a coworker replied, "[T]he same as usual, he just talked about Trish."

Rod's obsessive possessiveness was generalized and diffuse rather than directed at any specific thing Trish had done that aroused his jealousy. Indeed, Trish told shelter staff in February 1993 that she had caught Rod cheating on her twice. It seems that after she became pregnant Rod began to behave differently toward her. His drug use also intensified to the point Trish felt it had "altered his mind." He had a long history of drug use, with a criminal record of drug-related offenses. Moreover, Rod had other demons, including what Trish described as a father who physically abused him, as well as a mother who committed suicide in 1987. On the night of the shooting a friend of Rod's gave him a ride to a gas station; the friend said he thought Rod bought marijuana there from "his supplier." Somehow, he then got a ride from the gas station to the concert. Before the concert Rod had attended a meeting of Alcoholics Anonymous.

*Prior Threats to Kill*   The significance of threatening to kill intimate female partners is socially situated amidst a plethora of patriarchal control maneuvers. Men's threats to kill women are potent precisely because a small number of men do in fact follow through.

In general, the more detailed the case files, the more likely I was to find evidence of batterers issuing threats to kill victims before the fatal episode. This observation is a reminder that the absence of threats to kill in a case file does not imply that they were not made. In all likelihood, many perpetrators of intimate-partner homicide utter such threats at some point in their violent relationships. In nearly half of the cases where men kill their present or former intimate female partners, threats to kill surface as a potent theme. However, it is also the case that many men threaten to kill women but never follow through. For the sociologist, this observation raises a question: What is it that makes some men more likely to follow up on their threats of lethal violence than the vast majority of men who make such threats but do not make good on them? One way of at least beginning to address this question is to consider the overall characteristics of the cases in which threats are made good. Indeed, case study approaches often lay the groundwork for other (more quantitative) styles of inquiry that might attempt to answer such a question, perhaps by comparing the characteristics of cases where men follow through with a "control" sample of cases where they do not. One of the strengths of case studies lies in how they provide "thick descriptions" and an array of information about possible differences between cases or sets of cases.

In the two cases that follow, women told batterers that they wanted to leave them. However, in both instances the women had not made a clean break from the men by moving to another residence. It seems as if this expressed desire to leave was a key reason why both men made death threats. These observations from the case files are consistent with the research of Wallace, who suggests that once women have communicated their desire to leave the relationship, regardless of whether they have actually left, their risk of being the victims of intimate-partner homicide increases considerably.[7]

Alfred Simpson, a white man aged 23, was angry that his girlfriend, Martha Ellis, a white woman aged 32, was leaving him. He confronted her when she went to pick up her 13-year-old son, Ralph Ellis, from a trailer park. As Martha got out of her car, Simpson pulled her by the hair and shot her twice in the head. Martha's 14-year-old daughter, Jenny Dale, got out of the car and started to punch Simpson with her fists. Simpson then cocked his gun and she ran toward a trailer. He fired at her but missed. Simpson then left the scene; he was later apprehended by police after a brief struggle. At his trial Alfred was found guilty of first-degree murder for killing Martha and received a mandatory life sentence of 25 years, with no possibility of parole.

Jenny Dale told investigators that Simpson had shattered the windshield on her mother's car the day before the killing. She noted that Simpson was enraged at Martha for recently breaking off their relationship of about three months. On the day of the killing, he was drinking beer and peppermint schnapps with his friend Bob Allen and Martha Ellis's young son, Ralph. According to Simpson, the last thing he could recall about the day of the homicide was sitting around with Bob Allen and Ralph Ellis, planning to "go out and steal a car." Alfred Simpson was a habitual felony offender who had been released from prison just four months before the murder. His criminal history included aggravated assault with a deadly weapon and aggravated battery. Indeed, the gun used to kill Martha Ellis was stolen from a trailer during a burglary just five days before her death.

Threats to kill were liberally sprinkled through the archival materials in this case. Janice Braithwaite met Alfred Simpson two days before the murder. On that same day she loaned him her car so that he could "go and pick up a joint." Janice reported Simpson talking about the woman he lived with and saying, "If that bitch messes with any more of my stuff, I'm going to kill her." Martha Ellis's old boyfriend Fred Dickson told police that Alfred called him one day and said, "Motherfucker, your days are numbered. I'm going to kill you, like I'm going to kill her." Fred also said that Martha told him that Alfred had threatened her life on a number of occasions.

There was a considerable age difference between 37-year-old Sally Westlake and Jimmy Westlake, aged 56. Both persons were white. Friends stated that the difference in their ages contributed to the problems in their relationship. The couple, who had three young children, had divorced and later remarried. Approximately four months before murdering her in June 1994, Jimmy discovered that Sally was having an affair. Subsequently, he left her to live in his hometown in Illinois. There, he had an accident, falling off the truck he owned and drove as a self-employed long-haul trucker. Unable to work, he got back in touch with Sally and asked if they could reconcile. She agreed, Jimmy returned to Florida, and the two of them set up a ceramics business.

On the night before the killing, Jimmy and Sally went out for drinks at the Best Western Inn and decided to stay over. They retired to a room in the inn and shortly thereafter began to argue. Eventually they returned home, where, according to Jimmy, Sally told him to leave and said that she did not want to carry on the relationship. Jimmy reported that he told Sally he was going to commit suicide because there was no point in living if she did not love him. The two continued to argue. Jimmy told police that at one point he got out his gun and sat at the base of the bed with the gun pointed at his head. Sally tried to wrest the pistol from him and it discharged. Jimmy showed the police how this happened and, at the time, his account did seem to mesh with the fact that Sally had apparently been shot through the chest at close range. During this interview with police Jimmy had bloodstains on his chest and hands. Samples from these were processed as he talked with the interviewer. The medical examiner later discounted Jimmy's report that the shooting occurred at close range, noting no signs of stippling and no visible burning or powder residue on Sally's skin or her nightgown.

The accounts given by other witnesses conflicted with Jimmy's story of an accidental shooting. Ember Richman, a niece of Sally's, was staying over at the house after baby-sitting for her aunt. She heard doors slamming and things being tossed around in the master bedroom at around 3:00 A.M. At one point she heard Sally say, "Why don't you just kill me?" Jimmy apparently responded, "All right, then." Next there was a loud noise, followed by Sally saying, "You shot me," and Jimmy responding, "I'm sorry, I'm sorry." During the period after the disturbance Ember reported being afraid that Jimmy might find out she overheard the argument and so pretended to be asleep. Jimmy then telephoned his mother-in-law and told her that Sally had been shot. Her parents, who lived next door, rushed to the scene. Sally's father told police Jimmy had said to him that "they were struggling over the gun when it went off." Both of Sally's parents informed officers that Sally was afraid of Jimmy and that he had been violent toward her in the past. Her mother stated that Jimmy had threatened to kill Sally on a number of occasions, in addition to threatening to shoot her. Several years before, Sally had run to her mother's house in a frantic state, saying that her husband had a gun and was going to kill her. Another time, Jimmy locked her in a room, only to pass out from intoxication; she eventually got out of the room and called her mother to collect her. Jimmy had also carried on a number of affairs with other women. After their separation in February 1994, Sally filed for divorce and also obtained a protection order.

The intensity of Sally's fear that Jimmy would kill her did not really surface until police interviewed three of Sally's women friends and the man with whom she had a brief affair. These interviews make it clear just how menacing and controlling Jimmy was. Doreen had known Sally for 14 years and Jimmy for 9. Sally's "big problems" with him began when she was pregnant with their second child. According to Doreen, Jimmy gave Sally genital herpes through the affairs he was having. He "had always been physically and mentally abusive toward Sally." However, Doreen communicated that her friend now feared contracting AIDS through Jimmy's infidelity. Two years before her death, Sally told Doreen that Jimmy wanted to take her to Las Vegas. Just before her husband made this suggestion, Sally found that her handgun was missing. She told Doreen that Jimmy had connections with the Mafia and that she feared he was planning to have her killed in Las Vegas. Doreen also pointed out that Jimmy was very controlling of Sally. When he was on the road as a long-haul truck driver, he would call her at a prearranged time every day and check on what she had been doing.

Jimmy constantly accused Sally of having affairs with other men, even though, according to Doreen, she never did. Moreover, he did not like Doreen and accused Sally of having a lesbian relationship with her. Around the time of the divorce, Sally became convinced that Jimmy would kill her or arrange for her murder. On one occasion, after he had throttled Sally in an attempt to strangle her, Sally stayed at Doreen's house for a while. Doreen told police that during this period Sally wanted sheets over the windows, fearing that Jimmy would try to shoot her from outside. At one point, about a month before her death, Jimmy sexually assaulted Sally. Doreen reported Sally told her that she was lying in bed one morning when Jimmy forced his finger into her vagina. Finding it moist, he accused her of "being with another man." He then began to yell at her and "told Sally that he would kill her if she was having sex with someone else." These seemingly new forms of sexual abuse appear just before the killing in the cases of a handful of women. However, I have reported this "gynecological surveillance" elsewhere[8] in cases of woman abuse that did not result in death so, this kind of abusive behavior would seem to have limited predictive power.

Sally's friend Amy, who had worked with her at one time, confided that Jimmy was "always calling Sally at work" and would "question her about what she was doing." She apparently told Amy that "Jimmy was driving her crazy." On one occasion he came to the workplace and created a disturbance, throwing filing cabinet drawers around.

Melissa, who had been friends with Sally for about 15 years, told investigators that Jimmy frequently slapped or punched Sally. Three months before the killing, Melissa asked Sally when she was going to leave her husband. She replied, "[P]robably when he kills me." Sally went on to tell Melissa that she was afraid to leave Jimmy because she honestly thought he would kill her.

Billy Bonds informed police that he had a brief affair with Sally. He said that she told him of how Jimmy abused her and remarked that she was terrified that her husband would kill her. Within a short time of the affair starting, Jimmy visited Billy and told him that if he continued to see Sally he would kill him. Billy wondered how Jimmy knew his address and shared his concerns with Sally. She told him that Jimmy had hired a private detective to keep an eye on her and that the detective was the source of the information. Several months later, Sally warned Billy that she had overheard Jimmy on the telephone setting up his murder.

*Prior Police Involvement*   As noted in earlier chapters, a number of studies reveal that intimate-partner homicide is preceded by contacts between the parties and various "helping" agencies.[9] One of the key front-line agencies is the police. In just over half of the cases in which men killed their present or former intimate female partners, the police had contact with the parties because of domestic violence at the residence. However, given that officers do not always document domestic calls, it is difficult to determine the precise extent of earlier police involvement. In the following two cases, the prior contact with police was extensive and the threat posed by both male batterers considerable. Both cases raise certain questions: Why was not more done to protect these women in the face of such obvious and terrifying violence? Why was not the batterer incarcerated for a longer period for earlier assaults?

Maria Rendon, a 39-year-old Latino woman, was shot and killed by her estranged husband, Felix Rendon, a 45-year-old Latino, as she was manicuring a client's nails in the living room of her home. The couple had come to Miami in the Mariel Boatlift from Cuba in 1980 and had been married at least 20 years. Felix burst into Maria's new apartment by smashing through the sliding glass door. The witness at the scene told police that he shot Maria three times and then pointed the gun at the side of his own head. Felix then mumbled something unintelligible before pointing the gun at his face. Finally, he left the scene, only to shoot himself later. Felix survived his self-inflicted gunshot wound.

The Rendons' relationship was marked by escalating woman battering, which led Maria to tell friends that she just had to leave. She had left several times before but returned after Felix threatened members of her family. As Anna Lorca, a neighbor and friend, explained, "Maria endured so much. He made her life impossible." According to a number of neighbors, police cars frequently visited the Rendon residence. As one put it, "I always said something was going to happen to her." The Rendons' son, Jose, confirmed that his father had threatened his and his mother's life a number of times. Jose remarked to police that Felix brazenly told Maria, "One day I'm going to kill you."

At the time of her death Maria had a protection order in place against her husband. According to neighbors, Felix broke the order with impunity. However, when police arrived he had always fled. One couple said that officers had been at the Rendon residence several times a week during the three months before Maria's death. Jose confirmed that his mother was constantly being stalked by Felix, who "kept coming by the residence every couple of hours since he found where they resided and had knocked on doors and windows often." Like the neighbors, Jose also stated in the homicide report that "police officers responded to that address on numerous occasions because of Felix's behavior."

Felix Rendon had a long history of committing domestic violence, as the police were well aware. Between June 1984 and January 1994 he was arrested at least seven times. Four of these arrests were for aggravated assaults and batteries on his wife and son. Two months before the killing, he was arrested for breaking the terms of the protective order. Other arrests included DUI, petty theft, and carrying a concealed weapon and firearm. Another witness noted that Felix frequently discharged his weapon in the backyard of the family home. A key question in this case is, to what extent did the failure of the criminal justice system to incarcerate Felix for any length of time contribute toward his escalating violence against Maria? Without knowing more about the quality of each police interaction with him, it is difficult to discern whether or how police or prosecutorial apathy reinforced the violence and contributed toward the fatality.

Perhaps compounding his violent tendencies, Felix had been using cocaine and drinking alcohol heavily for years. He also suffered from depression, and Maria had tried to obtain psychiatric treatment for him. However, after numerous bouts of drunkenness, violence, and abuse, she finally gave up and moved out. When she started dating someone else, Felix was enraged. The catalyst for the homicide seems to have been Felix's discovery that Maria planned to divorce him.

There was also extensive police involvement before the murder of Jessica McKain, a 41-year-old black woman, by her live-in boyfriend, Ron Gemmil, a 26-year-old black man from Jamaica. The couple were the sole occupants of the boardinghouse room they rented and, according to Gemmil, had been living together for 10 years. McKain, a fruit picker, was found to have been strangled to death by Gemmil with a black necktie. Apparently, he struck her unconscious at the boardinghouse and then strangled her. At the crime scene Gemmil told officers that he did not intend to kill her but wanted her to "feel his pain." A police spokesman told reporters, "The victim made 11 complaints to the Police Department since 1991, including at least one since the first of the year." A resident of the boardinghouse where McKain and Gemmil cohabited reported that the police had been called to intervene in the couple's fights numerous times in the six months before the fatality. An officer working the crime scene remembered arresting Gemmil for an aggravated battery on McKain in 1993.

Gemmil told investigators that Jessica McKain was arranging to have him killed so that she could collect on the $500,000 insurance policy that she had taken out on him. His brother Steve reported that Gemmil was jealous of McKain talking with other men, but that she was also possessive of him.

According to his brother, Gemmil had threatened to kill McKain several times. A number of witnesses attested to having seen Gemmil at a mental health facility on several different occasions.[10] Alan, Ron's other brother, told police that Gemmil "has got mental problems, he's just sick in the head." Mimi Timms, a witness who also lived at the boardinghouse, told investigators that on one occasion Ron Gemmil's brother had to call the police because Ron was walking around in the street swinging a bunch of butcher knives in the air. He was apparently on medication of some kind to control his mood swings. It also seems Ron might have been dealing crack cocaine from the yard of the house. Mimi Timms told police that he showed her a vial one day with 15 to 20 rocks of cocaine in it.

Just two weeks before the killing, Jessica McKain called police to her residence because Ron had tried to hit her with a stick. The responding officer spoke with Gemmil, who told him that he refused to take his medication. The officer noted that Ron had a short temper and placed him in cuffs to protect everyone else at the scene. He was later taken to a mental health facility and confined under the Baker Act.[11] Police documentation of earlier visits to the residence include Jessica calling them on April 21, 1991. During this incident of battering, Ron hurled a concrete block through the windshield of a car that Jessica was sitting in. Police responded to the scene; Jessica said she did not want to press charges. The officer noted the two had been drinking and the parties went their separate ways for the evening. Police also came to their residence on March 13, 1993, because Ron had threatened her with a knife. The responding officer advised Jessica that she could have Gemmil legally evicted from the premises. Ron denied the threatening behavior; again, Jessica stated that she did not want to file charges against him. However, on March 21, 1993, Ron threw a glass jar at Jessica, cutting the back of her head. When police arrived she was picking glass out of her hair. Jessica was treated for a large laceration on the back of her head, and Ron was charged with aggravated battery. This time Jessica signed an affidavit saying that she wanted Ron prosecuted for aggravated battery. The state's attorney's office later dropped the charges. Jessica said she did not want Ron prosecuted.

*Escaping: Separation, Estrangement, Divorce* The Florida case studies are entirely consistent with the extant literature reviewed in Chapter 1, which showed an elevated risk of lethal violence for women who leave their abusers. Most of those Florida women killed in intimate-partner homicides who attempted to "break away" from their batterers had been physically separated from them at some point. Nearly three-fifths of women killed by present or former intimate male partners were either estranged, separated, or in the process of leaving the relationship. This figure includes a small number of cases in which women broke away from men while continuing to share the same physical space. Among such women are those who pursued an education, obtained employment or a different job, or engaged in a new intimate relationship.

Two weeks before she was killed by her husband, Lucinda Aguila, a 41-year-old Latino woman, sued Jiminez Aguila, a 61-year-old Latino man, for divorce. In her divorce suit Lucinda alleged that Jiminez had beaten her. The family, originally from New York, had accumulated around $500,000 in assets, and Lucinda had sued for alimony, the house, and a share of a monthly $2,777 payment her husband received from a gas station in Brooklyn. The couple had married in 1987. Just five days before the murder police answered a domestic call at the residence and spoke with both parties. Lucinda told them that her husband had become more abusive toward her since she had filed for divorce. On one occasion, she stated, he had punched a hole in the bedroom door because she was going out. Jiminez reported that his wife had filed for a divorce and had started a new job at a nursing home. He also said that "she was going out with friends from work all the time and that he could not tolerate that kind of behavior from his wife as long as she still lived in his house." The night of this domestic call, Lucinda stayed in a hotel and Jiminez remained at the house. Five days later, Jiminez locked himself in a room with his wife and shot her four times, killing her. During the shooting Lucinda called out to one of her daughters to help her. The daughter summoned help and tried to break down the door. She heard the shots that killed her mother. Jiminez then walked out of the room and eventually gave himself up to police. As he passed his daughter he told her, "I can't go on without her."

*Protection Orders*    As Table 4.3 indicates, at least 19 women (28.4 percent of the sample) were murdered by their present or former intimate partners while in possession of an order of protection. This fact should not lead one to conclude that protection orders are not worth the paper they are written on. On the contrary, the majority of abusers who are the subjects of protection orders are generally deterred from repeating both physical and psychological abuse.[12] However, in cases of intimate-partner homicide it appears as if the protection order made little difference. Sometimes, as in the Tosca and Felicia Perez homicide-suicide, the issuance of the protection order was akin to baiting a bear (see Chapter 2). However, in most instances where women die, it seems that the protective order is either ignored or flouted with impunity by abusers, rather than serving to spur them on to lethal violence. I have already discussed the etiologies of several cases where women were killed while in possession of protection orders. The case that follows is even more unusual insofar as the victim, over a number of years, had obtained three to five protection orders against her abusive husband. An abuser's flagrant disregard for the letter and spirit of the conditions laid down in a series of protective orders could indicate an increased likelihood of committing lethal violence.

Billie Lee, an African-American woman aged 38, was murdered by her husband, Carl Lee, an African-American man aged 39. Carl suffered from cancer of the spine, which witnesses thought to be in remission at the time he killed his wife. However, it was later found that his cancer had returned, and he died in jail awaiting trial for Billie's murder. Whether Carl knew his cancer had returned before he killed his wife is not clear from the case files. The couple lived at home with their two daughters, Bess and Evelyn, and with Bess's 6-week-old son. The Lees' turbulent 21-year relationship was punctuated with a series of violent assaults on Billie by Carl. She was hospitalized at least once because of his battering. Carl, who had been a truck driver, was on disability due to his cancer. Billie worked at a drug treatment facility and also attended community college. On the night of the killing, Carl and Billie had apparently agreed to go to a pajama party. He was angry when she returned home late from classes and told him she did not want to attend the party. Their daughter Bess advised investigators that Carl did not support Billie attending community college and that he kept very close watch on his wife. This scrutiny was the root cause of their fights, which, according to Bess, her father always started. Carl himself admitted to police that he pointed his gun at Billie on numerous occasions "just to scare her." In the front yard of their house, the couple argued about her lateness and her refusal to attend the pajama party. Billie came inside and locked the door. Carl used a key to get in and followed Billie to her bedroom. On the way, he called out to her, "Bitch, why did you lock the door?" Bess heard her mother scream, "Bess, help me!" She then heard her father kill her mother by shooting her five times.

The exact number of protective orders that had been issued in the Lees' case is unclear. Some witnesses attested to three, others to five. From the record it appears that Billie obtained an order against Carl when the couple were living in Georgia in 1980 and he broke into her residence and beat her up. The attorney who acted for Billie in her attempts to divorce Carl in 1989 noted that he received a copy of a restraining order served on Carl in that year after a particularly violent abusive episode. The attorney told police that Billie felt sorry for Carl because of his diagnosis of cancer. Consequently, she did not follow through with her plans to divorce him in 1989 or at any other time. It seems that another protection order was issued against Carl sometime in the spring of 1992 after he had "shot up" Billie's car and beaten her so badly she required hospitalization. In August 1993 she also procured an injunction against her husband, forcing him to leave their residence. On this occasion Carl stayed away until just before Christmas. Again, it seems from witnesses that Billie invited Carl back into the residence out of pity for him because of his cancer. If there is any pattern in these protective orders, it is that the intervals between their issuance decrease as the time of the fatality approaches. This might be a coincidence, although it seems logical and consistent with other cases to conclude that the abusive episodes became increasingly violent and more frequent.

*Perceptions of Betrayal*   As noted in Chapter 2, I use the term "betrayal" to refer to the abuser's sense that his female partner has committed certain acts tantamount to emotional treachery. These acts involve more than calling the police to the scene of a domestic dispute, even though the man may see treachery in such an action. Perpetrators who feel betrayed seem to experience a particularly acute sense of rejection that appears to transcend the obsessive-possessive desire to hold on to a partner. Since the perpetrator has placed the victim at the center of his projected hopes and dreams for the future, her decision to extricate herself from the relationship may lead some men to intense homicidal rage. Feelings of betrayal are therefore often associated with the victim attempting to break away from the perpetrator. It might seem at first that feelings of betrayal might be likely to arise in relationships of long standing. In Chapter 2, for example, the Perez homicide-suicide highlighted the festering sense of having been betrayed that seemed to eat away at Tosca Perez before he killed his 14-year-old daughter and then took his own life outside his estranged wife's new residence. Tosca and his wife had been married many years. In fact, however, feelings of betrayal appear among perpetrators who have been in relationships of varying durations with victims. In the case study under this subheading, I discuss the role of betrayal in the killing of Kristen Levingston, who had been in an intimate relationship with Evander Lewis for just 18 months before her death.

Brad Levingston, a 44-year-old black man, left the house where he and his family had lived for at least 18 years at 4:30 A.M. to bicycle to work, a ride that took him about 30 minutes. While he was sitting down having an early morning cup of coffee, the telephone rang and he was informed that his daughter had been shot. Brad borrowed a friend's truck and returned to his home. He arrived just in time to see Kristen, a 19-year-old black woman, being taken by stretcher into an ambulance. His wife, Jocelyn, who witnessed the shooting, filled him in on the details. At around 4:45 A.M. his daughter's former boyfriend, Evander, broke down the front door to their residence. He passed by Kristen's 9-year-old sister, who was lying on the couch, and entered Kristen's bedroom, where he fired one shot. He then left the residence. Kristen struggled into her mother's bedroom to get help. While she was assisting Kristen with the first gunshot wound, to her calf, Evander came back into the house and shot Kristen in the chest. She later died in hospital.

In many ways this case fits the typical "stalking" pattern. Kristen and Evander started dating in October 1992. According to witnesses, both were accepted into each other's families as a couple. However, in April 1994, Kristen found out that he had got another woman pregnant and had arranged for her to have an abortion. This incident led Kristen to end her relationship with Evander. Her decision may also have been influenced by the fact that she was leaving south Florida to attend Alabama State University in fall 1994. Throughout their relationship Evander tried to persuade Kristen to stay in south Florida and complete her education at Florida International University in Miami. However, Kristen wanted to attend Alabama State. She had made arrangements with her good friend of many years, Cedrica Maimo, to share an apartment in Montgomery. Evander's feelings of having been betrayed increased from April 1994 up until the killing on July 28 of that year. He stalked Kristen at her home, and on a number of occasions she reported tapping sounds on her windows at night. Since the family dog patrolled the fenced backyard, Kristen surmised the tapper must have been someone known to the dog. She told a new boyfriend, Michael Mitchell, that throughout her relationship with Evander he would always "pet the dog and . . . the dog would not bark at him when he came to the house or entered the back yard."

The stalking continued. Kristen's mother, Jocelyn, told police that on one occasion after the separation Evander came to the house and was sitting at the table with Kristen. She observed him "about to strike Kristen" and intervened. Kristen was afraid and crying and asked her mother to remove Evander from the house. She did so, forcibly, but reported he tried to "get around her and get back at Kristen." Jocelyn added that she was "afraid of Evander because of the look on his face, and felt as if he was about to inflict harm on both her and her daughter." After this incident Evander also began to stalk Kristen at the department store where she worked. In May 1994, she obtained a temporary restraining order against Evander, which became permanent on June 23, 1994. It seems, however, that he broke the conditions attached to the order a number of times. Within a few days of the issuance of the permanent order, Evander observed Kristen with Michael Mitchell on a double date with her future roommate and a second black man at the Grand Prix Race-o-Rama in Hollywood. In their inquiries, police asked Michael about this incident. He replied that when Kristen saw Evander watching the foursome she became very nervous and requested they all leave the Race-o-Rama. Other witnesses attested that Kristen thought Evander was almost continuously watching her.

Doubtless, incidents where Evander observed Kristen dating another man amplified his intense jealousy. However, Jocelyn told investigators she felt that her daughter's decision to leave Florida to attend Alabama State University lay at the heart of Evander's perception that he had been betrayed. Jocelyn advised police that her daughter was due to leave for Montgomery on August 5, 1994. She specifically told investigators that Evander was traumatized by the breakup of his relationship with Kristen, especially because she would leave the state. He turned his growing sense of being betrayed into a sophisticated surveillance and stalking strategy. However, for all his cunning, Evander's anger eventually took over. On the day he killed Kristen, it seems as if he waited until her father left for work before breaking down the door to the residence. Before the fatal shot into Kristen's chest, he said to her, "I told you I'll get you, bitch."

*Alcohol, Drugs, or Both*  Roughly two-fifths of the female intimate-partner fatalities were preceded or accompanied by the use of intoxicants. As I noted in Chapter 2, this does not mean that the drugs and alcohol actually caused the deaths. Many persons use drugs, alcohol, or both and do not become violent. Likewise, a large number of domestic fatalities occurred in the Florida sample without the reported presence of intoxicants. However, as I have stressed, these thematic continuities in the killings are best seen as interwoven rather than distinctive phenomena. Consequently, there will be times when drug and alcohol abuse is part of a broader lifestyle that is more likely to result in domestic homicide. In the cases that follow I present the use of intoxicants as a factor associated with other lifestyle characteristics, which, when taken as a whole, seem to render some women more vulnerable to being killed by their intimate partners.

Jason Rawlings, a black man aged 31, walked into a police station in Washington, D.C., and turned himself in for stabbing his girlfriend, Andrea Lynch, a black woman aged 29, in Florida. Police there found Andrea's body in an advanced state of decomposition at her apartment. The evidence at the crime scene suggested that she died after a struggle. Broken glass was scattered around the floor, the center of the couch was stained with blood, Uno playing cards lay on the living room floor, and a number of beer and liquor containers, some partially filled, were strewn around the apartment. Andrea's corpse displayed multiple stab wounds.

Jason apparently worked as a cook at a pancake house before fleeing to Washington. He told coworkers that he had to go to DC because his brother had been killed there in a gang fight. Investigators tried to learn about Jason by questioning his fellow workers. One part of an interview with Jennifer Dough proceeded as follows:

> *Investigator*   What type of person would you consider Mr. Rawlings?
> *Dough*   I took him to be rude, mean, and I was afraid of him.
> *Investigator*   Was anything brought to your attention about what Mr. Rawlings had said to another coworker about you?
> *Dough*   Yes. The coworker came to me and told me that Jason Rawlings said that he's gonna get me on [the] graveyard [shift] and rape me.
> *Investigator*   Now, when that was told to you did it seem like a credible statement? Did Jason try hitting on you before or anything like that?
> *Dough*   When he started working there he kept asking me if I was married and had kids. I told him yes, you know, just so I wouldn't be bothered by him. Just the way he looked at me . . . it scared me.

Apparently, Jason Rawlings had been engaged in an ongoing dispute with the assistant manager of the pancake house, Bud Chimmel. On one occasion, Rawlings had brought a firearm to the workplace and kept it in his pants pocket as he argued with Chimmel. Bud told police that Jason had "a very cold, cold look to him all the time, like the slightest little thing could trigger him." He also told them that he had seen Jason walking in a neighborhood known for drug dealing. Later, one of the employees told Bud that Jason had asked to be dropped off in the neighborhood so that he could buy drugs. The employee refused, telling Bud later that he was afraid to go to the area.

Johnny Lucid, a onetime policeman from Chicago, lived in the same apartment complex as Jason and Andrea. Lucid told investigators that Jason approached him on New Year's Day 1994 to borrow $10. The day was cool, but Lucid observed that Jason was sweating profusely and his eyes were jittery. When he refused to lend Jason $10, Jason told him that Andrea would be home soon and would repay him with $15. Lucid also remarked to investigators that he worked in the evening and spent a lot of time in his apartment during the day. He reported that he often saw Jason coming and going from the apartment during the day on his bicycle, usually carrying a back pack. When investigators asked what he thought Jason was up to during the day, Lucid replied, "I figured he was dealing crack and selling it on his bicycle." Certainly his behavior and demeanor were consistent with someone who was using and dealing crack. Through the witness statements one sees evidence of a man who is extremely volatile and irritable, who enters drug neighborhoods with unusual confidence, and who exhibits craving behavior, high anxiety, and perhaps paranoia. Jason's use of his bicycle and back pack is consistent with my own observations of street dealers in Miami. If Jason was smoking crack, it raises an important question: To what extent did his use of crack cocaine contribute to the killing of Andrea Lynch? Was it a mere epiphenomenon, a secondary component of an otherwise conflictual relationship? Or was the drug use more central to his employment of lethal violence? The research literature is adamant that drug use is of peripheral concern, or a correlative rather than causal factor in domestic violence. However, is this still the case with lethal violence when possible abusers are using drugs well known to produce paranoid psychoses as well as very violent and aggressive behaviors in general?

There is no evidence of prior domestic violence or any escalating abuse in the case of Andrea Lynch. The police never responded to a domestic call at the residence, and the investigative file contains a question mark beside the issue of a prior history of domestic abuse. The landlords, a married couple, reported no disturbances from the residence. However, one of them mentioned to investigators that the apartment complex "was built in the old days with cinder block, so you could not hear through the walls anyway." Both landlords informed officers that Andrea had lived in the apartment for about three months and that she told them she had a 10-year-old daughter living elsewhere.

Andrea had no friends that the landlords knew of and appeared to be very isolated. Indeed, if the observations of Johnny Lucid and Jason's coworkers that he was involved in the drug scene are to be believed, then it is possible that Andrea was also using drugs. This case seems to leave two possibilities. Either Jason murdered Andrea during an angry outburst brought on by his excessive drug use, or her killing was the culmination of woman battering that few, if any, persons knew about and that may have been fueled in some way by drug-related rage.

In the next case involving intoxicants, Rob Greaves, a 48-year-old white man, murdered his 45-year-old white girlfriend, Angela Newland, at their residence on the Seminole Indian Reservation. Rob performed odd jobs on the reservation and Angela was unemployed. Both were chronic alcoholics. When police found Angela's body it was covered with bruises. The medical examiner determined the cause of death to be blunt trauma to the abdomen causing laceration to the intestines and internal bleeding. When officers questioned Rob Greaves, he informed them that he and Angela had argued when he got home from work around 7:30 P.M. He wanted to watch a tape and could not get the videocassette recorder to work. Angela was drunk. According to Greaves she was the kind of person "who would never give him any peace." His problems with the VCR compounded the fact that Greaves was "not in a real good mood." He told police that he threw the machine at Angela, hitting her in the abdomen. He tried to reassure officers that he did not use great force: "It wasn't like I slung it at her with killer strength or something, you know." After throwing the VCR at Angela, Rob left for a bar to get some "peace and quiet." He returned home at 1:30 A.M. and Angela was still alive. When the two got up in the morning Angela complained of aches and pains. Rob remarked to investigators that she "always had aches and pains, . . . always complained about aches and pains." At breakfast he apparently took his first drink of the day: "I sat down and I had a drink. Normally, I have a morning beer, or two beers. Then I feel a little better and I can go to work. But I didn't have any beer in the refrigerator. I still had some gin that I hid so that she wouldn't get into it. I brought it out and made a drink." Angela had a drink herself. Rob left for work. When he returned at around 11:30 A.M. Angela was dead on the couch. On finding her, he immediately reached for the gin bottle and began to drink.

When asked to explain the bruises on Angela's body, Rob remarked that "she just gets drunk and falls all over the place." However, he did concede that "some of 'em's from hassles." Other witnesses filled in the picture. One man who found Rob at the scene told police that Rob admitted "beat[ing] her before he left for work" but "she was all right." When he returned he found her dead. The same witness, who knew Rob, said under oath that "Rob slapped her around a few times and I've seen her with black eyes." Angela's daughter, who knew Rob well, said he beat her mother frequently, to the point that she "had bruises on her all the time." She added that her mother told her that Rob gave her the bruises. Significantly, the daughter also remarked to officers that Rob had thrown the VCR at Angela before, along with a number of other objects.

If one is to believe Rob's statements, Angela had a significant problem with alcohol before the two of them got together. At one point in his interview with investigators he speaks of her ability to drink excessive amounts of alcohol.

> Now let me tell you something about how she could slug shit down. I remember the first Christmas together, we were at my buddy's house and he's got a half-gallon of Jack Daniel's for Christmas. Angela got up in the morning and goes, "[T]hat's what I need is one of those." And my buddy fills it, like this big, and she takes that son of a bitch and she goes glug, glug, glug, like it was water and goes, "[T]hat was dandy, can I have another?"

Other witnesses corroborated Angela's long relationship with alcohol. My point in mentioning it is that her alcoholism certainly antedated her relationship with Rob. It is therefore unlikely that her addiction to alcohol was simply a response to his battering, although it is possible that her alcoholism grew worse as his battering increased. It is also possible that her addiction stemmed from an earlier battering relationship or, perhaps more distally, from having been abused in childhood. However, the files remain silent on these matters, and the roots of Angela's alcoholism may well be buried with her.

*Mental Illness*  As noted in Chapter 2, most batterers are not mentally deranged and most rapists are not mentally ill.[13] Likewise, there are few examples of documented mental illness among the ranks of men who kill their intimate female partners, in the sense that perpetrators had what is rather imprecisely referred to as "disorganized personalities." My impression from reading the multiagency files is that men who commit intimate-partner homicide are no more likely to suffer from mental illness than are other men with the same demographic characteristics. According to the archival data, only 4 men out of the 67 were experiencing some kind of documented mental illness at the time they killed their intimate female partners. One suffered from dementia apparently brought on by a brain tumor, another appears to have been a paranoid schizophrenic, the third suffered from manic depression, and the last was driven by some kind of disorder that gave him an uncontrollable desire to beat women. I will discuss these last two cases in some depth. The documentation of mental illness in the investigative files does not mean that perpetrators can use the mental illness as grounds for a successful plea of insanity. In fact, the insanity defense is used in only a small percentage of cases, and in those the perpetrator is acquitted because of insanity only about 22 percent of the time.[14]

According to a number of family members and friends, Chuck Bradshaw, a 46-year-old African-American man, apparently suffered from a mental disorder that caused him to inflict bodily harm upon women. On July 3, 1994, between 2:00 and 3:00 A.M., he killed his girlfriend, Priscilla Johns, an African-American woman aged 43. Bradshaw spontaneously told police at the scene, "I beat the bitch to death." Officers found him with injuries to both hands and with his body covered in blood. Priscilla died of "multiple sharp and blunt force injuries." She sustained 18 such injuries to the face and head and 1 laceration to the left arm just above the wrist that cut through to the bone. One neighbor reported that Priscilla came across to his house at around 7:00 P.M. on July 2, 1994, and asked for a ride home "before Chuck killed her." Apparently the neighbor, Johnny Roach, an African-American man aged 61, told her it was a "domestic situation and he did not want to get involved." He added that Chuck had mental problems and a history of seizures; these problems had resulted in Bradshaw being confined in mental institutions on a number of occasions. Several other relatives and friends confirmed these mental problems. Apparently, he had beaten a number of his female relatives, including his sister and an aunt. His cousin Red Gates, a 32-year-old African-American man, told investigators that Bradshaw had been placed in crisis centers from time to time and that "he would beat up on women constantly." Red informed officers that "whenever one of the sisters wanted to visit the residence where Chuck lived, he would have to [go] with them in order to keep them safe from Chuck."

However, despite the talk of seizures and madness, it is also clear that Bradshaw called the police at around 8:00 A.M. on July 3, 1994, to report a domestic disturbance. Chuck reported that Priscilla was throwing furniture around and had refused to leave his residence. Officers responded within five minutes of this call from northwest Miami and found Priscilla's corpse in full rigor mortis. The morphological state of the body told police that she had been dead for a number of hours and that the domestic dispute, if there was one, was long over. Apparently, Chuck said to investigators that "he was going to cut the victim up and throw her out of the front door because he had told her to leave."

Priscilla's sister Cynthia reported that she had told her to stay away from Bradshaw because she thought he was "crazy." Cynthia informed police that her sister had been going out with him for about two years. Apparently, Priscilla lived with another boyfriend, Earl Gray, in Miami and saw Chuck at the same time. When they first started to date, he hit her on the head with a hammer, causing Priscilla to be hospitalized.

When so-called mental illness is implicated in a domestic homicide it is easy to lose sight of the similarities between that homicide and the other intimate killings of women. Although Chuck Bradshaw was diagnosed as mentally ill, he did exhibit a number of behaviors similar to those of other perpetrators. At times he was very controlling of Priscilla, he had seriously assaulted her previously, and he had a record of assault against other women. However, one cannot easily understand Chuck's violence through the acts of power and control typical of many male perpetrators of intimate-partner homicide. There are, though, a number of other ways of interpreting his bizarre behavior. A forensic psychologist would likely diagnose Bradshaw as having some kind of "impulse control disorder."[15] For forensic psychologists, such a disorder, although only meaningful when looked at in the context of prevailing cultural mores, is physiological in origin. It is also often accompanied by amnesia, delirium, or both. These symptoms are consistent with the fact that when officers questioned Chuck he was covered in blood, but apparently (according to police) did not know he had killed Priscilla.

To use the language of psychology, Chuck's behavior was not inconsistent with that of an antisocial personality who shows no guilt or remorse. Indeed, police officers at the scene noted that once they had communicated to him that he had killed Priscilla, Chuck showed no remorse. However, if the killing of Priscilla Johns is interpreted using the language of psychology, it does not necessarily lessen the role of misogyny in the case. Put differently, clinical analyses still allow one to link this kind of much rarer intimate-partner homicide to the acts of the larger body of male perpetrators who do not show evidence of the psychotic behavior displayed by Chuck. Persons suffering from impulse control disorder target different things. Bradshaw's focus was women, particularly those he was related to or in an intimate relationship with. Commonly in these cases, men like Chuck have met with some kind of egregious abuse in their childhood that promotes a hatred of certain women. If he suffered from an impulse control disorder, then Bradshaw was totally out of control vis-à-vis Priscilla, and he was not simply attempting to gain control and assert his will in the way the average batterer might do.

Libby Peru, a white woman aged 21, and Duke Tifano, a white man aged 24, had been dating for about eight months. He told officers that Libby wanted more out of their relationship than he was willing to give. For example, she wanted him to spend more time with her instead of going on motorcycle outings. On the evening of May 23, 1994, Libby called Duke, and he apparently told her he was unavailable that evening since a female friend, Betsy, was coming to his house. Tifano reported that Libby became angry and told him to return all the gifts she had given him during their courtship. Duke packed up the gifts and took them over to Libby Peru's apartment. She met him outside and the two argued for about 30 minutes. According to Duke, Libby slapped him in the face, spat at him, flicked her cigarette at him, and told him he was worthless. A number of neighbors heard the altercation. In a subsequent interview with police, Tifano said these slaps reminded him of the way his father used to treat him. He added that after Libby's assault he "blacked out" and did not remember his actions. He could only recall "yelling at her," the sound of his own "labored breathing," getting "weirded out," and then experiencing a sensation which made him feel he had to "haul ass" out of the area. At one point Duke remarked to police, "I can't fucking believe I bashed her head in."

Piecing the evidence together, it seems that Tifano terminated the altercation by banging Libby's head onto a concrete curb, killing her. He then fled the scene. During the ensuing investigation it emerged that Duke had been confined in four different mental hospitals on a number of different occasions. He was also taking lithium, although about a week before the killing he ceased taking it so that he could feel "normal." He told police that he had been experiencing considerable anxiety as a result of not being medicated.

Duke Tifano's mental illness and violent tendencies seem to have been channeled in certain directions only. His neighbors and coworkers knew him as a kind and pleasant man and reported no problems. When police informed neighbors of his arrest they were "shocked." Duke had not used violence in the workplace, although a couple of coworkers had reported a fascination with death on his part. For example, on one occasion a railroad accident resulted in a person being killed. A witness remarked to police that Duke "jumped for joy, making [a] comment how that was the greatest thing he had seen. He also made a comment about wanting to have his picture taken with the deceased." Several fellow employees reported hearing Tifano say on other occasions that he "would like to kill someone and watch them die." Duke had been violent toward himself and had attempted suicide once. He also said to police that he heard voices telling him to hurt other persons or himself and that he had assaulted a bouncer at a bar in the weeks before he killed Libby.

One officer I spoke with told me he interviewed Duke the night of the killing.[16] Apparently, he followed the officer's questions perfectly well and understood what was going on. However, other medical records reveal that Tifano's mental health was deteriorating. Notes from a mental hospital describe him as increasingly violent and as suffering from auditory hallucinations and paranoid schizophrenia. However, Duke was found mentally fit to stand trial and was charged with first-degree murder. In 1996 a jury found him guilty of second-degree murder, and the judge sentenced him to 22 years in the Florida State Prison.

It is impossible to identify the precise role played by mental illness in the killing of Libby Peru. It appears from the case file that there was no history of domestic violence. Likewise, there were no earlier police calls concerning domestic strife between the two and no history of protection orders taken out by either party. In this sense, the killing of Libby Peru differs from the killing of Priscilla Johns, since in the latter case there was a clear history of domestic violence and controlling behavior, as well as other well-documented acts of violence against women.

*Prior Criminal History*　Of the 67 men who killed their intimate female partners, at least 29 (43 percent) had criminal histories (see Appendix 1). This percentage recalls the work by Klein reported in Chapter 1, who found that 43 percent of 644 batterers arrested in Quincy, Massachusetts, had criminal histories.[17] Of the 29 Florida men with criminal histories, only four had convictions for misdemeanor domestic-violence offenses alone. The remainder had more substantial criminal histories, with at least 15 of the perpetrators having prior convictions for domestic-violence offenses, usually aggravated assaults, as one component of their criminal biographies. As Appendix 1 shows, although only 15 men had earlier convictions for domestic violence, the multiagency files document that 27 of the 29 perpetrators had battered their partners at some point before killing them. In one of the remaining two cases, an examination of the files was unable to confirm that the murdered intimate female partner had previously been battered by her killer. In the other case, the available evidence from all witness statements suggests the victim was not beaten, although, as I have pointed out before, it is difficult to know how accurate such a conclusion is. Given that it is difficult to obtain precise information on the criminal histories of all 67 perpetrators, and given that authorities are aware of only about half of all violent crime that is committed outside the home,[18] it is likely that more than 29 of the men had criminal histories.

It seems that male perpetrators of intimate-partner homicide have a much greater involvement in prior criminal behavior, especially criminal violence, than do the male perpetrators of multiple killings.[19] This difference is an important finding: it raises the question of whether the intimate-partner homicides committed by these criminally violent offenders are best seen as manifestations or extensions of their violent tendencies in general, as part of a more classic assertion of power and control over the women they partnered, or both. Put differently, in cases where perpetrators of single acts of intimate-partner homicide had histories of criminal violence, is it not possible to see their violence toward their partner as yet another expression of violent behavior in general? On the other hand, rather than looking at these men as different from those who do not have biographies punctuated by acts of criminal violence, could it not also be argued that their histories of violence are entirely consistent with the kinds of behavior involving power and control that lie at the root of classic battering relationships? That 27 of the 29 perpetrators with criminal histories had battered their partners in the past suggests that such behavior is a near-universal correlate in the lead-up to the use of lethal intimate-partner violence, regardless of what other violent crimes these perpetrators had committed.

Tiana Marino, a 37-year-old black woman, was murdered by her husband, Pete Marino, a black man aged 52, on August 5, 1994. The couple had recently separated, and Tiana had moved back to her mother's residence after living with Pete for three or four years. He had taken out a protection order against her, which was dated August 1, 1994. Pete alleged that on July 30, 1994, Tiana broke into his home and threatened to kill him. The order also states that on July 29, 1994, Tiana hit him with a stick on his lower arm and upper shoulder and that she had doused him with gasoline and tried to poke his eyes out. Pete stated that in 1991 Tiana threatened to kill him at knife point and tried to shoot at him. Finally, his petition also said that Tiana was on crack cocaine and that she needed help.

According to a number of witnesses, Pete Marino had violently abused Tiana for at least two years; as Appendix 1 reveals, he had an extensive criminal history of violence. Zach Crisp, Pete's nephew, said he had "become violent in the past and on one occasion knocked Tiana's teeth out." In general, Zach Crisp described his uncle "as a violent man with a history of harming people." For his part, Billy Bragg, Tiana's nephew, informed police that he thought jealousy lay behind Pete's anger, although Billy said his aunt was not having an affair. Billy also told officers that Pete had threatened to kill Tiana many times. Two days before the killing witnesses overheard Pete say he was "gonna get her ass." At approximately 2:00 A.M. on August 5, 1994, a family member reported that Pete came to his residence and told his nephew "I'm going to look for that bitch" and then left. He apparently caught up with Tiana at her new home and the two argued. The argument spilled out into the street, where Pete slashed her throat. Apparently he used a knife that several witnesses said he carried with him all the time.

Pete Marino's criminal history was extensive, including numerous arrests for aggravated assault, four for homicide, several firearms offenses, loitering and prowling, and gambling. He was sentenced to 10 years in prison for the homicide he committed in 1962. To say that Pete was a seasoned violent criminal, with all the connections that entails, would be an understatement. One must ask what his purpose was in taking out the protective order against Tiana. Pete states, among other things, that he was trying to get her help for her crack cocaine problem. However, the police file also shows that he himself used drugs. Was he afraid that his wife would kill him? Given his proclivity for violence and his well-documented earlier assaults on Tiana, it is reasonable to suggest that if she was violent toward Pete it was in self-defense. Another possibility is that there was mutual offensive violence between Pete and Tiana. One might also ask why he went looking for his wife if he was so afraid of her. The autopsy revealed that Tiana had a number of front teeth missing, a finding consistent with the statement of Zach Crisp that Pete had knocked them out. It seems the likely sequence of events here was similar to that in other cases. Tiana was separating from a very violent man after what was probably a series of increasingly violent domestic assaults. It also seems that she used resistive violence against Pete, including perhaps assaulting him with a stick and pouring gasoline over him. Tiana's own criminal history showed indictments for disorderly conduct (1975) and an aggravated assault (1978) in which she attempted to knife an unidentified black man. However, in neither case is it clear in what context the offense took place.

Pete openly stated he was going to kill Tiana. Why he took out the protective order is a mystery, although it is possible he hoped to use it as part of a self-defense plea after the homicide. Given that he was well versed in the workings of the criminal justice system, this is not an unlikely possibility. His familiarity with violence and the world of street crime is clear from his rap sheet and other archival details. It seems that this familiarity, his street sense, the folding pocket knife with the five-inch blade he always carried with him, and his awareness that Tiana would try to defend herself if attacked primed him to kill her as the final act in his assertion of control and hostility. However, his pedigree as a violent criminal does not mark him off as different from other men who murdered their intimate female partners.

Eric Farnsworth, a black man aged 34, is another example of a male perpetrator whose biography is steeped in acts of criminal violence. Unlike Pete Marino, he killed his wife, Janis, a black woman aged 29, and then continued his violent behavior in public, wounding three persons as he fired his Uzi assault rifle into a crowd at a Riviera Beach shopping center. Farnsworth had prior convictions for aggravated assault, forgery, and possession of marijuana. At the time of the shooting, police sources noted that he was involved with drug dealers in West Palm Beach and Riviera Beach. On the morning of the killing, officers came to the residence where the couple lived three times. On the first two occasions they escorted Janis and her belongings from the residence. Eric was present and was protesting her leaving. During the second police visit he warned Janis, "If you leave you will be dead in two days." On her third visit a few hours later to collect belongings, her husband emerged from a place of hiding close to the residence. As Janis pleaded for her life, he shot her and said, "You thought I was joking." Although Eric fled the scene he later turned himself in to sheriff's deputies.

As in the killing of Tiana Marino, one must ask about the extent to which the killing of Janis Farnsworth was an outcome of the generalized violent tendencies of a well-armed man who was involved in the local drug trade. Or, is it more plausible to look at the Farnsworth homicide as just one more domestic killing in which an obsessively possessive abuser wanted to maintain some semblance of control over his love object? What can be said with some certainty is that Eric's access to the Uzi almost certainly stemmed from his drug-dealing connections, and it was possessing this rifle that may have increased his confidence to such an extent that he could follow through on his threats to kill.

*Self-Defense* Traditionally, the criminal law allows persons under threat of violence to use justifiable defensive force to protect their lives or the lives of others. There are several factors that courts consider before deeming the defensive force justifiable. First, the potential or actual victims must have reasonably perceived themselves to be in danger. Second, the victims are only permitted to use force proportionate to that directed at them in order to counter and repel the threat. Typically, a threatened person who uses a weapon against an unarmed attacker cannot claim justifiable force. Similarly, deadly defensive force can only be used if the potential victim perceives an "imminent" threat of death, serious injury, kidnapping, or forcible rape.

In the 67 Florida cases of male-perpetrated intimate-partner homicide, only Steve Kray, a white man aged 37, seriously asserted that he feared for his life from his abusive partner, Samantha Rook, a white woman aged 25, and claimed that he felt compelled to kill her before she killed him. This case warrants attention, if only because it is unique among the Florida sample. Steve and Samantha had lived together off and on as a couple at his house for several years. There was a history of domestic violence in this case; unusually for the Florida sample, it was Samantha who was charged with aggravated assault after an incident in August 1993. Steve alleged she bit him on his arm during an argument and stabbed him in the face and head with a pair of scissors. He later dropped the charges against her. However, the evidence does not necessarily suggest that Samantha was the aggressor in the relationship. A number of witnesses reported seeing Steve threaten her with a gun several different times. The couple started arguing on the night of March 7, 1994, just hours before the killing. Steve later told police that they were arguing about his stepdaughter but would give no other details. He also said to investigators that Samantha attacked him on several occasions with a poker and an ash shovel from his fireplace set. As a consequence, Steve left the residence on three separate occasions during that evening to visit a nearby bar to drink more beer. He returned three times, on the last occasion armed with a nine-millimeter handgun. Another altercation ensued and he fired the pistol into the floor at one point as a warning to Samantha. At another point, Steve reported, she followed him into the bathroom and tried to force the handgun into his mouth and persuade him to commit suicide. He then retreated to his bedroom until Samantha came and asked him to sit in the living room with her. He agreed, but carried the handgun with him. Samantha asked him to put it down, but he refused. Another physical fight ensued. According to Steve, Samantha cornered him and began striking him with the ash shovel. He then shot her dead.

The case was local front-page news. One of the major points of interest was that Steve Kray might have been a "battered man."[20] This revelation opened the doors to a possible self-defense claim like the ones successfully used by some battered women who killed their abusers in situations that did not meet the traditional legal criteria of self-defense.[21] However, further police investigation of the Kray-Rook relationship revealed it to be more complicated than it seemed. First, the local sheriff's department reported that about a month before the homicide a teenager contacted them alleging that Kray had been sexually abusing her for eight years, plying her with drugs and alcohol prior to the sexual acts. Was this teenager Kray's de facto stepdaughter and Rook's biological daughter from another relationship? Had the daughter recently publicized the sexual abuse? If so, was this what made Samantha Rook so angry? Second, police questioned Kray's reason for returning to the residence three separate times if he indeed feared Samantha might be capable of lethal violence. Third, why did Kray not call the police before returning to his house? He had taken out a criminal complaint against Samantha in August 1993; why could he have not done the same thing again, thus defusing the situation? Finally, Steve Kray argued that he shot Samantha after she had backed him into a corner and held an ash shovel up to him. However, the crime scene investigation showed that he was actually standing over Samantha when he fired the fatal shot and that she had not backed him into a corner at all. Subsequently, as the full story emerged after detailed investigation, the talk of "battered husbands" subsided.

Even if Samantha Rook had regularly assaulted Steve, which she may indeed have done,[22] I contend it is inappropriate to use the term "battered husband" or "battered-husband syndrome" to capture the apparent plight of this man. Physical acts of violence only assume meaning when they are considered in a social context. The reason behind the use of the violence is of paramount importance here. The soldier who kills in war often uses socially sanctioned and therefore "appropriate" violence. For many, on the other hand, the IRA bomber who kills civilians uses terroristic violence that is widely condemned as "inappropriate." Put simply, the social meaning of violence does not depend upon the nature of the violent act itself. When men assault women in interpersonal relationships, the magnitude, import, and effects of their violence is backed by the patriarchal domination of many men over many women. In other words, male violence cannot be evaluated just by the injury it causes or by the immediate interpersonal or situational benefits that accrue to the men who use it. Rather, such male violence must be understood against the welter of social forces that accompany the act and limit women's range of resistive responses to that act. Just because a man is regularly assaulted by a woman does not make him a battered man, at least not in the same way that a woman who is physically victimized in a similar manner becomes a "battered woman." The difference is that the regular physical violence of men in interpersonal relationships is backed by a social power that cannot be overcome by women's mere use of more heinous forms of violence against men.

## Family Homicides

The etiology of killings within families differs from that of intimate-partner homicides. The former do not usually involve the same range and type of situational antecedents stemming from the conflict and antagonism associated with intimate-partner relationships. Perpetrators of domestic killings committed family homicide if they were related to their victim by blood or by marriage or cohabitation, but were not in an intimate-partner relationship with them. A typical example here would be a daughter's live-in boyfriend who murders the daughter's mother or father. As noted in Table 4.1 among the 78 single domestic killings of women in Florida in 1994, only 11 were family homicides. In addition to being much less frequent than intimate female partner homicides, the 11 family homicides involving female victims showed different etiologies. I will now touch briefly upon a few of the salient themes. Table 4.4 summarizes the relationships between the perpetrators and victims of the family killing of the 11 women.

Only 3 of these 11 killings exhibited signs of escalating domestic violence. In 2 cases the violent aggressor was a woman and not a man. In one of these, Bee Maine, a 60-year-old black woman, was murdered by her daughter, Elouise Griffith, aged 34. Police reported the two had been fighting for three or four years, with Elouise the aggressor. Eventually she stabbed her mother to death with a knife during an argument about a dress.

In the second case, Alice Richards, a 60-year-old white woman, was shot

### TABLE 4.4
Perpetrators and victims in the family killing of women

| Relationship | No. |
| --- | --- |
| Son kills mother | 2 |
| Brother kills sister | 2 |
| Brother-in-law kills sister-in-law | 1 |
| Sister's boyfriend kills sister | 1 |
| Nephew kills aunt | 1 |
| Daughter's boyfriend kills his girlfriend's mother | 1 |
| Daughter kills mother | 1 |
| Stepfather kills stepdaughter | 1 |
| Sister kills sister | 1 |
| Total | 11 |

in the back by her sister, Jane Robaret, a white woman aged 53. According to a key informant, Jane Robaret had been beaten regularly by her sister. At the time of the killing the two were engaged in a bitter dispute over whether Jane should continue to live with Alice and their mother. This observation is consistent with Ewing's observation that disputes about living arrangements often lie at the heart of family killings.[22] At the time of writing, Jane is in prison for murder.

The last case with clear evidence of domestic violence involved a stepfather, Brandon Peachy, an African-American man in his late 30s, who murdered his stepdaughter, Karen Pugil, an African-American woman aged 18, after years of sexually abusing her. He was convicted in 1992 of 11 counts of attempted sexual battery against Karen. I interviewed the detective who worked this case, and he told me that Brandon had also violently victimized his wife, Karen's mother, for many years. Although legally restrained from going near Karen, he abducted her one day from a supermarket in Miami where she worked. He took her to a remote rural part of Dade County and murdered her.

Mental illness seems to have played a central role in 2 of the 11 family homicides. Randall Johnson, a white man aged 47, called 911 to report that he had killed his mother by stabbing her. He claimed he had planned to kill her. Randall had recently been released from a veterans hospital. After the killing he remained in his mother's apartment with her body for nine days. Randall had also tried to stab himself in the stomach and slit his wrists. He claimed that he remembered killing his mother, but not why. Apparently, Randall choked her until she was dead and then stabbed her. She had a broken neck, as well. He said he had been having thoughts about killing his mother for a while and had checked himself into a mental hospital because of them. Randall said, however, that he did not receive the care he needed. This is reminiscent of the case of Terrance O'Brien, described by Ewing. On the day he stabbed his sister, O'Brien had checked himself into the same mental health facility that he had been released from just four days earlier. Having become impatient, O'Brien had left the facility against medical advice before killing his sister.[23]

In the other case involving mental illness, Bertha Pangel, a Latino woman aged 58, had been living with her daughter Rosa Pangel, aged 22, and her boyfriend, Angel Liaza, a Latino man aged 34, for five years. According to the multiagency files, both younger parties were developmentally disabled. Rosa reported that she awoke in the middle of the night to find Angel staring at the ceiling. She told investigators this gave her a "bad feeling." He then left their bedroom, returned with a machete, and attempted to assault Rosa. She ran away and then heard her mother screaming as Angel killed Bertha with the machete. According to the investigative files, Angel had never been violent before. He was on medication, however, having been diagnosed as a paranoid schizophrenic. Angel was later deemed unfit to stand trial.

In two other instances of family homicide, men killed women connected to them by marriage or affiliation after an argument. In one case, Brad Reese, a white man in his early 20s, was living with his brother Nigel and his sister-in-law Katrina, a 20-year-old white woman. Brad called the police to report that someone had killed Katrina while he was sleeping. She was found to have died of stab wounds, but the autopsy also showed she had been sexually assaulted. Several witnesses had seen Brad Reese intoxicated the night before, and he had also "fondled" a woman in a bar. Brad was charged with murder, but the murder weapon was never found and the motive never really became clear. In the second case, Bugsy Jacques, a 38-year-old black man, was dating Gena Mason's sister, Angela, who lived with her. On the night Gena was killed Bugsy was intoxicated. He argued with Gena, and she apparently kicked or pushed his dog with her foot. Bugsy pulled out a gun and said, "As long as you live, don't you ever put your foot on my dog." He then shot Gena and fled. Bugsy later contacted Angela to apologize for hurting her family. He said that he did mean to shoot Gena, but not to kill her. Bugsy was charged with murder.

Two final cases involve men killing older female relatives. One son killed his mother as she tried to intervene during a family fight. Clint Worm, a black man aged 43, was fighting with his son Reggie Worm when his mother, Clarissa Worm, aged 67, tried to separate them. She had just undergone heart surgery and the struggle killed her. In a similar case, a fight between a nephew, Rapheal Ardilles, a Latino man aged 33, and his niece was interrupted by Rapheal's aunt, Bella Rubio, a 73-year-old Latino woman. Rapheal shoved Bella into a wall, killing her.

## Conclusion

By far the majority of individual women killed in domestic homicides die at the hands of their intimate male partners. African Americans are significantly overrepresented among the ranks of perpetrators and victims. Note that twice as many black victims were unmarried as were married, a demographic detail that differs from white and Latino homicides. These killings of individual women are highly stylized. Moreover, they are often preceded by various permutations and combinations of several factors: a history of woman battering, accompanied by increasing threats to kill and an extreme possessiveness; attempts to separate from the abusive partner; and prior involvement with agencies such as the police and the courts. Even though almost half of the male perpetrators had criminal histories at the time they killed, few suffered from demonstrable mental illness that took the form of a disorganized personality. These etiologies reflect a much broader power relationship between men and women, with the former at least attempting to assert some control over their partners, who they may have perceived to be slipping away from them or simply betraying them. I will return to the role of this dynamic of domination and subordination in Chapter 7.

    As in the intimate-partner killings, the women who died in family homicides of various kinds had typically been embroiled in long-standing disputes with their killers. Consistent with the extant literature, men typically committed these homicides, although it is important to note that women, as the case studies reveal, were also capable of using lethal violence.

# 5. The Death of Men
# in Single Killings

I now turn to how men are killed by intimate partners, love triangle antagonists or sexual competitors, and family members. Consistent with the findings presented in the extant literature, intimate male partners were killed
largely by women, whereas love triangle antagonists and family members
were killed, in all but one case, by men. As in previous chapters, my approach
is one of "thick description," flavored by the ecology of the street and the
microprocesses of human interaction. Before embarking on this archival
analysis, I outline the main numerical patterns in the 58 homicides, showing
the distribution of killing by intimates, family members, love triangle antagonists, and others (Table 5.1). Intimate partners, 24 of whom were women,
killed 26 men. Nine men killed other men during love triangle disputes.
Another 20 men perished in family disputes between those related by blood,
marriage, or cohabitation; of these 20, 19 were killed by men and 1 by a woman.
Two men died after they refused to put down their weapons when confronted
by police at a domestic disturbance. The remaining man to die was a bystander
during a domestic dispute.

## The Intimate-Partner Killing of Men by Women

The death of men at the hands of their intimate female partners forms the
principal subject of this chapter. Among the nonmultiple killings in the Florida
sample, only 24 women killed their intimate male partners, as opposed to the
67 men who killed their female intimates. The intimate-partner homicides
reveal specific patterns involving the sex, race or ethnicity, and marital status
of perpetrators and victims. As in previous forms of intimate-partner killing,
the fatalities are almost exclusively intersexual and intraracial or intra-ethnic
phenomena. As Table 5.2 shows, black women perpetrated 16 of the 24 killings
of male intimate partners by women. Of these sixteen black women, 5 were

### TABLE 5.1

Breakdown of men killed

| Adult male victim's relationship to perpetrator | Male perpetrator | Female perpetrator | Totals |
|---|---|---|---|
| Intimate partner | 2 | 24 | 26 |
| Family member | 19 | 1 | 20 |
| Love triangle antagonist | 9 | 0 | 9 |
| Police domestic shooting | 2 | 0 | 2 |
| Friend/bystander | 1 | 0 | 1 |
| Total adult male victims | 33 | 25 | 58 |

### TABLE 5.2

Breakdown of intimate-partner killing with one male victim

| Perpetrator | Victim | Partners married | Partners unmarried | Totals |
|---|---|---|---|---|
| WM | WM | 0 | 2 | 2 |
| WF | WM | 5 | 2 | 7 |
| BM | BM | 0 | 0 | 0 |
| BF | BM | 5 | 10 | 15 |
| LM | LM | 0 | 0 | 0 |
| LF | LM | 1 | 0 | 1 |
| BL F | LM | 0 | 1 | 1 |
| Totals | | 11 | 15 | 26 |

Code: W = White; B = Black; L = Latino; M = Male; F = Female

married to the men they killed and 11 were not. This vast overrepresentation of black women (especially unmarried ones) among the ranks of women who kill men is entirely consistent with the results found in the extant research literature. Of the 7 white women who killed their intimate male partners, 5 were married to them and 2 were cohabiting with them. Again, the findings that white women kill fewer intimate male partners than black women, and that white women who do so are more likely to be married than not married to those partners, are consistent with the literature. Only 2 Latino women (1 white, 1 black) killed their male partners. Both these women were of Cuban descent.

## Microdynamics

It is not just the difference in numbers that stands out when comparing the intimate killings committed by men and women. There is also a profound difference in motive, etiology, and context. Women typically kill their intimate male partners in self-defense and within the confines of an increasingly abusive relationship. As noted in Chapter 1, Wolfgang uses the term "victim precipitation" to capture that interactional process whereby a victim of a crime engages in an act that elicits or partially elicits a violent response on the part of the perpetrator.[1] In his study of 588 criminal homicides in Philadelphia, Wolfgang was keen to demonstrate that many killings do not occur randomly, but rather are the outcome of a series of interactions between persons who often know each other.[2] Although the victim may not have intended his actions to elicit a lethal response, and although juries may not deem the precipitation to be sufficient to acquit the perpetrator of charges of murder, the killer nevertheless felt endangered to the point of responding in a manner that resulted in the death of the precipitant.

The concept of "victim precipitation" helps explain most of the 24 intimate-partner killings of men by women. However, as Luckenbill points out, it is necessary when using the term "victim precipitation" not to ignore all the complex interactions that precede and surround the homicide, interactions that may involve more parties than the killer and the victim.[3] Indeed, in the case of the 24 Florida killings, "victim precipitation" amounts to more than just the acts of violence directed at the perpetrator by the victim. Rather, one must explore the constellation of controls used by men in an attempt to regulate women's lives. Furthermore, the archival files clearly show that women resist male violence not only with violence of their own but with other countermeasures. Amidst this ebb and flow of power between those who are soon to be dead and those who are to survive, one must also explore the gendered manifestation of obsessive-possessive behavior, threats to kill, resort to support services, and attempts to leave or end tumultuous relationships. In short, to understand why women kill their intimate male partners, one must transcend the logic of the criminal law and its concern with appropriate defensive force, retreat rules, and perceptions of imminent danger, and instead socially situate the use of lethal violence amidst that panoply of relationship microdynamics and political forces that precedes and accompanies the homicide. Tables 5.3 and 5.4 address some of these microdynamics by exploring the interrelated

## TABLE 5.3
### Female perpetrators and antecedents to the intimate killing of men

| Antecedent | No. cases | % of 24 |
|---|---|---|
| Evidence of female perpetrator offensively assaulting victim during relationship | 5 | 20.8 |
| Evidence of female perpetrator and male victim both using offensive intimate violence during relationship | 4 | 16.7 |
| Evidence suggesting that female perpetrator was only party to have used offensive intimate violence during relationship | 1 | 4.2 |
| Female has left male partner or is in process of separating | 4 | 16.7 |
| Female perpetrator displayed jealousy of victim's activities | 5 | 20.8 |
| Female perpetrator made threats to kill male victim during relationship | 1 | 4.2 |
| Prior police contact in cases where women used offensive violence against male partner | 2 | 8.3 |
| Female perpetrator has prior criminal history | 7 | 29.2 |
| Alcohol and/or drug consumption by female perpetrator preceding fatality | 8 | 33.3 |
| Female perpetrator obtained restraining order(s) against male victim at some point during relationship | 2 | 8.3 |
| Female perpetrator deeply distressed over ongoing child custody dispute | 1 | 4.2 |

antecedents of the Florida killings from the standpoint of the female perpetrator and the male victim.

One of the outstanding characteristics of the relationship between women who kill and men who are killed that emerges from Tables 5.3 and 5.4 is the deeply compromised and entrapped position of women. This acute entrapment comes into sharper focus if we compare the situation here with that of the women who were killed by intimate male partners. In cases of male-perpetrated multiple killings, the intimate partners were separated in 7 relationships out of 10 (see Table 2.5). Likewise, when men killed female intimates in nonmultiple killings, the partners were separated in 6 of 10 cases (see Table 4.3). However, in the 24 female killings of male intimates, the parties were in the process of separating, or actually separated, in only 4 cases (16.7 percent). In 21 out of 24 cases (87.5 percent) there was clear evidence of a history of domestic violence.

## TABLE 5.4
### Male victims and the precipitation of the intimate killing of men

| Antecedent | No. cases | % of 24 |
|---|---|---|
| Evidence of male victim offensively assaulting perpetrator during relationship | 20 | 83.3 |
| Evidence of male victim and female perpetrator both using offensive intimate violence during relationship | 4 | 16.7 |
| Evidence suggesting that male victim was only party to have used offensive intimate violence during relationship | 16 | 66.7 |
| Male has left female partner or is in process of separating | 0 | 0.0 |
| Male victim displayed jealousy of perpetrator's activities | 6 | 25.0 |
| Male victim made threats to kill female perpetrator prior to homicide | 8 | 33.3 |
| Prior police contact in cases where men used offensive violence against female partner | 8 | 33.3 |
| Male victim had prior criminal history | 5 | 20.8 |
| Drug and/or alcohol consumption by perpetrator and/or victim preceding fatality | 13 | 54.2 |
| Male victim obtained restraining order(s) against female perpetrator at some point during relationship | 0 | 0.0 |
| Female perpetrator obtained restraining order(s) against male victim at some point during relationship | 2 | 8.3 |
| Male perpetrator deeply distressed over ongoing child custody dispute | 1 | 4.2 |

The multiagency archival materials most often point to men as the aggressors; in only 1 homicide where sufficient archival material was available was I able to find no history of male violence. Even in this case, the killing of Victor Green by his girlfriend Kelly Krish, Kelly was the recipient of acute emotional abuse. Police noted their involvement with the parties before the homicide in about one-third of the 24 cases. Notably, only 2 of the 24 women had acquired protection orders against their abusers during the course of their conflictual relationships. Like the "separation" factor, the very low proportion of women with protection orders contrasts markedly with those cases where men killed women. In both multiple and nonmultiple intimate-partner killings of women by men, about a quarter of the female victims had obtained orders of protection at some point in their relationship (see Tables 2.5 and 4.3). What this may indicate is that women in violent relationships who end up killing their abusers may be unable, for whatever reasons, to call on the courts for protection. Likewise, for whatever reasons, nearly all those women who killed had not left their abusers and were not in the process of leaving them. Of the 2 women who had prior protection orders against violent men, 1 was separated and in a new intimate relationship and the other had obtained a temporary ex parte order on the morning she killed her husband. The lives of both were being threatened by their male partners on an ongoing basis. My point here is that the overall analysis of the interrelated antecedents suggests that most women who killed were backed into a corner and could not escape. Their entrapment was acute and intense. Some of them were also profoundly frustrated with and angered by the behavior of their male partners. Notably, and unlike women who died in multiple and nonmultiple intimate-partner killings, 5 of the 24 women who killed (20.8 percent) articulated a jealousy at the infidelity of their partners. However, I contend that they handled their jealousy differently than did men, not letting it escalate to obsessive possessiveness and its accompanying proprietary claims, stalking, and threats to kill.

Consistent with my analytical schema in earlier chapters, I explore these socially situated and interrelated antecedents to women's use of lethal violence.[4] My main concern is with the issue of domestic violence and victim precipitation. Although I begin this section with a discussion of woman battering and victim precipitation, intimate-partner violence pervades nearly all the cases. Nevertheless, for organizational reasons, I present some cases to illustrate such attendant themes as the crack subculture, the difficulties associated with leaving, the antagonisms surrounding child custody, the issue of women's own feelings of envy, and the role of mental illness.

*Woman Battering and Victim Precipitation*   As noted in Table 5.4, among the 24 cases, 20 evidenced a clear history of woman battering. According to the archival sources, in 16 cases the man was the only perpetrator of violence in the relationship. In 4 other cases the archival data present mixed and at times conflicting accounts from witnesses and the parties; I coded these as showing evidence of both male and female offensive violence. In most cases woman battering was the principal precipitant of the killing. That violence usually punctuated the history of the relationship and directly preceded the fatal episode. In this sense, most of the 24 intimate-partner killings committed by women were consistent with Angela Browne's findings, in which she notes,

"Typically the killing of an abuser was unplanned and occurred in the midst of an attack against the woman, during the warning phase when it became apparent that an attack was about to begin, or during an escape attempt by the woman."[5] Violence immediately prior to the killing, and long-standing battering, likely both contributed to the precipitation of the homicide; it is impossible to distinguish between the roles of each form, or even, perhaps, to argue that they are discrete categories at all. For analytical purposes, I find it useful to draw a distinction between what I will call "proximal" and "distal" precipitating violence. By "proximal precipitating violence," I refer to the violence that immediately precedes the killing and seems to have played a pivotal role in triggering the lethal act. By "distal precipitating violence," I mean violence of long standing, whose grinding, cumulative effect likely fed into the homicide. In most cases of "victim precipitation by violence or intimidation," proximal and distal violence are both present. In only two cases of victim precipitation by violence does the archival material point to distal violence alone. In both these cases women clearly calculated the killing of their intimate male partners. One woman is currently serving life in prison after having been convicted of first-degree murder. The other, although charged with murder in the first degree, pled to second-degree murder and was given a six-year prison sentence followed by probation. I will return to the former of these cases a little later.

June Day, an African American aged 32, shot and killed her live-in boyfriend, Ralph Culpepper, an African American aged 49, after he had attacked her with a knife. The two had been together for three years, having met at the burial of June's brother, which was conducted by the funeral home where Ralph worked as a mortician. When police arrived she was holding their child in her arms; he was lying on the floor, with a knife in his right hand. She told officers that when he attacked her she feared for her life and was forced to kill him. Celeste Green, Ralph's mother, a 65-year-old African American, told police that her son had been living with June for some time, although he had another girlfriend, Vanda Beacon, a 35-year-old African American, with whom he had fathered three children. According to Vanda, she and Ralph had an "on-again, off-again relationship," until he met June. Ralph had long since separated from his first wife, Genie Culpepper, an African American aged 50, with whom he fathered two children. Genie lived in Oakland, California, and played an integral part in this case. On the day of the killing, June called Ralph's mother to find out where he was. According to Celeste the call irritated Ralph, who had told June not to call his mother's house and inquire into his whereabouts.

Indeed, the victim's mother told police she was "sick of his girlfriends calling her house to see where Ralph was."

A number of witnesses attested to Ralph's propensity for battering June. Bill Murdock, an African American aged 45, said he had known Ralph since 1965 and that on one occasion he had heard June tell Ralph, "You're not going to dog me for Vanda. You're not going to do that. You will die first." Having conveyed this to police, Bill also made it clear that his friend battered June. Specifically, Bill reported that Ralph had a "very strong temper" and that he had seen him "knock the hell out of June before." June herself remarked to investigators that she had previously been battered by Ralph and that she only struck him in retaliation. As a corrections officer, June knew how to defend herself. Just before the killing the two had been arguing, and Ralph knocked her down. He then left the apartment and returned a short time later and fixed himself a drink. June told police that he next appeared holding a kitchen knife, saying that as a mortician he could "kill her in a second" because "he knew where to cut." Ralph then approached June, and they struggled over the knife. During the struggle June cut her hand on the blade. When Ralph pushed her to the ground, she grabbed the gun and shot him twice.

The other woman in this love triangle, Vanda Beacon, also reported that Ralph "had a very bad temper." However, she said he had never struck her offensively, although he was "verbally argumentative." Vanda refused to let Ralph live with her and their three children until he made up his mind who he wanted to be with—her, or June Day. Genie Culpepper, Ralph's first wife, said he had beaten her during the time they were married and this was the reason she left him. She also reported that, in general, "Ralph fought with women."

In the Culpepper case, the police did not appear convinced that June had shot Ralph in self-defense and at least implied the possible existence of an ulterior motive. Investigators contacted the Prudential Insurance Company, which held an upgraded policy on Ralph Culpepper's life that named June Day as the sole beneficiary. Apparently the coverage had been raised from $25,000 to $100,000 in May 1994, just two months before the homicide. This is the only one of the 24 cases in which women killed their intimate male partners where insurance payouts are mentioned in the archival data as a possible motive. However, when the state's attorney's office put all of the information together, prosecutors cleared the case as justifiable homicide, recognizing the role of Ralph's precipitating violence.

This case is unusual among those involving the intimate killing of men in the African-American community because the perpetrator and victim both had well-paying jobs with benefits. June Day was entitled to legal counsel by virtue of her job with the federal prison system. Ralph Culpepper, a mortician of long standing, had good insurance coverage, including separate policies naming his mother and his girlfriend Vanda Beacon as beneficiaries. However, Ralph resembled a number of the other African-American men who died in domestic homicides in that he had fathered children with different women and was not married to the woman who killed him.

Joanna Bronte, a white woman aged 26, is currently serving 18 years in prison after a jury found her guilty of second-degree murder for shooting to death her husband, Jasper Bronte, a white man aged 26.[6] The fatal incident occurred just seven weeks after Joanna had given birth to her first child. She had just returned to her job as a bartender after maternity leave. Jasper worked as a mechanic. On the night of the killing the couple argued. Jasper was angry with Joanna because she was out drinking and partying while he was looking after the baby. He was expecting her to come home at 4:00 P.M., but she did not return until after 9:00 P.M. The argument escalated and Joanna reported that Jasper choked her unconscious on the kitchen floor. When she regained consciousness she chased her husband into the bathroom. Joanna broke the blades on two knives before using a butcher knife to hack a hole in the bathroom door. According to Joanna, Jasper then came out of the bathroom and attacked her with a towel rack. At this point, she pulled a gun. He fled to their bedroom. Joanna followed and fired two shots, one of which passed through the bedroom door and struck Jasper in the head, eventually killing him.

Jasper had prior convictions for battering other women he had been in relationships with. In 1989 he assaulted his first wife, the mother of his first child, with whom he lived for three years. He had also beaten Joanna on a number of occasions, and in 1992 he was convicted of assaulting her. In that same year police arrested them both for domestic violence, although charges were later dropped. Apparently, just weeks before the killing, sheriffs deputies were called to the residence for a domestic disturbance. However, departmental records show the complaint was not deemed serious enough to warrant a report.

For police and prosecutors, Joanna appeared to be the aggressor during the episode that led to the fatality. They clearly did not accept her account that she felt backed into a corner where she had to shoot Jasper. Joanna's own history of violence made it easier for prosecutors to see her as the aggressor and therefore to pursue first-degree murder charges. Her criminal record dates back to 1982 and contains 19 offenses. Most are minor charges, but her record does show arrests for disorderly conduct, burglary, damaging private property, and resisting arrest. This history, with its elements of violence, enabled prosecutors to present Joanna as a heavy-drinking, ill-tempered, and strong-willed woman who understood perfectly well what she was doing when she killed her husband. Indeed, in her closing argument the prosecutor told the jury, "This is a woman who can get pretty pissed off when she's been drinking."

Although the crime scene evidence is open to many interpretations, I think it perfectly reasonable to argue, contrary to the jury's findings, that Jasper used proximal precipitating violence that led to his demise. Put differently, a reasonable argument could be made that Joanna killed her husband without planning and also without malice aforethought. This kind of killing would qualify as manslaughter rather than murder. Indeed, prior to trial, the state offered a plea bargain of manslaughter with eight years in prison as an alternative to proceeding with first-degree murder charges.[7] The fact that Jasper also used violence throughout this relationship to exert control over Joanna—who by all accounts could, at least to some extent, take care of herself—is also suggestive of self-defense or manslaughter rather than murder.

Through the testimony of witnesses, relatives, and friends, Joanna's master status emerged at trial as that of a tough young woman who did not fit the mold of dutiful and submissive wife. Rather, she drank alcohol, hung out in bars, and seemed to feel very much at home in the bar subculture. Given that she came from a small town in Wisconsin with a high density of drinking establishments and plenty of dark, cold time, her proclivity for frequenting bars and enjoying that subculture is not surprising. The record also shows Joanna sometimes expressed her anger in a violent or destructive way. A former boyfriend mentioned to police that back in Wisconsin Joanna had "knocked a guy's teeth out" during a physical fight in a tavern. Her defense attorney told me of another incident in a bar in which Joanna hit Jasper with a cue stick in an unprovoked assault. Another witness described her as a "little on the wild side" and a "heavy drinker." The owner of her local tavern in Wisconsin said Joanna had to be asked to leave on one occasion for falsely accusing a man of not paying up on a debt. She had to be removed forcibly and once in the parking lot used a knife to slash the tires on two vehicles. Joanna was arrested for this offense and found guilty of damaging private property (November 13,

1990). However, these seemingly negative characteristics did not prevent the Florida Department of Health and Rehabilitative Services from deeming her to be a "fit mother," nor the judge in the Florida murder case from releasing her before trial on only $5,000 bond, stating that she did not pose a threat to the community.

Other evidence suggests that Joanna was a battered woman who was merely defending herself in the way she knew best. She told a sheriff's deputy at the scene, "He treated me like fucking dirt. . . . A person can only be pushed so far." These words point to a relationship punctuated by Jasper's attempts to control Joanna. In one earlier incident leading to arrest, he knocked her from their vehicle, skinning her knees. She walked home. When she got there Jasper shoved her into a bedroom, removed the phone that was there, and locked her in. Rather than submit to his control, Joanna knocked out the bedroom window, walked to a friend's house, and called the police. When officers arrived they arrested Jasper for disorderly conduct.

After eight hours of testing and interviews with Joanna and analysis of prior police reports, Lenore Walker, a clinical and forensic psychologist and author of *The Battered-Woman Syndrome,* concluded in her expert testimony that Joanna indeed suffered from the syndrome at the time she killed Jasper. Walker told the jury that it was her professional opinion that Joanna "believed Jasper was going to kill her." She also carefully laid out an escalating history of violence directed by Jasper at his wife, further bolstering her claims that Joanna was a battered woman. Joanna herself testified that Jasper lost interest in their unborn child once he found it was to be a girl and that he was mean to her during the birthing. The manager of the Brontes' apartment complex reported seeing bruises on Joanna's upper arms about a month before the homicide.

During her argument with Jasper on the night of the killing, Joanna called her mother and told her to expect her to come home because she could not stand to live with her husband any more. One reason for the call was to ask her mother for money in order to get out of the relationship. She then told Jasper that she was leaving and taking their baby as well; by her account, this enraged him further. As I have pointed out in connection with other cases, communicating to the batterer the decision to leave a violent relationship is dangerous for women.

Joanna knew her position with Jasper was untenable, and she clearly expressed her depression and disenchantment to others. She told a younger woman who worked with her at the bar, "[N]ever get married and never have kids." Other witnesses told police that Jasper was not happy with Joanna going back to work at the bar after the birth of their daughter. Indeed, the issue of her returning to work seems to have been central to the argument that resulted in the fatality. According to the archival data, two days before the homicide Jasper told one of his supervisors from work that "he and his wife were arguing about her going back to work at the bar as he did not want her to go back to work. Jasper was also unhappy about having to leave work to take care of the baby while she was at work at the bar."

Although she was indicted for first-degree murder, Joanna was found guilty of murder in the second degree. This means that the jury rejected the state's claim that she had planned the murder, whereas it accepted the prosecutor's arguments that she intentionally killed Jasper with malice aforethought. The jury rejected the expert testimony, which asserted that because of battered-woman syndrome Joanna thought her life to be in danger and therefore acted in self-defense. In reaching this conclusion the jury likely perceived Joanna to have been capable of using offensive as well as defensive violence. Given her history of violent behavior this is hardly surprising. I will return to the issue of women's use of violence. Suffice it to say here that, even if Joanna used offensive violence from time to time in her relationship with Jasper, it does not negate the fact that Jasper contributed to his own death. His contribution was both proximal and distal. Proximally, he choked her into a state of unconsciousness, and he was otherwise threatening and controlling immediately before his demise. Distally, he battered Joanna, rejected their child, and attempted to introduce a regime of ever closer controls into the life of a woman who was prepared to resist them physically.

I now present two subheadings that illustrate the difficulties faced by three black women before they killed their intimate partners. Under the first sub-heading, *Escaping,* I consider the case of a woman who killed her abuser while she was physically trying to leave the relationship. The second subheading, *Crack Subculture,* explores the neighborhood and subcultural influences upon the dynamics of relationships characterized by intimate violence. At least some police and criminal justice players in these three cases portrayed the black women involved as aggressors. To suggest a context for understanding not only the dynamics of these cases, but also how the label of "aggressor" emerges, I preface the three narratives with insights from bell hooks.[8]

hooks argues that black women are a more acutely oppressed group than black men. Before being forced to America on slave ships, black men exerted a powerful patriarchal domination over black women. As hooks puts it:

> White male observers of African culture in the 18th and 19th centuries were astounded and impressed by the African male's subjugation of the African female. They were not accustomed to a patriarchal social order that demanded not only that women accept an inferior status, but that they participate actively in the community labor force.[9]

This style of domination in which African women actively worked beyond the domestic sphere appealed to slaveowners, who needed docile agricultural workers but also wanted women to perform loyal work in the household. Masters did not want to use in their homes black women who threatened the safety and security thereof. Consequently, it was essential to make doubly sure that female house slaves were especially submissive. As a partial result of this need, the subordinate status of African women was constantly reasserted on the slave ships through sexual assault and rape. These ceremonies of degradation constituted a deliberate attempt to reinforce the traditional subjugation of black women. The only difference on the slave ships and the plantations was that the direct oppressors of black women were, first and foremost, white men.

Under the slave-based system of plantation agriculture, female slaves occupied the lowest positions in society. Not only were they raped and ritually whipped by white men, they were also the sexual targets of male slaves, who, as hooks points out, imitated the behavior of white men by raping black women.[10] Insofar as black women and girls produced new slaves, they were useful to slaveholders in a way black men were not. However, even during pregnancy, female slaves were not spared the wrath of punishment. To protect the fetus, pregnant black women and girls were placed naked into holes in the ground. Then they were whipped or beaten about the head, shoulders, and upper back and arms.

At first, slaveowners forced black women to mate indiscriminately. However, after a while it was easier to manage slave culture if partners "chose" their own mates. A system of patriarchy developed among slaves akin to that lived out by whites. Although black men were never in the position to be the complete patriarchs white men were, a system of nuclear families emerged, with already enslaved females now also playing out subservient roles in their own households.

Demographic evidence suggests that the rise of single-parent families headed by women in the black community dates from the 1960s. Many scholars have argued, dubiously, that the institution of slavery psychologically and emotionally emasculated black men, thus leading to the rise of pathological families that came to be headed by black women.[11] Some investigators confused matriarchy with matrilineality and matrifocality. This notion of the black matriarch has its roots in slavery, where two competing stereotypes of black women emerged. The first, "Aunt Jemima," was the happy, loyal, aged "mammy" who loved her work with white families. A number of writers have exposed the falsity of this image. The opposite stereotype portrays some black women as what hooks calls "Sapphires." She notes, "As Sapphires, black women were depicted as evil, treacherous, bitchy, stubborn, and hateful, in short all that the mammy figure was not."[12] There are clear parallels here between the polarities of Aunt Jemimas and Sapphires, and the dichotomy between the "true woman," morally pure and pristine, and the growing ranks of nineteenth-century prostitutes, whose evil and seductive influence rose increasingly in the growing cities of America with the rise of industrial capitalism.[13] The image of the Sapphire is of central importance to my task of making sense of the commission of intimate-partner homicide by black women. hooks elucidates the matter:

> The Sapphire identity has been projected onto any black woman who overtly expresses bitterness, anger, and rage about her lot. . . . The "evilness" of a given black woman may merely be the facade she presents to a sexist-racist world that she realizes would only exploit her if she were to appear vulnerable.[14]

Now I turn to narratives of three cases in which black women kill their intimate partners. For some readers, all three perpetrators may qualify as Sapphires. Certainly there is more than a hint of this belief among some of the police and prosecutors working their cases. However, as the narratives unfold, I evoke black women's collective historical experience and contemporary social condition as a foil to those possible explanations that might lay blame for murder or manslaughter at the feet of Sapphires and their seeming hatefulness. The historical legacy of slavery and oppression cannot be underestimated as a context for explaining how it is that African-American women appear to be differentially entrapped in violent domestic relationships to the point that they are compelled to kill. Notwithstanding the unique difficulties faced by Latino, Caucasian, and Asian women, none of these groups seems to contain anything like the number of deeply entrapped victims of domestic violence as is found among their black counterparts.

*Escaping: Separation, Estrangement, Divorce*  Rochelle Hunter, a black woman aged 44, had lived with Bernard Russ, a black man aged 42, for about a year and a half. A native of Jamaica, Russ had come to Florida in 1974 and worked as a plumber. Rochelle was temporarily unemployed due to a recent surgery, although she had earlier worked in restaurants as a cook and then a supervisor. On the day of the killing Rochelle was attempting to leave the relationship, and the apartment the couple shared. Both her daughter and her church had given her money to find a new place to live. As she was leaving, she told police, Bernard confronted her in the driveway and threatened to cut her throat. Rochelle picked up a brick and hit him in the head, killing him.

There appears to have been no history of Bernard beating Rochelle. Although he directed some violence at her just before the killing, in essence this case is one of proximal precipitating threat. The menace seemed all the more real to Rochelle because of the distal violence that she understood Bernard to have employed in his earlier relationships with women. Excerpts from her interrogation by police provide information on the nature of the precipitation process.

> *Rochelle*  He said, "I'm going to cut your throat." He was sitting inside the van.
> *Police Officer*  Did you see a knife?
> *Rochelle*  I didn't see it. I didn't give him a chance. . . . I was afraid of Bernard. I thought he was going to cut me, 'cos' he brags about how he beat his wife.
> *Police Officer*  Have you known him to carry a knife on his person, or in his vehicle?
> *Rochelle*  Yes. . . . It's a switchblade knife with a white, pearl-type handle.

Investigators found a switchblade in one of Bernard Russ's pockets after he was taken to the hospital. Friends described him to police as a peaceful man who enjoyed playing cricket. According to them, Bernard carried a knife as one of his tools as a plumber. None of the friends said they knew about his history of abusing women. When confronted with Bernard's penchant for battering, one of them remarked: "I have no recollection of that. . . . That is not what I know of him. If that were true I would be more than surprised. I know him to be a very peaceful man. He was involved in helping the woman find a new apartment."

In his interview, a detective began to ask Rochelle about her ability to cope with anger. However, the conversation took a different turn.

> *Detective* People get angry. . . . Has anybody ever scared you before or anything like that?
>
> *Rochelle* I have had men beat me all my life. Ever since I was 15 years old I've been beaten by men. I was married to a man for 8 months and he was kicking me in my face and everything. I got away from that. I'd been working and taking care of myself and I met Bernard. I had known him for 12 years but we just only been together for a couple of years. I didn't know he had a history of fighting nobody.

At one point in the investigation, an anonymous employee of a restaurant where Rochelle had worked called police and informed them that she was a "mean person." Investigators went to the workplace and found and interviewed one employee, Carl Coke, who said he once got into an altercation with Rochelle about who should clean some pots and pans. By his account, she threw a knife at him and it stuck into the wall beside him. The exchange between the detective and Carl Coke proceeded as follows.

> *Detective* What kind of reputation did she have amongst the employees? Was she a company person or was she a short-tempered person or . . . ?
>
> *Coke* She was very much a company person. She was a corps instructor, which means she would go to new units when they opened up and train people, work there for a couple of weeks, help get things under way. She had a reputation as very stern. You couldn't tell her anything. She knew everything there was to know about making pies and I don't know if she had a reputation for being short tempered, I mean, she was a big girl and you knew not to upset her, push an issue with her.
>
> *Detective* Was that because of her physical size?
>
> *Coke* I would say so, yeah.

With access to only part of the information in this case, it is not difficult to understand how Rochelle could be seen as someone approaching the Sapphire stereotype. One unidentified caller had labeled her a "mean person." Another coworker had borne the brunt of her temper as she supposedly threw a knife at him. A local newspaper reported the respective body sizes of Rochelle and Bernard in the very first lines of the initial article on the case: "Bernard Russ was slim, 5 feet tall and Rochelle Hunter's boyfriend. Rochelle weighs 250 pounds, is 5 feet 4 inches tall."[15] The reader is left with the image of a rather large size discrepancy between the partners, in a story involving a woman who is potentially mean and capable of using a knife.

However, I contend that a more accurate interpretation puts forward an oppressed black woman, brutalized since adolescence by men, but surviving on her own and rising to a supervisory job. There is no doubt that Bernard Russ had a history of brutalizing women. He was arrested in 1986 for spousal battery and improper exhibition of a weapon. Between 1989 and 1992 his girlfriend at the time made four other reports of domestic violence perpetrated by him to police. Given black women's collective experience of violent victimization at the hands of both black and white men, it is not hard to see how their use of violence may have evolved as a resistive strategy that is passed across generations of mothers, aunts, sisters, and other female relatives. Rochelle was in a vulnerable position. She was temporarily sidelined from work by surgery and was short of cash. She was also acutely aware of Bernard's propensity for battering women. In fact, Bernard bragged to Rochelle about how he beat his wife. If we combine the historic vulnerability of black women with Rochelle's own susceptibility in her personal relationship, we begin to see the onerous forces compelling her toward a preemptive strike with the brick.

Rochelle was a physically strong woman. The brick she hit Bernard with was 2 feet long and weighed 19 pounds. Put simply, she did not give him a chance to get the knife out or mess with her. In many ways her case recalls that of Joanna Bronte, who killed Jasper Bronte. Neither woman fits the mold of submissive partner. Joanna Bronte is white, and there are few cases of white women behaving as she did among the sample where intimate male partners are killed. As noted earlier, this is probably because proportionately fewer white women are entrapped in domestic relationships that are so violent that they are compelled to kill. However, in essence, both Rochelle and Joanna were deeply entrapped and both likely saw the defensive actions they took as their only options.

As in the killing of Jasper Bronte, prosecutors sought a murder conviction. However, although she was charged with second-degree murder, Rochelle Hunter (like Joanna) was offered a plea bargain of negligent manslaughter.

Unlike Joanna, she was offered credit for the 212 days she had served in jail, and she agreed to be released under a five-year suspended sentence. Comparisons aside, the two cases are fundamentally different. Although one might argue that Joanna Bronte's provocation seemed greater and more immediate, it was Rochelle Hunter who ended up with the lighter sentence. However, even if both women had been offered the same sentence under a manslaughter plea bargain, Rochelle, without a child to care for, may have been much better placed to take it, since Joanna had a young daughter whom she did not want to give up.

*Crack Subculture*   The increased role of crack cocaine in the lives of girls and women in inner cities beginning in the mid-1980s has been well documented.[16] Rather than demonizing the use of this drug, Bourgois and Dunlap observe that crack is simply the "latest medium through which the already desperate are expressing publicly their suffering and hopelessness."[17] Based upon their interviews with 14 female crack users in Harlem, most of them African Americans, Fullilove, Lown, and Fullilove argue that the general trauma and abuse these women experienced propelled them into drug use.[18] As they became drug dependent, the women became less able to meet "culturally defined gender roles" (e.g., mothering). This failure created a different kind of trauma, which further fed the need to dampen the pain, which thereby exacerbated drug abuse. Once fully enmeshed in the male-dominated crack subculture, the women were further ensnared and victimized by an unusual and highly exploitative form of prostitution in which they traded their bodies for crack. According to Fullilove, Lown, and Fullilove, women consume crack in binges where "pursuit and use of the drug outweight other concerns."[19] Often this consumption occurs in crack houses run by men, and as addiction develops it is accompanied by the "degradation of women within crack culture."[20] Phillipe Bourgois puts it this way:

> The spectacle of publicly addicted women is exacerbated by the misogyny of street culture. The male-dominated ranks of the underground economy exclude females from the more profitable, autonomous entrepreneurial niches such as dealing, mugging, and burglarizing. . . . [W]omen are still forced disproportionately to rely on prostitution to finance their habits and to support what remains of their families. . . . Crack addicts are also particularly vulnerable to public sexual humiliation, as they tolerate

extreme levels of verbal and physical abuse in their pursuit of the initial sixty- to ninety-second ecstatic rush provided by smoking the drug.[21]

Joyce Cameron, a black woman aged 19, fatally stabbed her boyfriend, Eugene Mosley, a black man aged 30, in the chest after he had knocked her down and tried to drag her up a flight of stairs into their apartment. The couple had been together for five years. According to a witness at the scene, Joyce stood beside the body saying, "I couldn't take it any more. I couldn't take him beating on me and I had to do it." A neighbor, Flora Hird, a black woman aged 45, said to officers that Eugene and Joyce fought constantly and that she had called the police to their residence a number of times. Flora Hird saw "Joyce as the aggressor in a majority of the disputes" and told investigators she had stabbed Eugene before. She also mentioned to officers that Eugene "ran over Joyce with a car, but she wasn't sure if it was intentional."

As the fatal incident began, Joyce was having her period and wanted Eugene to buy her some tampons. He refused. She went out to make the purchase and returned to find him smoking crack cocaine with a friend, Anton Michaels, a black man in his early thirties. Joyce reported that "Eugene was in the bathroom and the whole house smelled like crack. When I walked in he had a crack pipe in his hand." According to her statement she told him, "You laying in bed fucking me . . . I need what I need. . . . [y]'all know what I'm saying? [A]nd you can't get me a box of tampons . . . but you can go buy a piece of God-damn rock. . . . You know I caught you smoking that God-damn rock." Eugene became enraged that she should challenge him about his use of crack. He replied to her, "You don't sit here and tell me my business." She left the apartment but took a knife with her, because "every time he smokes that stuff he gets angry." Joyce felt sure that Eugene would follow her downstairs and attack her. As she was knocking at the door of another apartment in order to telephone the police, he apparently threatened her. Joyce told investigators Eugene said, "I'm gonna drag you right back up them damn stairs." She reported warning him, "You come close to me and I'm gonna cut you." In spite of having the knife, Joyce was afraid of Eugene. By her account, on one occasion he'd "dangled her over the balcony rail."

Investigators gathered information from persons at the scene very quickly. Although a number of witnesses were uncooperative and told the police little, others were more forthcoming. They suggested that Joyce was an aggressive young woman who enjoyed hanging out in the area. The patrol officer at the scene also suspected that both Eugene Mosley and Joyce Cameron used crack. This overall image of her became a part of the language of interrogation almost instantly.

> *Detective*   What kind of relationship did you and Eugene have?
>
> *Joyce*   We been together five years. . . . I always been abused.
>
> *Detective*   But you've also abused him, 'cause there are reports where you stabbed him once.
>
> *Joyce*   Yeah, I cut him, 'cos' I don't know what he do to me.
>
> *Detective*   How many times have you stabbed him before?
>
> *Joyce*   Just once . . . just once. . . . I never stabbed him that bad like I did tonight.

The detective asked Joyce why she did not leave the relationship. He used her experience of abuse as a bridge into the question about leaving. Perhaps the detective was simply insensitive to the plight of battered women and unaware of the complex difficulties of "just leaving." Or perhaps he posed the question in this way to get some sense of just how intimidated Joyce was by Eugene. Whatever the detective's motive, the persona presented by Joyce changes from that of a tough aggressor to someone oppressed and very afraid of being subjected to more serious forms of violence.

> *Detective*   Now during this whole time, he's abused you, why didn't you leave the relationship?
>
> *Joyce*   I loved him and he had told me nobody could have me if he couldn't have me.
>
> *Detective*   So you didn't leave 'cos' he was threatening you? I need to hear you say that.
>
> *Joyce*   He got more violent.
>
> *Detective*   How did he abuse you?
>
> *Joyce*   He ran me over. We just got through arguing.
>
> *Detective*   Just to note, Joyce is showing me a large scar area on the inside of her left leg and thigh. . . . What else has he done to you?
>
> *Joyce*   He bit me on my finger. He beat my head against the wall. He put a dent in the wall. And he pulled my hair out. When we first met, he was buying me and giving me things . . . jewelry and everything. Then things changed. . . . You see that black eye right there . . . I done had plenty of them. . . . [S]ee my lip . . . I done had plenty of them.

Neighbors placed a number of calls to police and emergency medical services immediately after Joyce had knifed Eugene. The dispatcher's log shows that a patrol car was sent to the scene at once, along with emergency medical services. Several other police cars arrived there within a few minutes of being dispatched. Emergency medical personnel arrived within 10 minutes and treated Eugene Mosley for the stab wound. He was pronounced dead at a nearby hospital within 40 minutes of the time the initial 911 call was received. The first patrol officer at the scene spent less than 30 seconds in the ambulance with Mosley. He was attempting to obtain information, but the medical personnel told him they had to go and that Mosley had only a faint pulse.

It lies beyond the scope of my research to comment on anything other than the timing of the delivery of medical services. Without much more extensive field research, it would be inappropriate to assess the quality of medical care received and how this may have contributed to whether Eugene Mosley survived and whether Joyce Cameron ended up being arrested for murder or merely aggravated assault. Superficially, it does seem as though police and medical services were dispatched as quickly as possible and that this call received priority over all others received in the same period. It also appears from the statements of witnesses that this was a poor, multi-unit apartment complex where a number of residents were known to police to use or deal crack cocaine. From my reading of the transcripts of conversations between officers and witnesses at the scene, relations between the police and the residents of the apartment complex might best be described as tense. It does not seem that this tension, in and of itself, resulted in delay or hesitation in the delivery of police or medical services.

Charlotte Rentry, an 18-year-old African American, lived with Fred Kemble, a 32-year-old African American. Their relationship began when she was 14 and had been put under his legal guardianship by her alcoholic mother. According to one key informant, Fred was a street-level cocaine dealer who had a lot of disposable cash. Charlotte apparently liked the fact that Fred enjoyed a reasonable standard of living. While she was still under his legal guardianship, they had a daughter together (aged 2 at the time of the homicide). On the night Charlotte stabbed Fred to death, he and his older brother, Ed, told her they were going to see a friend, Barry Humper. Within 30 minutes of the two brothers' leaving the residence, Barry Humper came to the house. He informed Charlotte that he had not seen either man that evening. Feeling as if her partner had lied to her and believing that he was seeing another woman, Charlotte became enraged. She had a long history of disputes with Fred.[22] Anticipating a confrontation when Fred returned, she hid a knife in the curtains near the headboard of their waterbed. She told police that she often hid knives or sticks in anticipation of fights with Fred, because displaying a knife was usually enough to stop his aggressive advances. When the two brothers returned, Fred and Charlotte argued through their daughter's bedroom window. Charlotte had locked all the doors to the residence to prevent Fred from entering. However, after their initial verbal exchange, he broke into the residence by pushing in a screen and climbing through the window. He then opened the front door for his brother. Ed took the daughter into another room while Fred and Charlotte argued for at least one hour. During the altercation, she apparently broke a beer bottle on the sidewalk and threatened to cut him with it. At another point, Charlotte picked up a knife and gestured toward Fred with it. She told police that this tactic had worked in the past, with Fred usually backing off from assaulting her. However, she said he came up to her and tried to wrestle the knife out of her hands. It was then, she claimed, that she accidentally stabbed him, going on to say that she did not realize she had injured him until she saw the blood on herself.

There does not appear to have been any proximal precipitating violence from Fred directed at Charlotte. Rather, the precipitation is through the distal battering and the sense of fear and intimidation that it produced.[23] Charlotte talked of this fear to investigators.

> *Detective*   All right, you went into your bedroom?
> *Charlotte*   Yeah.
> *Detective*   And then you looked around and you saw Fred standing in the doorway?
> *Charlotte*   Yeah.
> *Detective*   And you could tell by the look on his face he wasn't going to let you out?
> *Charlotte*   He wasn't going to let me out.
> *Detective:*   Did he say anything about not letting you out?
> *Charlotte*   No, no. . . . When I see him looking how he was looking and he was just blocking the doorway . . . I just grabbed the knife and hid. And it wasn't like "I'm going to stab you and everything," I wasn't planning to use it or nothing. I just was trying to scare him to make him move out of the way so I can go on out.

*Detective*   What did he say when he saw that you grabbed the knife?

*Charlotte*   He was just looking all crazy and everything. We were just looking at each other.

*Detective*   Now what do you mean when you say he was looking crazy? What did he look like?

*Charlotte*   He had this mean look on his face. Anger.

As Lee Bowker observes, battered women are extremely sensitive to subtle behavioral changes in their abusers that signal impending violence.[24] As such a woman, Charlotte was cueing into Fred's anger and reading it for what it predicted—the likelihood of her getting hurt. For police and prosecutors, Charlotte was the aggressor in the fatal incident. Consequently, she is charged with second-degree murder. The basis of the state's case derives from both physical evidence at the crime scene and police and prosecutors' interpretation of Charlotte's demeanor. Obviously not wanting to compromise the state's position at trial, the prosecuting attorney refused to discuss the case with me or any of her prior dealings with Charlotte. According to police, Fred was killed by a stab wound that would have required a downward motion of the knife. In their eyes, such a deep stab wound, which penetrated his heart and lungs, could not have been accidental or inadvertent and was therefore inconsistent with Charlotte's description of events. Officers also questioned why Charlotte hid the knife when, if she anticipated trouble, she could have left the apartment or called the police.

In addition, investigators I talked with who knew both the case and Charlotte told me that in their opinion she was capable of the kind of offensive violence required to kill her partner. One of them pointed out to me that while she was awaiting trial Charlotte was charged with aggravated assault. When I asked the officer why she was not prosecuted, he said he did not know. However, as is clear from her rap sheet, she was charged with aggravated assault in 1996, but the prosecutor declined to proceed against her. Although the prosecutor would not explain why the state did not take the aggravated assault case against Charlotte to trial, another key informant told me that the incident involved several black men who approached Charlotte in a parking lot and asked her if she wanted some crack cocaine. She felt threatened by one of them and shoved him. Another man in the group called police, complaining about her aggressive demeanor. The responding officer arrested Charlotte, and she was eventually charged with disorderly conduct and aggravated assault. Yet another source told me that Charlotte felt very threatened by the men, that she did not use crack cocaine, and that the charges were spurious.

Here is what she had to say to investigators about her experience of abuse at the hands of Fred and her search for some "respect."

> *Detective*   What are the fights mostly about?
> *Charlotte*   If it ain't something that he want me to do [it's] he start cursing me out and I start to curse him out. I want him, you know, to respect me. . . . I knew him before and I knew he was messing with a lot of females.
> *Detective*   So you suspect he's still messing with other females?
> *Charlotte*   Yeah.

As noted earlier, one of the reasons the state is taking the case to trial is that prosecutors believe Charlotte failed to call the police or take other actions to avoid a confrontation with Fred. In her conversations with investigators, Charlotte explained that she did not call the police because she and Fred had "been fighting ever since we met and I'd called the police before. When I called them before about him, we was fighting and he hit me. He punched me and everything and they told me that the only thing I can do is just leave, you know, get my stuff and leave."

Charlotte had a young child, few skills to earn an independent living, and no family support network. Consequently, calling the police on a batterer who was dealing cocaine on the street was always about much more than just stopping her personal victimization. To have involved officers risked not only the possibility of police doing nothing and the violence continuing and perhaps escalating, it also invoked the specter of poverty for Charlotte and her daughter. She put it as follows:

> *Detective*   So you've never filed charges against him for beating you up?
> *Charlotte*   No, because he was taking care of me and my baby and he was the only thing I had.

*Child Custody*   Charlotte Rentry's case is one of the few intimate-partner killings of men in which there was no apparent proximal precipitating violence. Another such case, but more unusual still because a woman planned to kill her former husband, involved Erin Newcombe. She murdered her estranged spouse, Bert Newcombe, while he was performing his job as a mailman. At the time of the killing in August 1994, Erin, aged 41, had been married to Bert, aged 47, for 22 years. Both persons were white. They had a 22-year-old daughter and a 9-year-old son. Eight months before the murder, Erin had filed for divorce and moved in with her new boyfriend. Records indicate that Bert told one of his coworkers that the new man in Erin's life had installed windows at their house after Hurricane Andrew. He also told his coworker that he was concerned about this man because he had a criminal history and was also involved in the adult bookstore business. Other witnesses informed officers that Bert had been outraged by Erin's departure and had threatened to kill the whole family, including himself. Bert's threats to kill his wife were clearly communicated to a number of persons and backed by statements that he knew how to commit homicide because of his military training. These threats were passed on to Erin, who, eight months before the killing, obtained a temporary restraining order against him. At one point, Bert tried to enlist the help of his son-in-law, Barry Bingo, to kill Erin. However, Barry promptly communicated these threats to Erin and her new boyfriend. In January 1994, Erin not only obtained the temporary restraining order, but also purchased two handguns from a store in Fort Walton Beach. Her mother said to police that Erin was terrified that Bert would kill her. The mother reported that she heard him tell Erin at one of the custody hearings, "[Y]ou'll never live to see the day you get custody of my kid."

Under the criminal law, Erin Newcombe's violence warranted an indictment for first-degree murder. She was found guilty and is currently serving life in prison. Erin tracked Bert down as he was delivering mail in South Miami. (He had worked for the postal service for 21 years.) She found him talking with one of the persons on his route, a man named Jessie Barnes. He informed officers that Erin approached Bert and said, "I got you now." She then fired several shots at her former husband, who fell to the ground. At this point her gun malfunctioned, so she walked back to her car and retrieved a second one. She then fired at him several more times. Bert died at the scene. According to Jessie Barnes, after the shooting Erin calmly walked back to her car and waited for the police. At one point Barnes approached her after checking Bert Newcombe and finding no pulse. He informed officers that Erin stated she was sorry for what had happened.

Barnes also told investigators that "she was not provoked at all" by her former husband. In the sense that Bert used no proximal precipitating violence,

Barnes's statement is accurate. However, digging a little deeper reveals a long history of battering and abuse directed at Erin by Bert. A number of other precipitating factors also appear, including a bitter custody dispute over their nine-year-old son, which Bert had recently won. Since this case is unusual among those in which women kill their intimate partners, the etiology and victim precipitation warrant close attention.

Stephanie Bingo, the couple's 22-year-old daughter, remarked to investigators that Bert was a very abusive husband and father. According to Stephanie, Bert would come home from work and not interact with either her or her mother. On a number of occasions he forced them out of the house, saying things like they were "no-good pieces of shit." Bert was also very possessive of all the household items and constantly reminded his family that he owned the possessions. This behavior was consistent with his broader misogynist leanings. He said to both Erin and Stephanie that "women were worthless and no good." Bert was an alcoholic, and he also sold marijuana and Quaaludes from the house. Erin took tranquilizers in an attempt to deal with Bert's abuse.[25] Aside from the battering of her mother, there were times Stephanie remembered watching her father sexually abuse her mother. She recalls falling asleep on the floor at a party and waking up to witness her mother giving her father oral sex while a number of other persons stood by and watched. She told police her mother later said that her father coerced her into this sexual act. These statements by Stephanie were consistent with evidence offered by Erin's own mother, who remarked that although her daughter always denied being battered by Bert, over the years "she observed Erin with black eyes and bruises on a number of occasions."

Stephanie told investigators that her father also beat her young brother, Albert Newcombe. Albert had been diagnosed with hyperactive attention deficit disorder and was taking Ritalin. After leaving the marriage, Erin was very concerned that Bert, with his superior earning potential, would be awarded custody of their son. Just before the killing, Bert and Erin had to undergo psychological testing as part of the process of deciding who would take custody of Albert. In conversations with her daughter, Erin apparently stated that she was "very concerned that Bert was going to get custody of Albert and that she did not want Albert to turn out like his father." Bert eventually won custody of the boy. According to Erin, her former husband faked his way through the psychological testing by telling a "pack of lies." Indeed, when police searched her car at the scene of the shooting, they found numerous documents in the back seat concerning the psychological evaluation of Erin herself, Bert, and their children. This, too, suggests the importance of the recent custody award as a prime inciting factor that augmented the lingering, deep-seated abuse or distal precipitating violence and intimidation that was an ongoing part of the Newcombes' marriage. Further questioning of Erin's boyfriend, Frank Stapleton, revealed that on the morning of the killing she read all the results from the psychological evaluations at her attorney's office. She had earlier been told over the phone by her attorney that the outcome of the tests was not favorable to her custody claims over Albert. Her affect changed after hearing this news, and Frank Stapleton told police that Erin never seemed the same again. After reading the reports and making a copy for herself, she left the attorney's office and disappeared. Frank Stapleton, who had accompanied Erin, was left stranded without a ride. He tried to page her but received no answer.

In the aftermath of the killing, the details of the psychological testing emerged. Dr. Sangster, a psychiatrist in this case, recommended that primary custody of Albert be granted to Bert. He based his decision on the finding that "although Bert may not have the psychological makeup to be very introspective to either his own feelings or try to connect with his son on a deeply emotional level, he most likely tends to bond with his son through common activities such as sports."[26] Dr. Sangster went on to advise that there was "no indication in any of the formal testing nor in the clinical interview of any signs of severe personality problems which would interfere with Bert being able to be a capable and loving parent." In contrast, Dr. Sangster advised that "Erin acknowledged removing Albert from his father, school, and friends in Miami without any prior preparation of Albert or his father." These actions were consistent with her personality traits as revealed through the testing. Erin's responses indicated "a high degree of self-involvement and self-concern and that her more passive dependent personality style may prevent her from taking any type of action which would be for the psychological benefit of the child, if it interfered with what she felt was for her own benefit or gratification." Dr. Sangster obviously did not know of the history of domestic violence and abuse in this case. If he did, he certainly did not factor it in to his recommendations. Had he known, or had he factored it in, he might have better understood why recommending Bert as primary custodian was not a good idea. To grant custody to a man who had beaten his wife, sexually abused her, and physically and emotionally abused his children for many years makes no sense. Add to this that Bert was an alcoholic and drug user of long standing, and it is quite remarkable he should be recommended as primary custodian. It is also remarkable that Dr. Sangster either missed these details of Bert's lifestyle or, perhaps, worse still, knew of them and did not consider them important. Had he known of the battering he might have been able to better understand Erin's swift and unilateral decision to remove Albert from school. Had he known of the death threats against Erin he might have been less certain in his conclusion that she was overly concerned with her own well-being.

*Women as Aggressors?*   As noted in Chapter 1, men commit the bulk of intimate violence in their relationships with women.[27] Men also inflict the majority of serious injuries and commit more intimate-partner homicides. When women use violence against male partners, it is neither reinforced by nor embedded in patriarchal privilege. Put another way, men and women may kill with the same kind of weapon and in the same kind of manner, but the social meaning and context of the killing is gendered and therefore different.

Among the 24 female-perpetrated intimate killings of men, it is possible that one woman used offensive acts of violence in her relationship with her male partner that do not appear to have been preceded by any documentable proximal or distal precipitating violence. In four other cases the archival data suggest that women used offensive intimate violence alongside men.

In this regard, I now turn to the killing of Victor Green, who appears not to have used any proximal or distal precipitating violence against his female partner, Kelly Krish, before she murdered him. When police pulled up to the residence shared by Green and Krish, both aged 39 and white, they found him stabbed twice in the chest. Victor later died of his wounds. According to Kelly, earlier that day he had stolen the battery charger to her wheelchair. She said this theft was part of an ongoing pattern of emotional abuse, which included him accusing her of going out with other men. Sheriff's deputies had apprehended Victor earlier that day in the theft of the battery charger, but they determined the offense did not happen. He was released after being interviewed. When Victor got home, the two argued and Kelly stabbed him in the chest. As he bent over in pain she then stabbed him in the back of the neck. Asked if Victor had threatened her, Kelly replied that he had not, but said that he was always "playing mind games with her" and that she "couldn't take it anymore."

The neighbors described Victor and Kelly as alcoholics. Rita Hart, who lived next door, remarked to investigators that she had never seen Victor strike Kelly, but she advised that she had seen her strike him "on numerous occasions." Apparently, on the morning of the homicide Kelly told her neighbors that she was going to kill Victor. Bob Hart tried to talk her out of it, although he later said to police that he thought she was "just talking." After the stabbing Kelly passed by Bob and Rita Hart on her way to the patrol vehicle. "You should have listened to me. I did it. I did it good," she told Rita.

When I talked with Kelly's defense attorney about any prior male violence in the case he replied that he thought there was none. Doubtless the absence of any apparent distal or proximal precipitating violence influenced the jury, which returned a guilty verdict for second-degree murder. Kelly is currently serving an 18-year sentence.

In the killing of Joshua Brown by his wife, Marion Brown, and in the killing of Marshall Murray by his wife, Alison Murray, the role of victim precipitation is unclear. I will discuss both cases and review the competing interpretations of claims makers.

Marion Brown, an African American aged 29, stabbed Joshua Brown, an African American aged 65, in an argument over money. She is currently serving 260 months in prison after being found guilty of second-degree murder. On the day of the killing Joshua had enraged Marion by threatening to take her off his social security so that she would not receive benefits if he died. The couple were recently married, although they had been together for 13 years. Marion was getting into her car with her 12-year-old son when she became enraged by his threat. She grabbed a steak knife that she kept in her handbag for personal protection and stabbed her husband in the back as he walked away from her toward the house. The knife wound to his upper middle back severed his aorta and he bled to death at the scene.

There is no evidence in the case files of Joshua's using either proximal or distal precipitating violence. Indeed, Marion's son from a previous relationship, Wilfred, reported that on only one occasion did he see his stepfather, Joshua, wield a weapon against Marion; even then, the display of the weapon was to warn her not to assault him. This argument, which took place a long time before the killing, resulted in Joshua's holding up a carpet cutter to Marion. She herself denied any domestic violence in their relationship, but stated that she and her husband did argue and curse at each other from time to time. Certainly her act at the scene was aggressive and unprovoked by any comparable or, to use the language of criminal law, "proportional" force. Nor is there any evidence that Marion had assaulted Joshua previously, although her son intimated that such violence may have occurred.

In Marion Brown's case, as in a number of others, the investigative file is limited in its scope. Her defense attorney told me that Marion's mother reported that there was a history of abuse by Joshua Brown. Apparently, he had isolated Marion, especially limiting her access to her own family. The attorney also told me what a number of other defense attorneys in these cases did: that investigators assume the women have murdered their male partners. As a consequence of this assumption, officers may not include information or follow up leads that might compromise the prosecution of the woman. Marion's attorney argued that police defend this practice by saying that they had acquired enough information to prosecute and did not need to investigate further.

The woman who prosecuted this case provided further insights that, as one might expect, differed from the perspective of Marion's defense attorney. In a telephone interview she told me: "Marion was the dominant personality in this relationship. It was Marion who abused Joshua, not the other way around. When I first took this case on I thought it was another case of a woman who had been abused all her life, fought back and got sent to the slammer for fighting back. It couldn't have been farther from the truth."

To my question whether it is realistic to think that a girl who entered an intimate relationship when she was 16 years old could dominate a man who had long been in the workforce, the prosecutor responded, "I agree that she was not always the dominant force. The relationship changed."

When I asked if she felt police and prosecutors sometimes left out or failed to inquire about information that was inconsistent with the prosecution's position, she told me: "I like to explore all the details in a case and get at the truth. In fact, there is not much worse than getting to trial and having some evidence of prior woman battering surface that might support the defendant and which is difficult to deal with. I consider it my ethical duty to search out all of the facts."[28]

Alison Murray, a black woman aged 33, stabbed her husband, Marshall Murray, a black man aged 34, to death by severing his carotid artery during an argument at their apartment. Charged with second-degree murder, she was found not guilty by a jury in April 1996. According to one of the police officers who was at the scene, "Marshall was a happy-go-lucky drunk who bled like a pig when she cut him." Again according to police, Alison had no cuts or scratches on her at the crime scene.

A former neighbor, Cassius Bogan, had known the couple since 1989. He said to officers that he had witnessed Alison throw Marshall out into the yard at least 10 times in the six years he lived next door. Cassius also reported that Marshall had shown him the scars from where Alison had stabbed him in 1990. She had also apparently interfered in Cassius's arguments with his wife. On one occasion Alison walked into his apartment and told him to leave. She was very aggressive on this occasion, and Cassius described her overall as "a very mean individual." In talking about the domestic violence between Marshall and Alison, Cassius said that on every occasion he witnessed the couple arguing it was Alison "who was the aggressor"; he had never seen or heard Marshall "raise his voice or do anything to the suspect." Omar Takir, an employee at the restaurant where Marshall worked, told investigators that Marshall would receive one to two phone calls a night from his wife. These calls upset Marshall. Omar reported that he felt Marshall was afraid of Alison and that she "might do something crazy." The restaurant workers who knew Marshall reported him to be personable, easygoing, and polite. All the other witnesses police interviewed who knew the couple remarked that Alison was the initiator and aggressor in the arguments they saw and that Marshall would just walk away. The principal cause of the disputes, according to a diverse group of witnesses, was Alison's jealousy of her husband and her accusations that he was sleeping with other women.

There were dozens of police calls to the Murrays' apartment. Responding officers reported that they felt Alison was manipulating the situation in an attempt to get Marshall arrested. He seems to have told a friend at one point, "[I]f I touch her, I'm going to jail, and even if I don't, I'm going to jail because she's gonna tell the police that I touched her." Sheriff's deputies answering one domestic call at the residence were told by Alison that "he was beating on her." However, the deputies concluded that "the call was a way to try and manipulate the Sheriff's Office into arresting her husband and that the call had no merit, therefore the call was coded out and a report was not required." Six other officers had similar experiences at earlier domestic calls to the residence; all concluded that Alison was manipulating the situation.

Alison's own words do not figure prominently in either of the police reports that were retroactively added to the homicide file. In one report, dated

March 26, 1994, officers wrote that Alison told them "she and her husband had argued and that she wanted him out of the apartment." In the same report, the deputy notes that "there were no indications of violence from either party." On this occasion deputies arranged for Marshall to go next door and stay the night with a friend. When they informed Alison of this arrangement, she replied that she was "afraid of what her husband would do to her if he came back over to their apartment." The other report of an earlier police call that was added to the homicide file describes a domestic disturbance just a month before the killing. This time, Alison reportedly said that Marshall had "thrown stuff all over the house." However, the responding officer, who I later interviewed over the phone, reported that he saw only a fan on its side in the hallway and some clothes that appeared to have fallen off a bed. Apart from this "the house was in perfect order." The implication in the officer's statement is that he thought Alison's description of the disarray was exaggerated. Farther on in the report the officer tells readers that he asked Alison if she had ever had her husband arrested for domestic violence. She replied yes. He then asked if Marshall had hit her that day. She replied no. The officer concludes, "It was apparent that Ms. Murray was familiar with domestic-violence law and that she was trying to manipulate the sheriff's office into arresting her husband when no crime was committed."

Alison did not testify at her trial. In his opening remarks her defense attorney made reference to her upcoming testimony. However, in the words of one observer from the local domestic-violence shelter, once Alison had heard all of the prosecution's evidence against her she became very tense and decided at the last minute not to testify.[29] According to the prosecutor, Alison "could give as good as she got. She was not a battered woman."[30] The prosecutor's opinion agreed with those of police officers, who argued that Alison was happy to have Marshall around when he was earning money, but wanted him out of the house when he was not. The prosecutor felt that she was not in imminent danger and could have responded to her husband in a manner other than knifing him. She told me that Marshall was stabbed a number of times, and the wounds were not consistent with a purely defensive response on Alison's part. The prosecutor went on to say that

> this kind of violence is more common in the African-American community. That is just the way those people deal with their problems. They have either learned it from their families or witnessed it elsewhere. We see

a lot of black women with knives and box cutters. They are completely lacking in the social graces. However, there is no doubt in my mind that they get beat up by their men more than white women do.

As in other cases, I quizzed the prosecutor about the death perhaps being attributable to tardy or poor emergency medical services. She said that the response was very quick and she did not think it was a factor in the death.

Predictably, my conversation with the director of the local domestic-violence shelter yielded a different perspective on the killing of Marshall Murray. The director told me that, although a number of earlier police calls to the residence were written off as "Marshall just being drunk," he had in fact beaten his wife. For the director, the witness statements attesting to Alison assaulting or being aggressive toward her husband refer to incidents where she was trying to get him out of the house when he was drunk and after he had assaulted her behind closed doors. Alison was also anxious to protect her son, then four years old. The fatal incident itself involved Marshall approaching Alison with a lighter in one hand and a can of charcoal lighter in the other, uttering words to the effect of "I'm going to burn you, bitch." This apparently was not the first time he had threatened to burn her. A can of charcoal lighter was found at the scene with his blood on it, which appears to have persuaded the jury of Marshall's attempts to set his wife on fire. At the least, for the director, his advances with the fluid and the lighter were sufficient for Alison to feel she was in imminent danger of losing her life and therefore warranted her stabbing him. In addition, she was also acutely concerned about the well-being of her son, who was at the scene of the homicide.

According to the counselor at the domestic-violence center who worked with Alison after the killing, she had been assaulted by her husband before his death. Just after the birth of the couple's child, Alison told the counselor, Marshall hit her and "busted her lip." When asked why the jury might have acquitted Alison, the counselor replied that the witnesses used by the prosecution were "not very impressive." Like Marshall, these men had criminal histories. As for Cassius Bogan, Alison told the counselor that he beat his partner. The counselor felt that the known criminal histories of these men who testified for the prosecution tainted its case in the eyes of the jury. I quizzed the counselor further about why it should be that black women figure so disproportionately among the ranks of those who kill their intimate male partners. Her response was the same as those I have received from many African-American women to whom I presented research findings in Florida: "More black women are into fighting back than leaving." The counselor went on to say, "In groups that I facilitate, black women voice the opinion that they will not tolerate the same levels of violence that white women will." She added that "black women are also less likely to use domestic-violence shelters in Florida."

Through intermediaries I got word to Alison that I wished to talk with her about her case. The two of us spoke for about an hour and a half on the phone.[31] She reported having an adversarial relationship with local police. According to Alison, Marshall had assaulted her on a number of occasions during their relationship. Usually, however, when police came to their residence they either simply arrested him for drunkenness or allowed him to move in overnight with a friend. Alison responded to charges that she had been the aggressor in the relationship by saying she had never struck her husband out of aggression and had never initiated violence against him. As she put it, "I'd never been so angry that I just hit him." Alison told me that she felt Marshall perceived that she would never defend herself against him. "He knew I feared him. When I struck back at him [on the night of the killing] I could see it was a shock for him. I could see it in his eyes. In fact, I was shocked. But I had my four-year-old son in the house with me. Marshall said he'd kill me and our son and then himself and that we were all going to die. He was going to ignite the whole place. He'd been drinking and he'd drugged himself into a state." Alison also reported that she had been planning to leave her husband and that "they were over." She went on, "I had a job offer. He was jealous of me. He thought he had built me up, but he hadn't."

Marshall had apparently not just been an alcoholic. According to Alison, his drug of choice was crack cocaine. She observed that

> crack use among black men aged 30–40 in [my] community is epidemic. Marshall never did crack around me, I would not tolerate it. But he was such a con artist. The police never knew of his crack use. The cops are so green around here. They are only interested in the crack dealers with the flashy cars. Most crack addicts can't even keep their hair cut. It's everywhere in the neighborhood. Marshall fought a lot of people. He came from a pimping, drug-dealing background. He probably came from previous homicides. I knew he was involved with robbing others for drugs. Crack addicts are good thieves. It is an expensive habit. They walk the neighborhoods and they'd steal from their mamas.

Alison feared her husband in part because of her knowledge of his crack-related activities. In general, she observed, black women knew of the potential of crack-dealing men for violence. She drew a number of connections between domestic violence and drug use in the African-American community, and her observations are directly relevant to the committing of homicide by black women:

> With crack dealers women see what they are capable of doing. Knowing he can cold-heartedly kill, rob, cheat, and lie, she can feel when it's getting dangerous. She knows people just disappear in the black community and they've been killed. No one cares. No one investigates. People assume these people have just gone somewhere else. When Marshall had been on crack he was crazy and that's what happened the night I killed him.

These remarks are a reminder that black women's perceptions of entrapment, threat, and danger in domestic relationships may differ significantly from those of Caucasian and Latino women.

But it was not just her fear of Marshall because of his earlier violence, or her sense that he had been mixing crack and alcohol, that alarmed Alison. She stated that if her son had not been in the house she would be dead. "In my case it was my son. If my son hadn't been in the bed Marshall would have killed me because I would not have fought back. What he was doing with the lighter and the lighter fluid was dangerous. I reacted the way I did because of my son."

I could not resist asking Alison Murray, as a black woman in her later thirties, for her opinions about why it was that African-American women are overrepresented among the ranks of those who kill their male intimate partners.

> *Websdale*  Alison, can you give me your opinion on why it might be that one-eighth of the population of Florida is black and five-eighths of those women who killed their intimate partners in 1994 were black?
>
> *Murray*  White girls are gullible. White girls will put up with centuries of abuse. They will not fight back. It is just the way they've been brought up. They are very soft. They are taught to be obedient. A lot of white girls even let their kids run all over them. Black women are a little smarter. But black women are also more reluctant to use shelters . . . to talk about what goes on in the privacy of their own homes. Black women are more likely to try to leave a relationship without their abus-

ers knowing about it. I wish I had done that. But then I might not have been alive today if I had.

For one last perspective, I called Alison's defense attorney, who provided additional insights into this interesting and very sad case.[32] When quizzed about her victimization prior to the fatal episode, her attorney told me that he felt the physical evidence from the crime scene, especially the victim's blood on both sides of the can of charcoal lighter, was sufficient to convince the jury that Marshall was threatening to set his wife on fire before she stabbed him. However, unlike Alison herself, her attorney said that acknowledging the existence of proximal precipitating violence "was as far as I was going to go." Pressed about what this meant, he commented:

> In my opinion she was just the opposite of a battered spouse. I think she dished out as much as she got back. When I heard her story [of proximal and distal precipitating violence] I went out to try to document it. I couldn't. One of the victim's friends told me of the time when he went to visit Marshall in the hospital after Alison had stabbed him a few years earlier. I then took what I found to a psychologist. If I could have shown battered-woman syndrome, then I would have. But we didn't have the evidence. I don't believe anybody anymore. People mix up the truth with lies. I don't believe my clients, victims, advocates, or police. I just get a case together and put it to the jury. Even though we got Alison acquitted I didn't have a good feeling after they left the courtroom. And as for the folks from the domestic-violence shelter—they came out in force at the trial. It was good to see them support Alison. But they lost a lot of credibility with me by jumping to all kinds of conclusions before knowing the facts of the case. Alison only contacted the shelter people after the killing.

Unlike the outcome in the Marion Brown case, the jury found Alison Murray not guilty of second-degree murder. Both cases speak poignantly to society's understanding of the role of woman battering in precipitating lethal defensive violence. The Alison Murray case is sufficient to remind one that when police arrive at the scene of domestic disturbances they are witnessing the public face of a private altercation. Things are not always what they appear to be. Although I do not want to suggest that women are incapable of using offensive violence, it seems impossible from reading the archival material in conjunction with interviews with the key players to rule out the fact that women like Alison

Murray suffered both proximal and distal brutalization at the hands of their male partners before finally killing them. Perhaps by the luck of the draw, in Alison's case the jurors apparently felt that she acted in self-defense. In the cases of Marion Brown and Kelly Krish, they saw the women as murderers.

*Women's Envy*   Male obsessive possessiveness is a common antecedent in the killing of intimate female partners. However, the archival materials point to only five women expressing jealousy about the activities of their male partners. And in only one of these cases does it seem that female jealousy may have played a central role in the killing. It is clear from the archival data and the work of other researchers that women's jealousy, as opposed to men's, is more likely to be based upon a partner's actual, rather than perceived, infidelity.[33] It is also clear that women's envy differs from men's obsessive possessiveness in the way it is expressed. Men are much more likely to engage in stalking behavior that is designed to intimidate and control women. Women's envy, even though in rare instances it may erupt in lethal violence, is generally much more tightly circumscribed, mirroring their more limited physical and social mobility in a patriarchal society.

Heather Clark, a 29-year-old black woman, had been living with her boyfriend, Roger Carlton, a 33-year-old black man, for a number of years. Clark was a nurses' assistant at a nursing home; Carlton worked for a newspaper, doing pasteup. Heather Clark's attorney told me that Carlton was "a ladies man," as did the prosecutor, who said that he was a handsome man who "liked women." Indeed, Carlton had left Clark at least once for another woman. His coworkers thought the world of him. One woman said, "He was such a sweet, well-mannered, likable person. Very soft-spoken. Very nice. . . . He was never the type of person to lose his temper. He was never mean to anybody."

The Clark-Carlton case is a classic example of how violent men can present themselves to the world in one way and yet behave entirely differently behind closed doors in their intimate relationships. Although it never came out in any of the archival documents and was never raised at trial, a number of sources, including Heather Clark's defense attorney, told me that Carlton had battered her on a number of occasions before the homicide. This history of violence is significant, since it places limits on the extent to which one might attach causal importance to Heather's envy or jealous rage.

It seems that Roger Carlton had begun an intimate relationship with Tabitha Jackson, a woman he had known in his native Jamaica. They had been dating for about six weeks prior to the homicide. She became suspicious that he was not being honest with her and called his home one night just before he was due to return from work. Heather answered, and the two women talked for about an hour. They learned that Roger had been lying to them both. Tabitha then called Roger at work around 1:10 A.M. and told him of her conversation with Heather. He left work early and got home about 2:00 A.M. He called Tabitha, with Heather listening in on an extension and joining the conversation at various points. Roger became enraged when confronted with his own dishonesty. He stormed into the kitchen, hung up the extension phone, and slapped Heather. He returned to the bedroom and then prevented her from calling Tabitha again. Heather went back into the kitchen to try to get the extension to work. At this point, Roger "came after her and she was fearful. She opened up a kitchen drawer, pulled out a knife, and stabbed him."

In her interrogation, Heather attributed the entire argument to Roger cheating on her.

> *Investigator*   This whole argument was about another girl that you thought he was cheating on you with?
> *Heather*   Yes, and not only thought, but she admitted it.

Heather's so-called envy and anger, however, seem to have been quite measured and not like the jealousy of most of the men I have discussed who have found themselves in the throes of a love triangle. While talking with Tabitha, Heather suggested that she come over to Roger and Heather's apartment to confront him about his dishonesty. Tabitha said she would not feel comfortable doing this, but she would call him at work. Trying to set up a three-way meeting in the manner Heather suggested hardly resembles the intense obsessive possessiveness that many male perpetrators of intimate-partner homicide had corroding their souls. Without generalizing about the nature of women's rage at discovering infidelity, it does seem, in this one clear-cut case of a love triangle involving two women, that Heather's jealousy—or, perhaps more accurately, her ability to deal with her feelings of jealousy—was such that she did not resort to violence against the "other woman." Tabitha also expressed disappointment in Roger's behavior, especially since he had told her he was not living with anyone. However, she was not enraged to any great degree, or, if she was, her anger does not surface in the archival material. Both women conversed in a seemingly amicable way with each other. Their hour-long talk on the phone was not punctuated with threats on each other's lives or warnings about backing off from the mutual love interest. The contrast here with the jealous homicidal rage of men who find themselves in a similar situation is marked.

Having noted the rather muted, neutral tenor of Heather and Tabitha's jealousy, I look to the prior violence in this relationship as a more likely precipitant of the homicide. As mentioned, both distal and proximal precipitating violence was directed at Heather. However, the state refused to see her actions as justifiable homicide and sought a second-degree murder conviction. Eventually, she was found guilty of manslaughter and was sentenced to six years in prison and six years of probation. Her perceived jealousy and anger at discovering that Roger was in another intimate relationship may have enticed the prosecution into seeing this as another murder rather than an act of self-defense. However, this case carries with it a caution against projecting the kinds of angry male proprietariness recounted in earlier chapters onto the behavior of women caught in love triangles but also faced with male violence. Heather Clark likely did not kill in a jealous rage. In fact, from my reading of the files she probably killed in self-defense.

*Mental Illness*  So-called derangement played a minor role in the killing of intimate male partners. Their deaths arose largely out of a rational adaptive response by women seeking to defend themselves. Only one case involves a woman killing her male partner and then being deemed incompetent to stand trial. In one other case, a nurse who stabbed her abusive husband to death by slashing his femoral artery was not prosecuted. She later tried to commit suicide and was confined to a mental health facility.

Lucia Cuevas, a black Cuban woman aged 56, knifed to death her boyfriend, Heraldo Limas, a white Cuban man aged 57. According to her defense attorney, the couple met in a Cuban mental health facility. On the day of the killing Lucia apparently followed Heraldo in a vehicle she had borrowed. She confronted him on the street and Heraldo attempted to run away. Lucia gave chase in the vehicle and ran him down on the sidewalk. She then got out of the vehicle and stabbed him repeatedly in the upper chest. Heraldo died of his injuries later that day in the hospital.

This case remains a mystery. Lucia is currently confined to the Florida State Mental Hospital. Although charged with first-degree murder, she was deemed incompetent to stand trial. When I talked with her defense attorney over the phone, he told me that she was suffering from some kind of schizophrenia. He did not know whether Lucia had been battered by Heraldo.

Indeed, the attorney told me that he was unable to get even the day or date from her because, as he put it, "[S]he's completely 'bonkers.'" Again, one cannot rule out that Lucia is a battered woman. As a number of authors have explained, mental illness and battering are often linked, with women who have been battered suffering a disproportionate amount of mental illness.[34]

*Killing the Competition*    Love triangle killings are domestic homicides. Unlike intimate-partner killings and family homicides, the antagonists are often not well acquainted with one another. In that part of the Florida sample involving single domestic homicides with male victims, nine men killed love triangle antagonists. Not one woman killed another woman involved in a love triangle, however. Competition between men over a woman is far more acute, dangerous, and potentially lethal than any such contest between women. This sex differential in love triangle antagonism also appears in the research literature from other cultures and in the research literature on lethal interpersonal competition in general.[35] As Daly and Wilson observe, "Lethal interpersonal competition is especially prevalent among young men."[36] One of the common threads that seems to run through family homicides and love triangles is that of men not being able or willing to "back down." These observations mirror a much larger literature on how men posture and fight over their perceived honor and social status and how they will sacrifice their lives over issues that may seem trivial to onlookers.[37] Rather than lose face, some men seek respect through their altercations with other men and will engage in potentially lethal violence, be it over a "love interest," as in love triangles, or between themselves, as participants in family homicides.

In five of the nine love triangle killings, the former partner had battered his female partner, who had since moved into another intimate relationship. In the other four cases, the evidence available is not sufficient to make such a determination. I illustrate some of the dynamics of love triangles by discussing two cases in which men killed their sexual antagonists.

Al Norton, aged 43, and Elizabeth Sorel, aged 30, became attracted to each other while she was in the process of leaving Larry Webb, aged 28. All three persons were white. During their relationship, Sorel and Webb had a child together. Larry Webb had a history of battering Elizabeth Sorel, especially when he was drunk. He also had a history of arrest for violent behavior in Illinois, Georgia, and Florida. According to a number of witnesses, including Elizabeth, Webb was extremely possessive of her. On the night Al Norton killed him, the three spent some time together at what had been Elizabeth and Larry's trailer. Three nights before the killing she had moved into a residence of her own. Larry had lived at Al's place for a couple of months, but about a month before his death he had moved into a trailer park. During the evening, Al and Larry went out to an Exxon gas station to buy beer and cigarettes. Upon returning they found that Elizabeth had left the trailer. Larry became angry and accused Al of interfering in his relationship with her. As Al was leaving the trailer to go home, Larry kicked and punched his vehicle. When Al got home Elizabeth came out of the shrubbery near his house and said that she did not want to spend any more time with Larry because he beat her. The two of them then went into Al's house. A short while later, Larry arrived at the residence and started banging on the door. Al heard him shouting, "I know she's in your house, let me in." Larry continued to beat and kick at the door and warned Al "not to fuck around." At one point, Al told him that Elizabeth was inside the residence and recommended that he go home and go to sleep. However, Larry continued to kick the door, eventually breaking it down and forcing his way inside. As Larry entered the house, Al shot him three times in the upper chest, killing him. Al told investigators that Larry had threatened to kill him before and that Larry carried a razor knife. The state declined to prosecute Al, the assistant state's attorney deeming the shooting to have been in self-defense.

It later emerged that the victim was aware his killer was armed. According to Al, "Larry knew I had a gun . . . and he knew I'd use it. He's been suicidal the last couple of days. He made a razor knife and was carrying it." As in similar cases, it seems that Larry was willing to risk life and limb in search of saving face, gaining some modicum of respect, or simply intimidating Al and Elizabeth. Like most men on the losing side of love triangles, Larry was extremely jealous and possessive of the woman who was in the process of leaving him.

Another kind of love triangle seems to have existed between Barney Rogers, a black man aged 38, Wilson Amenda, a black man aged 43, and Helena Bennedy, a black woman aged 39. Wilson Amenda, Helena Bennedy's current boyfriend, apparently stayed with her two to three times a week. Barney Rogers was her former boyfriend and the stepfather of her two sons, whom she had with another man. Although Barney and Helena had separated two years earlier, he continued to come around and "cause problems." Helena told investigators that since their breakup "there had been ongoing disputes. She had to call police on numerous occasions." On the night of the killing, Barney came around to borrow money for gas. Helena told him to leave the premises.

According to her 11-year-old son, Brad, Wilson came out of the house and confronted Barney. Wilson allegedly said to Barney as he was pulling away in his car, "What's up, pay nigger?" He then taunted Barney, saying, "Let's fight. Come on then, me and you, one on one." When Barney eventually turned around to face Wilson, he shot Barney in the neck and then several more times, killing him.

The killings of Larry Webb and Barney Rogers differ. In the former, Larry was the putative aggressor; in the latter, it seems that Barney was the victim of aggressive violence from the new man on the scene, Wilson Amenda. Fundamentally however, both fatal shootings grew out of competition, possessiveness, and the need to assert one's ownership of a woman. Both victims had abused the woman in the triangle, and both paid for it with their lives.

### Family Homicides

In 19 of the 20 instances of killings within families in the Florida sample, men killed other men they were related to through blood, marriage, or cohabitation. Table 5.5 summarizes the relationships between the perpetrators and victims in these family killings of men. Most numerous are killings between brothers (4), sons killing their fathers (3), and killings between brothers-in-law (2).

Table 5.6 shows the sex and racial or ethnic background of these perpetrators and victims. Black men and white men killed male family members in equal numbers in Florida in 1994. However, given that African Americans comprise only 13.6 percent of the state's population, compared with the 83.1 percent made up of whites, blacks are heavily overrepresented. Latinos committed 3 of the 20 family killings of men, a proportion consistent with their roughly 12.0 percent share of the population.

Joe Newman, a black man aged 29, shot his brother Buster Newman, a black man aged 26, to death following a disagreement during a card game. After the disagreement, Joe left the house where the game was being played and went to retrieve a rifle from his parents' residence. Upon his return Joe and Buster fired shots at each other. Buster apparently was wounded and managed to get away into the backyard of the house, where his dead body was later found. Both men had criminal histories, although Buster's was the more extensive. Joe had a number of charges for aggravated battery on a police officer, resisting arrest, and loitering and prowling. In 1988, Buster was sentenced to

### TABLE 5.5
### Perpetrators and victims in the family killing of men

| Relationship | No. |
| --- | --- |
| Brother kills brother | 4 |
| Son kills father | 3 |
| Brother-in-law kills brother-in-law | 2 |
| Nephew kills uncle | 1 |
| Son-in-law kills father-in-law | 1 |
| Uncle kills nephew | 1 |
| Boyfriend kills his girlfriend's son | 1 |
| Girlfriend's sister kills boyfriend | 1 |
| Boyfriend kills girlfriend's father | 1 |
| Stepson kills stepfather | 1 |
| Father kills son | 1 |
| Brother kills sister's boyfriend | 1 |
| Girlfriend's son kills boyfriend | 1 |
| Father-in-law kills son-in-law | 1 |
| Total | 20 |

### TABLE 5.6
### Breakdown of perpetrators and victims of family homicide

| Perpetrator | Victim | No. |
| --- | --- | --- |
| WM | WM | 8 |
| BM | BM | 8 |
| BF | BM | 1 |
| LM | LM | 3 |
| Total | | 20 |

*Code:* W = White; B = Black; L = Latino; M = Male; F = Female six years for manslaughter; he also had a number of other convictions for possession of crack cocaine, resisting a police officer, possession of marijuana, and possession, sale, and manufacture of dangerous drugs.

The police report in this case notes that investigating officers received very little information at the crime scene. In fact, witnesses and various other parties there were described in both the press and the homicide file as uncooperative. Given the criminal histories of these two men, the lack of cooperation is hardly surprising.

The archival data reveal nothing of a history of violence between the brothers or of any domestic violence within the families they grew up in. It may be significant that their parents lived apart, with Joe living with his mother and Buster with his father. Absent more information, it is impossible to take these leads any further. What is clear is that the altercation escalated to the point where neither man could back down and both men seemed to become deeply invested in what several authors have dubbed "the search for respect."[38] I will return to this matter of the search for respect, street subcultures, and mainstream values in Chapter 7.

Not all family homicides are so dramatic, confrontational, and bloody. The killing of Jack Glover, a 49-year-old white man, is perhaps best described as "inadvertent." Jack and his wife, Martha, were visiting their son, Terry Glover, a 23-year-old white man, when the two men got into an argument. Terry hit his father three times on the side of his head. Jack, who suffered from poorly managed diabetes, alcohol abuse, and hypertension, later died. The state declined to prosecute in this case.

Terry's assault on his father evolved from an argument that Jack Glover had with Terry's wife, Teresa Glover. Terry and Teresa accompanied Jack and Martha to Cape Canaveral to visit the Kennedy Space Center. Jack, keen to be one of the first ones at the center that day, insisted that they leave early in the morning. While they were traveling, Teresa wanted to take a break to eat a sandwich. Jack insisted that she snack in the car in order to save time. Jack and his daughter-in-law argued, and, to use Terry Glover's words, "the rest of the ride home was extremely quiet because everyone seemed to be agitated and no one spoke to each other." Terry and Teresa refused to go out to Treasure Island with Jack and Martha that evening when the couples got back to Tampa. Their refusal enraged Jack Glover. When Jack returned to his son's house later that evening from Treasure Island, Terry confronted him about his argument in the car with Teresa over the sandwich. The younger Glover informed officers that he "got into a shouting match with the victim and they became very angry with each other." Terry reported that Jack "got in his face and they were nose to nose." Terry then hit him three times. By his account, this physical fight was the first time he had ever struck his father. Terry described Jack Glover as "an asshole." Terry's wife, Teresa, described him as "a chauvinist" who was "always in a hurry."

In a case involving two 31-year-old Latino men, Fernando Sifuentes killed his brother-in-law Antonio Santiago after Antonio woke him up after the killer had drunk a bottle of liquor. According to Fernando, the victim awakened him very abruptly and proceeded to utter profanities about his mother. The two men argued, and Antonio threw two plates at Fernando. In referring to their respective firearms, Fernando seems to have told Antonio, "If you want to get it out, get it out, and I'll get mine out." The two men then left the scene, only to meet up again on the street. Fernando fired his shotgun at Antonio while his brother-in-law was sitting in a car. Antonio died at the scene, and Fernando was charged with first-degree murder.

As in other cases of family homicide, neither of these two men could back off from a showdown with the other. It is likely that this male dyad had fought before, although the reasons for antagonism remain obscure and do not appear directly related to competition over, or to the violent victimization of, a woman.

In only two cases does it appear that the violent victimization of a woman lay at the heart of the etiology of the family homicides. I will mention these cases briefly, since they are not the norm among the killings in the Florida sample. Pedro Morales, a Latino man aged 23, punched his father-in-law, Joseph Rosa, a Latino man aged 46, who consequently fell over and hit his head, causing a fatal blunt trauma injury. Numerous witnesses attending the family birthday party for a year-old niece attested that Pedro was a jealous and angry man who had beaten his wife, Lucinda Morales, a Latino woman aged 23. During one period of separation from Pedro, Lucinda had an affair with Leonardo Casis; it ended three years before her father's death. When Pedro found out about the affair he beat her so badly she nearly died. For this beating he was found guilty of domestic violence and aggravated battery. The couple were separated for a while, but Lucinda reported that she was so afraid her husband would kill her that she went back to live with him. Just before punching Joseph Rosa many times, Pedro had grabbed his wife's hair and accused her of looking at Leonardo. Lucinda slapped him around the face. It was then that he took off and attacked Joseph, Lucinda's father. After assaulting him, Pedro also approached Leonardo Casis and struck him in the face with his closed fist. Lucinda later told investigators that her husband had recently gotten a girl pregnant and that he was always "messing around with other women." Pedro was charged with second-degree murder after Joseph's death. Lucinda's mother, with whom she and her two children were living at the time of the killing, told police that she would live in fear of Pedro, because if he "got out of jail he would be directly over to her house."

In the second homicide, a father-in-law took justice into his own hands after learning of his daughter being beaten by her husband. Louis Sharavi, a 64-year-old white man, shot his son-in-law, Kevin Hanks, a 41-year-old white man, six times, killing him. The shooting occurred outside a tavern owned by Barbara Hanks, Sharavi's daughter, a 35-year-old white woman. Barbara watched as her husband was gunned down. She then ran to his aid as her father fled the scene. Sharavi had a criminal history, including a 1986 conviction for trafficking marijuana. One witness interviewed by investigators reported "trouble" at the bar for the last few weeks. The witness went so far as to remark, "[Y]ou won't believe it, but I said just last week that someone was going to be murdered in that tavern." It later emerged that Sharavi killed Kevin Hanks to protect his daughter, Barbara, from being beaten.

## Conclusion

In Florida in 1994, there were far fewer women who killed intimate male partners (24) than men who killed intimate female partners (67). Whereas no women killed other women in love triangles, 9 men killed male love triangle antagonists. When men died in family homicides it was nearly always at the hands of other men. These highly significant dissimilarities between the sexes are matched by profound differences in the motives and etiology of the killing of men. Male victims of intimate-partner homicide almost always precipitate the killing through proximal violence, distal violence, or both. Even though this process of precipitation is not always apparent in the homicide files, when one looks beyond them to such other sources as trial transcripts, the comments of defense attorneys, and news reports, a history of battering emerges. This observation does not mean that female perpetrators, most of them battered women, are found innocent of murder or manslaughter by the courts. Indeed, a number of women are serving considerable prison time in Florida for defending themselves in a manner that does not meet the criteria of self-defense under an androcentric legal code.

That black persons represent roughly one-eighth of Florida's population and yet account for two-thirds (16 of the 24) women who killed male intimates points to their heavy overrepresentation among this group of perpetrators. Using the work of bell hooks as a touchstone, I argue that this overrepresentation has nothing to do with any innate aggressive characteristics of black women. Instead, their acute and multiple oppression as black, female, and poor plays a significant role. The limited available evidence does not support the argument that tardy police and emergency medical responses resulted in a shooting or a stabbing becoming a fatal injury. However, without more evidence on the quality of medical services, or, better still, the precise delivery of medical aid in each of the fatalities under scrutiny, this impression means little.

It might be argued that the overrepresentation of black women among the killers of men may be a product of social class rather than race. Put differently, black women in the Florida sample are, disproportionately, very poor, and it could be that poverty, not race, is the more appropriate correlate of lethal violence. However, as I will argue in Chapter 7, it is impossible to isolate poverty and control for it in such a way as to pinpoint the precise workings of class as opposed to race. Perhaps more important, to argue that one can somehow arbitrarily separate race from class is to minimize or ignore the ways in which these forms of oppression are intimately interwoven.

Another possibility is that more black women are trapped in violent domestic relationships that force them to kill than are their Caucasian and Latino counterparts. It could also be that—due to the chronic and acute economic problems in the black community, the existence of the crack cocaine subculture, and the overarching legacy of slavery and its attendant brutality and misogyny—black women perceive a greater sense of entrapment and interpersonal hopelessness, thus rendering them more likely to kill their male partners. I will return to these issues in Chapter 7.

The underrepresentation of Latino women among female perpetrators of intimate-partner homicide is also consistent with other research findings mentioned in Chapter 1. Although the numbers are very small, it may be significant that both Latino women who killed male intimate partners were Cuban. As a general rule, Cuban women tend to be better off economically than other Latino women (especially those of Mexican descent in Florida), have fewer children, and as such perhaps experience patriarchal domination in different ways. Any kind of generalizing from a sample of two cases is deeply problematic. One of the Cuban women was mentally ill, and there is no information on how she perceived her entrapment. The other Cuban woman was middle class, had resorted to the police and the courts, and still killed. Suffice it to say that much more research is needed on the low Latino Sex Ratio of Killing (SROK). This research needs to take into account that Latino culture is not monolithic and that Latino women are subject to different degrees of entrapment. As I will show in Chapter 6, it is difficult to argue that Latino migrant farmworkers in Florida are not entrapped by their lack of citizenship, their itinerant lifestyles, and their abject poverty to a degree that is typically greater than their usually better off Cuban peers. However, once again, one must note the importance of the perception of entrapment and its social meaning to women, rather than what some might like to call the "empirical reality" of entrapment.

One of the threads running through the intimate-partner homicides and the love triangle killings is the notion of women as the property or possession of men. In the killing of male intimate partners one sees women defending themselves against this suffocating possessiveness and ownership that they perceived was quite literally about to kill them. As for the love triangle homicides, men killed other men who were seen as either usurping or trying to usurp their property rights or love interests in women. Five of the nine such killings involve a history of woman battering by the usurped male in the triangle.

The family killing of men typically involved arguments between related men who could not back down or lose face. Again, black men are overrepresented among the ranks of perpetrators and victims, although the reasons for this remain obscure. (In Chapter 7, I present possible explanations for these racial disparities.) Fewer cases involve woman battering as a factor of some importance in the etiology of family homicides. Indeed, among the 20 cases of men dying in family killings, I describe 2 in which violence against women figured prominently amidst a number of other factors.

# 6. The Death of Children

Although the literature on the abuse and neglect of girls and boys is massive, few studies explore the interpersonal dynamics and socially situated etiologies of domestic child fatalities. As noted in Chapter 1, most of the research into such killings reports basic demographic information about victims and perpetrators, the cause of death, the involvement of drugs and alcohol, and other discrete phenomena. There is practically nothing empirical written about the relationship between adult interpersonal violence and child fatalities, although a number of studies imply a connection between the two.[1] There may be many reasons for the failure to examine the domestic killings of boys and girls in great detail. Child protection agencies maintain case files on children suffering from abuse and neglect. If they later die as a result of a domestic homicide, the information from these records might become part of a death review. However, researchers generally do not have access to these highly confidential files. Additionally, the same child protection agencies do not always keep a record of children killed by family members in homicide-suicides and familicides. In these cases, unless there is a history of child abuse and neglect that is known to the agencies, the children's deaths often go unrecorded. Official records of deaths involving child abuse and neglect from the Department of Children and Families (DCF) in Florida usually do not list girls and boys who perish during homicide-suicides and familicides unless the department had prior of knowledge of their abuse and neglect. Such record-keeping practices result in a serious underestimation of domestic child fatalities across the country. Likewise, police departments in Florida regularly underreport child domestic deaths, or instead categorize them under a heading that is not considered a domestic killing.

In 1994, children constituted over one-quarter of all domestic-homicide victims in Florida. Seventeen boys and girls died in homicide-suicides and familicides. I have discussed some of these cases in Chapters 2 and 3. Usually the

DCF had no prior contact with children who were victims in multiple domestic killings. The lack of contact, however, does not mean that these children did not suffer abuse, neglect, or both before being killed. Fifty-six other children died in situations where they had previously been abused, neglected, or both, and many of these cases were known to the DCF.

This chapter introduces some of the patterns evident in these child fatalities. Through a series of tables, I explore the perpetrator's relationship to child victims; the relationship between the parents or caretakers of the child; the cause of death; the racial or ethnic background of the victims; the presence of prior child abuse, neglect, or both; the presence of domestic violence in the relationship between the caretakers of the child; any earlier contact between the family and such agencies as the police, courts, or the DCF; any criminal history of the perpetrator; the involvement of drugs, alcohol, or both; and the role of weaponry. Having provided a statistical sketch of the cases as a whole, I make the central characteristics of child domestic death concrete by using case histories to illustrate the themes enumerated in the introductory tables.

The identity of the perpetrator is known in all but 3 of the 83 cases of domestic child homicide in Florida in 1994. The Florida findings on the sex of the 80 known perpetrators and their relationship to the victim are very similar to those of Schlosser, Pierpont, and Poertner.[2] Table 6.1 shows the perpetrator's relationship to the child victim. In 62.1 percent of cases the perpetrator is male, and in 34.5 percent, female. Biological fathers committed 27.6 percent of the child killings, and the boyfriends of the children's mother another 21.8 percent. Some boyfriends were formally identified as stepfathers, although the majority were not. Taken together, boyfriends and stepfathers killed 23 children (26.4 percent). Biological mothers were responsible for 27.6 percent of the fatalities. In contrast to the findings of some other researchers who have emphasized the disproportionate importance of nonbiological parents in the commission of domestic child homicides,[3] analysis of the Florida sample shows that biologically linked caretakers (largely biological mothers and fathers) constitute the majority of perpetrators of child homicide. If the 8 children killed by their biological fathers during the commission of multiple domestic killings are excluded, then mother's boyfriends or stepfathers assume first place among male offenders.

As Table 6.2 indicates, in 30.1 percent of cases the parents or caretakers of children who died were married and living together. In 22.9 percent of cases the parents or caretakers lived together but were not married.

| TABLE 6.1 | | |
|---|---|---|
| Perpetrator's relationship to victim | | |
| Male perpetrator | No. | % of 87 |
| Biological father | 24 | 27.6 |
| Mother's boyfriend | 19 | 21.8 |
| Stepfather | 4 | 4.6 |
| Cousin | 2 | 2.3 |
| Uncle | 3 | 3.4 |
| Stepbrother | 1 | 1.1 |
| Brother | 1 | 1.1 |
| Total | 54 | 62.1 |
| Female perpetrator | | |
| Biological mother | 24 | 27.6 |
| Aunt | 2 | 2.3 |
| Girlfriend | 1 | 1.1 |
| Stepmother | 1 | 1.1 |
| Mother's girlfriend | 1 | 1.1 |
| Friend's mother | 1 | 1.1 |
| Total | 30 | 34.5 |
| Unknown perpetrator[a] | 3 | 3.4 |
| Totals | 87 | 100.0 |

*Note:* In four cases 2 perpetrators were identified. Hence the above table shows 87 perpetrators for 83 child victims.

[a]Even when the perpetrator is unknown, police still see one of the family members as the prime suspect. In these three cases family members were the only persons in the home at the time the child died under suspicious circumstances.

Table 6.3 reports the method of killing by the sex of the perpetrator. Of the 54 men and boys who caused child deaths, 14 (25.9 percent) did so by shooting. Among the 30 women who killed children, 7 (23.3 percent) shot them. Although twice as many male as female perpetrators used a firearm, similar proportions of males and females shot boys and girls. Consistent with the work of Schloesser, Pierpont, and Poertner,[4] the data on Florida child fatalities reveal that men are much more likely than women to inflict lethal head injuries upon children. The only cause of death disproportionately associated with female offenders is drug or alcohol abuse that medical authorities conclude effected

### TABLE 6.2
Relationship between child's parent(s)/caretaker(s)

| Status | No. cases | % of 83 |
|---|---|---|
| Parents/caretakers married and living together | 25 | 30.1 |
| Parents/caretakers unmarried and not living together (e.g., separated, divorced) | 13 | 15.7 |
| Parents/caretakers unmarried and living together | 19 | 22.9 |
| Single mothers with no intimate partners documented in the multiagency files | 14 | 16.9 |
| Relative is primary caretaker of child (2 aunts, 1 grandmother) | 3 | 3.6 |
| Relationship status between parents/caretakers not known | 9 | 10.8 |
| Totals | 83 | 100.0 |

Note: Combining the number of relationships in which parents or caretakers were married and living together (25), separated or divorced and not living together (13), and unmarried and living together (19) yield 57 cases where domestic violence was possible between parents or caretakers. This figure of 57 relationships forms the basis for the calculations on the proportion of parental or caretaker relationships that exhibited domestic violence (see Table 6.6).

neonaticide. In four of the five deaths of newborns involving drugs or alcohol, the autopsy identified the mother's excessive use of cocaine prior to birth as a major contributor to the fatality. In the other case, a mother consumed excessive amounts of alcohol that led to the death of her newborn. I will return to the phenomenon of drug-related neonaticide later.

The findings in Table 6.3 differ somewhat from those offered in other published research. As Hicks and Gaughan note, many of the published studies indicate that children killed in the home die from blunt impact (usually head) injury inflicted by a parent.[5] In their analysis of child abuse deaths in Kansas from 1975 to 1978 and 1983 to 1985, Schloesser, Pierpont, and Poertner found that 57.7 percent of such deaths were attributed to "head injury."[6] Krugman's analysis of 24 child abuse fatalities attributed 17 (70.8 percent) to head injuries.[7] My own examination of child deaths includes homicide-suicides and familicides, multiple killings usually effected with a gun. In consequence, I report higher numbers of children dying from gunshot wounds than do researchers whose data sets do not include multiple killings. Fully one-quarter of domestic child fatalities in Florida stemmed from gunshot wounds. Only one-fifth resulted from head injuries, and one-tenth each from abdominal trauma and shaken-baby syndrome.

I noted in Chapter 1 that the relationship between race and domestic

**TABLE 6.3**

Cause of death

| Means | Male perpetrator | Female perpetrator | Perpetrator unknown family member | Totals |
|---|---|---|---|---|
| Shooting | 14 | 7 | 0 | 21 (24.1%) |
| Head injury | 14 | 1 | 2 | 17 (19.5%) |
| Abdominal trauma | 6 | 3 | 1 | 10 (11.5%) |
| Shaken-baby syndrome[a] | 4 | 4 | 0 | 8 (9.2%) |
| Asphyxiation[b] | 3 | 3 | 0 | 6 (6.9%) |
| Knifing | 2 | 3 | 0 | 5 (5.7%) |
| Multiple[c] | 4 | 1 | 0 | 5 (5.7%) |
| Drug/alcohol abuse | 0 | 5 | 0 | 5 (5.7%) |
| Severe neglect[d] | 1 | 1 | 0 | 2 (2.3%) |
| Machete wounds | 2 | 0 | 0 | 2 (2.3%) |
| Burns | 1 | 0 | 0 | 1 (1.1%) |
| Arson | 0 | 1 | 0 | 1 (1.1%) |
| Suffocation | 0 | 1 | 0 | 1 (1.1%) |
| Cardiac failure[e] | 1 | 0 | 0 | 1 (1.1%) |
| Unknown cause | 2 | 0 | 0 | 2 (2.3%) |
| Totals | 54 | 30 | 3 | 87 (99.6%) |

*Note:* In four cases two perpetrators were identified. Hence the above table shows 87 "causes of death" for 83 child victims.

[a]Both parents were deemed to have contributed to the death of one child by shaken-baby syndrome.

[b]Both parents were deemed to have contributed to the death of one child by asphyxiation.

[c]Both parents were deemed to have contributed to the death of one child by multiple causes, which involved a severe beating of the entire body.

[d]Both parents were deemed to have contributed to the death of one child by severe neglect.

[e]The cardiac failure in this case was due to blunt force injury to the rectum, probably from the insertion of a finger or penis.

homicide needs to be approached with considerable caution. It is not sufficient to simply argue that race differentials in child homicides reflect the cultural characteristics of different racial groups and their respective tendencies to use lethal violence against children. Instead, there is evidence to suggest that socio-economic status is a more significant factor than race in generating higher rates of domestic homicide in the African-American community.[8] Table 6.4 indicates that black youngsters constituted 41 percent of the 83 child homicide vic-

### TABLE 6.4
Characteristics of the 83 child victims

| Characteristic | No. | % of 83 |
|---|---|---|
| **Sex of child** | | |
| Male | 39 | 47.0 |
| Female | 44 | 53.0 |
| Total | 83 | 100.0 |
| **Race/ethnicity of child** | | |
| White | 31 | 37.3 |
| White-Asian | 2 | 2.4 |
| Black | 34 | 41.0 |
| Latino | 16 | 19.3 |
| Total | 83 | 100.0 |
| **Age of child** | | |
| < 1 year | 24 | 28.9 |
| 1–2 | 9 | 10.8 |
| 2–3 | 17 | 20.5 |
| 3–4 | 5 | 6.0 |
| 4–5 | 4 | 4.8 |
| 5–10 | 12 | 14.5 |
| 10–17 | 11 | 13.3 |
| Missing data | 1 | 1.2 |
| Total | 83 | 100.0 |

tims in Florida. Given that African Americans only constitute 13.6 percent of the state's population, black children are significantly overrepresented among the ranks of victims. However, since the data on income, occupations, and socioeconomic status among the families in which child fatalities occur is incomplete, it is difficult to assess the significance of race differentials.

The Florida findings show that younger children are more vulnerable to homicide. As Table 6.4 indicates, just over three-fifths of girls and boys killed were less than 3 years old, with nearly a third under 1 year old.[9] The reasons for this vulnerability lie not only in very young children's physical fragility, particularly their relatively large head size and their inability to control head movements, but also in their less frequent contact with agencies such as day care centers and schools that may identify abuse and neglect problems before they escalate. Additionally, these children are less able than their older counterparts to communicate verbally the abuse they experience.

## Interrelated Antecedents to the Death of Children

As in adult domestic killings, a number of etiological themes or situational antecedents characterize the domestic child homicide cases. These themes provide an important context for understanding the deaths of the 83 boys and girls. Prominent among them are a history of child abuse; a history of domestic violence (typically woman battering) in the relationship between caretakers or parents; prior contact with various agencies; poverty, inequality, and unemployment; a criminal history on the part of the perpetrator; the use of drugs, alcohol, or both; and the easy availability of weapons.

Although I did not directly interview family members, friends, relatives, and others close to victims and perpetrators, the evidence amassed through multiple agency files and numerous contacts with agency personnel—detectives, prosecutors, defense attorneys, child protection workers, administrators of child protection programs, physicians, and judges among them—still provides rich details for constructing etiologic patterns. As in the earlier chapters, I examine the extent to which the etiologic themes and situational antecedents pervade the 83 cases. I emphasize again here that these themes are linked to each other and appear in the case histories as richly interwoven phenomena.

*The Role of Prior Child Abuse*   A number of studies indicate that children known to have been abused or neglected are more likely than those not known to have been abused or neglected to become the victims of homicides.[10] Nearly half of the 83 boy and girls killed in Florida had experienced prior abuse, neglect, or both at the hands of the perpetrator. Most of these cases revealed the child had been violently victimized by the perpetrator. In this sense my findings are similar to those reported by Wilczynski.[11] As Table 6.5 indicates, this abuse or neglect often occurred in tandem with parental or caretaker domestic violence. This linkage, one not hitherto explored in the research literature, is very important. As I will argue later, it not only enables one to better grasp the finer nuances of child deaths, but also has broad implications for policy interventions aimed at reducing child fatalities.

### TABLE 6.5
Prior abuse or neglect and child homicide

| Situational antecedent | No. cases | % of 83 |
| --- | --- | --- |
| Children abused or neglected by perpetrator | 41 | 49.4 |
| Children abused or neglected by perpetrator in combination with domestic violence between parents/caretakers | 18 | 21.7 |
| Child abused or neglected by perpetrator without domestic violence between parents/caretakers | 23 | 27.7 |

Table 6.5 identifies those cases of prior child abuse accompanied by domestic violence between the child's parents or caretakers. Since so much adult domestic violence is hidden from the gaze of authorities and the official record, it is very difficult to state with any certainty whether such adult interpersonal violence was present in cases of child homicide.

In the death of Anja Belton, three years old, there is no available evidence pointing to a history of domestic violence between her parents. Anja was sodomized and then strangled to death with the wire of an alarm clock by her father, Richard Phelps, after she had threatened to tell her mother about him sexually abusing her. After strangling his daughter, Richard returned to the living room of their house and resumed watching television. He later told police that he laid Anja's body on the floor of the bedroom she shared with her one-year-old brother to make it look as though she had fallen out of bed and broken her neck.

Anja Belton's death appears quite straightforward insofar as the father, fearing exposure as a child molester, killed his daughter in an attempt to elude detection. Here, the child abuse preceding the killing and the three-year-old's stated intention to tell her mother of her victimization directly led to the use of lethal violence.

In cases where a history of child abuse exists alongside adult interpersonal violence, child protection files are sometimes quick to point to the mother for failing to offer protection from the abuse dispensed by her male partner. Child protective agency narratives on these types of child homicides raise important questions about the responsibility of mothers to defend their children in the face of their own fear of sublethal or lethal battering. In those cases where women killed their children, no comparable discourse of blame is directed at fathers, stepfathers, boyfriends, or other men who may have been involved. This is an important finding, because it implies that sometimes child protection workers consciously or subconsciously expect mothers, but not fathers, to intervene in cases of child abuse. Such a double standard punishes women all the more because it fails to acknowledge that it is mothers rather than fathers whose failure to protect is often influenced by their fear of battering. At some level, mothers can invoke the intimidation factor, whereas fathers who fail to safeguard children have no such "duress justification" to resort to.

Immokalee is the center of agribusiness in Collier County, Florida. Its population of 16,000 swells to more than 30,000 during the winter harvest as migrant workers arrive to bring in tomatoes, peppers, citrus, and other crops. The community is very diverse, with migrants coming from Puerto Rico and the countries of Central and South America. Edgar and Magdalena Benitez lived in Immokalee, where they worked as farm laborers, tying and picking tomatoes. Edgar had a permit to work in the United States; Magdalena, his wife, did not. The couple, both migrants from Mexico, lived together with their son, Jose, who was 11 months old, and their two young daughters. Jose had been born in Flagstaff, Arizona, in March 1993, and the family moved to Immokalee the following month to work in the fields. On February 23, 1994, Jose disappeared after going out with Edgar in his truck.

Some time later a family fishing in a canal saw a skull floating in the water. (Until seeing the eye sockets they thought it was a buoy). Police identified the skull as that of a child between five and nine months old, but there were few leads in the case. Investigators found a Sears Die Hard battery near where the child's corpse had been discovered. They suspected the battery had been used to weight the small body down. They also found a pocket knife and some bone fragments. Nearly two months passed before Magdalena Benitez contacted police to tell them that her husband, Edgar, had murdered Jose. The Benitez family was then living in North Carolina, the adults again working a harvest. Magdalena ended up talking with officers only after Edgar had assaulted her within earshot of neighbors. The neighbors contacted the migrants' crew leader at the North Carolina camp, who then called the local authorities. Once in the company of police, Magdalena reported how Edgar had gone off with Jose and how the child had never returned. Speaking only in Spanish, she told officers that her husband was an abusive man who beat their infant son regularly. Magdalena reported a long history of Edgar hitting Jose on his legs, hands, and back with a cable, and hitting him in the face in a manner that left bruises.

Magdalena reported to investigators that she lied to child care workers when they asked about the bruises on her son. She also said to police that her husband had abused her, including punching her in the stomach while she was pregnant with Jose. The Benitez family followed the harvests, and Edgar would keep a tight rein on Magdalena's movements. At times he would beat her for going outside their trailer to hang out the washing. Edgar told her that he did not want other persons looking at her. When her husband assaulted her he would cover her face with a pillow so that no one could hear her cry out.

Sometime before the young boy's death, a child assessment worker employed on a federal grant program in Collier County, Florida, was referred to the Benitez family by a worker from a Christian migrant association. She conducted a developmental assessment of Jose Benitez in a domestic-violence shelter in Naples, Florida. As well as finding the boy developmentally slow in motor skills, the worker described Magdalena's affect as "scared."

Members of the migrant farmworker community also knew of Edgar's abusiveness toward Magdalena. On one occasion in Immokalee a number of workers witnessed him beating her with his fists in the field where the couple was picking tomatoes. Elsior Cardenas, whose brother was a crew leader there, described the situation.

> They were tying and picking tomatoes. It was about three years ago [1991]. My brother seen him [Edgar] beating her. We ran . . . and they were about two ditches behind where we were picking. . . . My brother picked him up with one arm and got him off her. He had already beaten on her because she was all scratched up where he would slam her towards the stakes, and had her on the ground. My brother told him, "Don't beat your wife." And she was just crying. She was pregnant because she was complaining that she had pains in her stomach. . . . She had dirt all over her where he had been beating on her on the ground and throwing her against the stakes and the tomatoes. At the time that my brother got him off of her, he was choking her. He had both his arms on her neck. And after that my brother told him he didn't want to see him in the fields no more 'cause, you know, that wasn't right for him to beat on his wife.

On the day of the killing, Edgar came home from work hungry and demanded that Magdalena cook his dinner. While she was preparing the food Jose fell over and Magdalena went to his aid. Edgar was incensed that his wife took time off from preparing his meal and insisted she leave Jose alone and get back to work. Magdalena said she ignored Edgar, which enraged him all the more and led to a beating. He then gestured toward their two daughters as if he was going to beat them. Magdalena intervened and pushed the two girls into the bathroom. While continuing to beat his wife, Edgar seized Jose and hit him in the face. The young boy started to vomit blood. He then took his son out of the trailer and threw him into his truck. As he left the trailer, Edgar locked the door, using a lock that he had installed to keep his wife and two daughters from going out. He drove off, returning several hours later with a 24-pack of beer but without Jose.

When Magdalena asked where her son was, Edgar beat her again. She was terrified of her husband and waited until the next week before confronting him a second time regarding Jose's whereabouts. The couple were in the process of applying for food stamps, and he had listed their son's name on the application. Magdalena asked Edgar why he had put down Jose's name if the boy was not in fact with them. She said to her husband that if he did not tell her where Jose was she would say to the clerk that Edgar had abducted their son. Magdalena's threat caused him to tear up the food stamp application and insist upon them leaving the building. When he got his wife into their truck he beat her. Edgar then admitted killing Jose and dumping his body, saying to her, "I'll kill you if you tell anyone what I'm going to tell you, but I killed your son." He went on, "If you tell the police, if I go to jail, I'll get out one day, and when I get out I will kill you and leave you without children also."

Eventually, police found evidence linking Edgar to the crime scene and he confessed to killing Jose. In a plea bargain, he was found guilty of manslaughter and sentenced to 55 months in prison. The two-month delay in reporting Jose's disappearance and subsequently identifying his skull reflects the fear Magdalena Benitez had of her husband. It also reflects her compromised status as an illegal immigrant. When asked by an investigator if she tried to leave Edgar, the conversation developed as follows:

> *Investigator*   Did you ever think of leaving your husband because of the physical abuse against you?
> *Magdalena*   Yes. I left. The police took me. I left, but I had no kind of help. A worker at a shelter in Naples [34 miles away] told me that I had to go back to Mexico because I wasn't legal here in the United States.

A day care worker who was involved with Jose in Immokalee, Sonya Vasquez, described some of the dilemmas Magdalena faced as a battered migrant woman:

And she [Magdalena] told me, "He hit me and he hit the baby too." And I said, "[Y]ou know this isn't right." She says, "I know, Sonya . . . but what can I do? I'm afraid of him. He says that I won't be able to do nothing, because I'm an illegal person, and they won't listen to me. They only listen to him, and he'll get all the kids."

Magdalena's plight, as a migrant worker and as a battered woman, is not unusual. Indeed, another child was killed in Immokalee in 1994 under circumstances very similar to those in which Jose Benitez died. In the eastern United States migrant farmworkers move from Florida through the Carolinas and even as far as New York State and Maine.[12] The women among them face a number of difficulties, including language barriers (Magdalena Benitez spoke only Spanish), cultural differences, and isolation. The transient lifestyle of moving from one harvest to the next makes it difficult to establish ties with local communities and to get to know what sources of assistance, if any, are available. It also seems that a very high number of migrant women experience interpersonal abuse. Orloff and Rodriguez cite a 1994 survey showing that one out of three migrant farmworker women reported experiencing physical abuse within the past year, with one in five reporting forced sexual activity.[13] In the same survey, just over a quarter of migrant farmworker women reported being afraid of their partner. Orloff and Rodriguez observe that, like Magdalena Benitez, many battered migrant women do not seek legal assistance because their husbands "use their immigrant spouses' dependence upon them to obtain legal immigration status as a means of controlling their wives and keeping them in isolation."[14] These observations arising out of the death of Jose Benitez remind one that the domestic killing of children can involve the complex intersection of child abuse, woman battering, economic deprivation, and cultural isolation, all intertwined with the apparent inaccessibility of important and potentially life-saving state services.

The compromised position of Magdalena Benitez also points to the vast differences in experience between migrant farmworker women, on the one hand, and other Latino women who have a much higher material standard of living and enjoy formal rights of citizenship. Magdalena Benitez and others like her are acutely entrapped compared with many Latino women. However, it appears that the entrapment of female migrant farmworkers tends not to produce the kind of lethal resistive violence used by some African-American women. And one must bear in mind that the meaning of entrapment to indi-

**TABLE 6.6**

Prior domestic violence between the 57 couples and child homicide

| Situational antecedent | No. cases | % of 57 |
|---|---|---|
| Total cases of prior domestic violence between parents/<br>caretakers | 30 | 52.6 |
| Domestic violence between parents/caretakers in<br>combination with child abuse/neglect | 18 | 31.6 |
| Domestic violence between parents/caretakers without<br>reports of child abuse/neglect | 12 | 21.1 |
| No domestic violence documented in multiagency files | 18 | 31.6 |
| Evidence from multiagency files is inconclusive<br>regarding presence of domestic violence between<br>parents/caretakers | 9 | 15.8 |

*Note:* In 26 cases there was only one caretaker of the child; that caretaker does not appear to have been in any intimate relationship.

vidual social actors who find themselves in variously compromised social situations is likely of greatest importance in generating lethal resistive interpersonal violence.

*The Role of Domestic Violence*   The death of Jose Benitez is a good example of just how difficult it is for battered mothers to report the abuse of their children and themselves. In Magdalena Benitez's case, the inability to complain to authorities was also intimately associated with her compromised position as a female migrant farmworker. My focus in this section remains firmly on the role of domestic violence between caretakers or parents. However, it is clear from Table 6.6 that in 18 of the 30 cases where adult domestic violence preceded a child homicide there was also a history of child abuse. In only 12 of the 30 cases did adult domestic violence appear by itself, without a known history of child abuse or neglect. Even though these numbers are small, they indicate that, when a history of domestic violence precedes a child homicide, it is one and one-half times as likely to occur in tandem with prior child abuse or neglect than on its own.

The role of domestic violence in the killing of boys and girls is complex and multifaceted. Table 6.6 shows that in just over half the cases of domestic child homicide where two parents or caretakers were involved in caring for the child, the woman was being beaten by the man before the homicide.[15] In some cases men kill children just to get back at their female partners, who they believe have betrayed them in some way. In other cases women seem to acquiesce in the abuse and eventual killing of their own children because they are terrified of their male intimate partners, who usually end up committing the final homicidal act. In still other cases, some examples of which I introduced in Chapter 2, men kill their female partners, children, or both in multiple homicides as the culmination of an abusive domestic relationship. In this section I offer examples of all these scenarios as a way of beginning to appreciate the complex links between child abuse, adult domestic violence, and child homicide.

Two-year-old Kathy DeLeon was murdered by her mother's boyfriend, Frankie Amin, a 27-year-old construction worker. Her mother, Carla DeLeon, a Latino female aged 20, and Amin were both immigrants from Honduras. At the time of the killing they lived in a run-down single-story apartment building in Miami's East Little Havana, a neighborhood in which newcomers from Central America often initially settle. The couple met in Miami about a year before Kathy's murder. Carla, Frankie, and Kathy shared a four-room living space with three other men and another woman. Frankie Amin, who did not have a job, had been angry with Carla DeLeon because she had found employment as a waitress at a restaurant and bar in north Miami. He was particularly upset that she would be serving other men. On the Thursday night before the killing he turned up at the restaurant and bar. During the argument that followed he struck Carla several times. Other employees then separated the couple and removed Frankie from the building. On his way out he called to her, "Be careful. Don't talk to the police or you'll regret it." Carla was so afraid that she did contact police; a patrol car escorted her back to her apartment. Carla's mother later told investigators that Frankie had beaten her daughter on many occasions and that she had advised her to call the police. When he saw Carla arrive with the patrol officer, Frankie yelled out to her, "You are going to regret this, you are going to cry tears of blood." He then ran back into the apartment and barricaded himself in. Officers pursued Amin and broke down the door. When they got inside they found Kathy dead on a bloody mattress with her throat cut. Frankie Amin was lying against a wall crying, holding a bloody knife and saying to police, "[K]ill me, kill me." Carla DeLeon had to appeal to the Honduran embassy for funds to bury her daughter.

This case recalls a homicide-suicide I discussed in Chapter 2, in which Tosca Perez, enraged at his estranged wife's affair with a new lover, took the life of his 14-year-old daughter, Felicia Perez, before killing himself. The major difference between the Perez and DeLeon killings is that in the former case the perpetrator was the biological father of the girl, whereas Frankie Amin was in effect a stepfather. Indeed, this difference may have had something to do with why Tosca Perez took his own life after killing his daughter, whereas Frankie Amin did not, although he was clearly suicidal. In both cases, the male perpetrator professed a deep and abiding love for the child he murdered. (Neighbors and friends told investigators that Frankie Amin loved Kathy DeLeon.) Both men, however, were obsessively jealous of their female partners. On the night Frankie confronted Carla DeLeon at the restaurant and bar, she was deeply concerned for her own safety. Carla informed police, though, that she was confident Frankie would not hurt Kathy, because he loved her. The Kathy DeLeon tragedy is a textbook example of a revenge killing designed to hurt a female partner and mother who the perpetrator believes has betrayed him in a profound way. Although the extent of the betrayal in this case was known only to Frankie Amin, it seemed to grow out of his patriarchal understanding of the role of women in intimate relationships.

In seven cases, I was unable to confirm whether mothers who were held responsible for the deaths of their children were being battered by male partners. There were only four child deaths in which mothers were deemed responsible and were known to have been battered by their intimate male partners. In one such case a drug-addicted, unemployed mother killed her blind five-year-old son, who suffered from cerebral palsy. The cause of death was acute ethanol poisoning. This homicide recalls those cross-cultural examples given by Daly and Wilson from 21 different societies in which parents killed deformed children. Making reference to the logic of evolutionary psychology, they comment, "Whatever our moral sympathies in the matter, we should recognize that the rejection of an unhealthy newborn could be an adaptive (fitness-promoting) parental response."[16] In two other cases in which mothers were deemed culpable in child deaths, the fathers were also found responsible. I now narrate a classic case in which both parents were found guilty of murdering their child and in which the mother alleged she was battered.

The death of Alice Tanner, a 7-year-old white girl, at the hands of her stepfather, 32-year-old Christian Maynard, and her mother, 24-year-old Libby Maynard, made news nationwide. On Saturday, October 22, 1994, the Broward County Sheriff's Department received a call from Libby Maynard saying that she and Alice had been in separate stalls in the restroom of a Fort Lauderdale swap shop. When Libby emerged from her stall, Alice was nowhere to be found. The sheriff's department conducted an extensive search of the area but could not find the child. The couple appealed to the general public for help in locating the girl, with Libby Maynard making a tearful plea on national television.

On October 24, 1994, the Broward County Sheriff's Department and the FBI began a follow-up investigation. Determining that no samples of the girl's hair or fingerprints were available, investigators went to the Maynard residence in order to obtain such samples. The couple consented to the search. Subsequently, law enforcement personnel found a pair of blue jeans believed to belong to Alice Tanner with what seemed to be blood on them. They also found a suspected bloodstain on a mattress located in the bedroom. After confirming the presence of blood, investigators became increasingly suspicious about inconsistencies in the Maynards' account of Alice's disappearance. On October 27, 1994, after having been read her *Miranda* rights, Libby Maynard agreed to take a polygraph test. The results of the exam suggested deception. Eventually she confessed to investigators that Alice had died over a month before and that the swap shop story was fabricated.

Libby said that her daughter died while being disciplined by Christian Maynard. She stated that he struck Alice several times on the face and buttocks; the girl then went into what Libby described as "seizures." According to her account, Christian then put a towel over Alice's mouth, as they had done in the past, so that no one would hear her cry out or scream. Although Libby and Christian attempted to administer first aid, within a few minutes Alice appeared dead. Christian put the child in a bath of cold water in an attempt to revive her. He then put the body in the bedroom and told Libby not to go in. By her account, Alice's body remained in the room in a closet for four days. The couple used blankets to hide it from Christian's sons, aged three and five. They burned strawberry incense for four days (September 16–20) to cover the smell of the rotting corpse. On the night of September 19, 1994, Christian removed Alice's body from the apartment and buried it behind a Kmart in a grave five and a half feet deep that he dug himself. He then returned and told Libby he had buried her daughter.

Investigators discovered a number of previously unknown details during their interview with Christian Maynard. He told them that he was questioning Alice about some sexual activity that he thought she had been involved in with one of his boys, who also lived at the residence. After Christian Maynard posed the question to Alice about the alleged sexual activity, he reported, she defecated. Christian admitted that this act enraged him and he started to hit her. Nevertheless, he said that he thought her death was an accident and he had not meant to kill her. Later he led police to the burial site, where officers dug up the "bundle" that once was Alice Tanner.

Neighbors confirmed that they had heard a disturbance on the day of the killing. The person living next door reported hearing screams and the sound of someone being hit. And it was not for the first time in that apartment, the neighbor added. She reported hearing a man's voice yell, "Why did you shit on the floor in front of me?" She then heard a woman yell, "That's enough, Christian!" A friend of Christian Maynard's went over to watch football one night while Alice's corpse was still in the apartment. Apparently, he told his friend that Alice had been banished to the bedroom. During the evening, the man reported, Christian would go into the room to check on how Alice was getting along with her homework. On other occasions Libby Maynard took in a tray of food, then came out and reported on how the girl was progressing. It was charades such as these, combined with Libby's tearful televised request for her (long dead) daughter to come home, that contributed to a widespread public perception that the couple were conniving child killers.

Other facts emerged that reinforced Libby's image as an uncaring mother. The press reported that Libby gave birth to Alice in 1987, but left her daughter when she was just a few months old. Alice's great-grandmother raised her until she was five. The girl then went to live with her adoptive mother, the new wife of Libby's former husband. This woman then decided that Alice should live with her natural mother, and she took her to Libby in June 1994. Reporters alleged that the Maynards apparently resented Alice being dropped on their doorstep. They already had two sons of their own, Libby was pregnant again, and she had given up her job as a waitress at a bar. Christian Maynard was making only eight dollars an hour working as a cook at a beach bar. The press also informed readers that Libby lied about her address in order to enroll her two boys in better schools a considerable distance from their Riviera Beach apartment.

It was perhaps unfortunate for Libby Maynard that she was arrested the day after Susan Smith of Union, South Carolina, was charged with killing her two sons, aged 14 months and 3 years, by drowning them in a lake. The media coverage of the case was extensive and sensational. Like Libby, Susan Smith went on national television, claiming tearfully that a black man had abducted her two sons and driven off in her car. Later she confessed to driving the car into a lake. The killing of the Smith boys overshadowed the killing of Alice Tanner, but the media discourse on the homicides reveals a number of convergences between the two cases. One of the central discursive themes in the presentation of both was that of the dishonest, unfit mother. Not only had she killed her own children; she had, through emotional pleas for their return, duped the authorities and the media, in effect cynically using the image of nurturing motherhood for her own wicked ends.[17]

This imagery did not serve Libby Maynard well as she came up for trial. Indeed, her defense attorney requested the proceedings be moved from Palm Beach County because she could not receive a fair trial there, given the widespread hatred of her. When news surfaced that her attorney was going to use battered-woman syndrome as a defense there was widespread outrage. One erstwhile friend of Libby's was quoted as saying, "That's bull. . . . [S]he had every chance in the world to tell people what happened. I don't care how much he beat her up. She had a month to get help. She was walking around here with her daughter dead." In the same newspaper article, a staff writer comments: "But in this part of the state, where Libby's name is still spat like a curse, most people aren't buying that argument [battered-woman syndrome]. 'It makes me want to throw up,' said Bruno Herff, who once worked with Libby and once liked her. Not anymore. 'I don't care how anybody feels,' he says, 'a mother is a mother.'"[18]

Prosecutors sought the death penalty for Libby Maynard for failing to protect her daughter and for also abusing her. The judge who presided over the sentencing decision (after Libby waived her right to have a jury recommend a punishment) gave her a term of life in prison without parole. Summing up, Circuit Judge Stephen Rapp noted that Libby Maynard did not want to take care of her daughter and felt that she was an "unnecessary expense." He went on to say, "She sold Alice's bicycle and toys before Alice was murdered. . . . Alice, who was soon to be murdered, would have no further use for them."[19]

At the time of writing, this case is going through the appeals process. Without Libby's own account of her relationship with Christian Maynard it is difficult to document the precise nature of her interpersonal victimization and what impact it had on the death of her daughter. Although her defense attorney alluded to Libby being a battered woman, the facts about her interpersonal victimization are not clear from her trial. One of the two appeals attorneys working the case told a key informant that Christian Maynard used to take the money that Libby, an epileptic, needed for medicine and buy marijuana. Another key informant familiar with Libby's social life in prison told me that her fellow prisoners described her, in unsolicited reports, as a very abused woman. Another account, from an inmate who had a lengthy romantic relationship with Libby, also reported that Christian Maynard brutalized her.[20]

As noted in Chapter 2, children also die during multiple domestic killings. Most of these homicides committed by men involve a history of violence toward intimate female partners. In the case narrative that follows, I show how a history of woman battering, a pending separation, earlier police involvement, and obsessive possessiveness preface the killing of three young children.

Pancho Casis, a Latino male aged 31, shot and killed his three children—Charlotte, aged 5, Pancho Jr., aged 4, and Helen, aged 1—and his wife's suspected boyfriend, Federico Nascimento, aged 34. He also shot but did not kill his wife, Marianna Nuevo, aged 22. He then committed suicide. The killing occurred in the family's one-room apartment in Little Havana, where the five of them lived with little furniture in a space of about 300 square feet. The couple paid $340 for this accommodation. Pancho Casis was a cook who came to Florida from Venezuela; Marianna was from Puerto Rico. The two had met in Miami seven years before the killings.

The apartment manager informed police that Marianna was preparing to leave Pancho and take the children with her. About 10 days before the multiple killing, he reported, the couple had a loud fight. After it had ended, Marianna packed all of Pancho's clothes into bags and placed them in the hallway. He moved back in the next day. The manager also said that Marianna had confided in him that Pancho had hit her.

The alleged boyfriend Pancho killed, Federico Nascimento, lived 20 blocks away with his sister, Maria, and her husband, Pablo. Federico was a Cuban refugee who had arrived in Florida just three months before on an inner tube with eight other rafters. Neighbors told investigators that Marianna had often been at the house where Federico lived, since she was an old friend of Maria, a Cuban woman who came to Miami during the Mariel Boatlift. The two were neighbors at one point, and Maria baby-sat Marianna's children from time to time. Maria informed police that the relationship between her brother Federico and Marianna was platonic, not romantic. Pancho obviously thought otherwise. Investigators told reporters that they thought Marianna and Federico were lovers. However, a detective I talked with who was close to the investigation later told me that there was no romance.

According to Marianna's relatives, up until 18 months before the killings Pancho was a "noble man." However, Marianna later told reporters that her husband began to get very jealous of her relationships with everyone, including her girlfriends, during this period. In the 18 months leading up to the homicides, Marianna said, Pancho attacked her with a knife and on another occasion attempted to strangle her. She reported the latter incident to the police. She told reporters that after the attempted strangulation they "stayed together." As Marianna put it, "[W]hen you don't have any money, what can you do?"[21]

*Prior Agency Contacts*    The Florida sample of 83 domestic child fatalities revealed child protective services had earlier involvement with caretakers or parents concerning child abuse or neglect in at least 21 cases (25.3 percent). This is consistent with the extant research mentioned in Chapter 1, which shows prior protective agency contact with 25 to 50 percent of children who were later killed and their families. In Florida, other agencies, including day care providers (1 case), hospitals (2 cases), and psychiatric facilities (1 case), also raised concerns about child abuse and neglect. The narratives that follow illustrate the different kinds of involvement of child protection services with the perpetrators of domestic child homicides.

Shaniece Fromm, an African-American girl aged two, died of traumatic asphyxiation when the lid on her crib fell on her neck and pinned her against the side railing. At the time, she was in the crib with her regular companion, a 3-year-old developmentally disabled white girl named Gloria Maltad. Shaniece was adopted by Alex and Birgit Fromm when she was 10 days old. When police arrived at the house, Alex had removed the crib's 15-pound lid and put it in the garage. Officers found the lid later in their investigation. The Fromms' crib was made of Plexiglas at one end so that they could see Shaniece and Gloria without lifting the lid. Investigators found the living conditions in the house to be "deplorable." There was trash everywhere and the rooms were infested with insects. As officers walked around, roaches crawled over their shoes. Shaniece's body—including her face, mouth, chest, stomach, arms, and legs—was covered with insect bites.

Records indicate that child protective services used the Fromms as foster care or shelter care parents.[22] They requested "special needs" children, and between February 1991 and October 1994 apparently received $65,616 in foster care and shelter care payments for the more than 40 boys and girls who passed through their residence. This is a high number of children for the period involved and meant that child placement or protection workers had considerable contact with the couple compared with their involvement with some of the other caretakers or parents in the sample. The press made a lot of the fact that the Department of Health and Rehabilitative Services (HRS) paid a higher board rate to the foster parents of so-called special needs children, as much as $1100 a month per child. The implication was that with so much state money going to the family, HRS should have known more about the conditions in the home.

Persons who lived nearby reported numerous loud arguments and signs of domestic violence between Alex and Birgit Fromm. On one occasion a neighbor reported Alex standing on his porch yelling, "I'm tired of these niggers in my house." This statement, made at 2:00 A.M., was apparently a reference to the foster children, and especially Shaniece, their black adopted daughter. Reporters did not miss noting that such an environment might be inconsistent with extending appropriate care to young children. As a result of press coverage, questions surfaced about how HRS supervised the placement and monitoring of girls and boys in foster care and shelter care. The state charged the Fromms with first-degree murder, relying on a statute that did not require proof of premeditation if felony child abuse was present. Prosecutors argued that the crib design constituted a "cage" and was therefore inherently abusive. The defense argued that the lid on the crib stopped the children from getting out and injuring themselves. At trial, the jury found the Fromms guilty of misdemeanor culpable negligence, which carried a maximum jail term of one year.

This case is a model of a child homicide in which child protective agencies had considerable contact with the parents. Here, however, the state's involvement did not prevent the fatality. Other cases run the gamut from extensive, ongoing contact to minimal contact that took place long before the fatality. Indeed, it would be useful to know more about the relationship between the nature, duration, and timing of the delivery of child protection and the killing of children in the home. Additionally, there is more to be learned about the nature of child protective services intervention and the prosecution of child homicide cases.

In the death of Andrew Regis, a 2-year-old black boy, one sees occasional as opposed to regular involvement with child protective services, with most of the contact taking place between 1988 and 1990, when four HRS reports were made on the family. Andrew died of a skull fracture and burns over a large portion of his body. A week before his death he was hospitalized for burns, only to be discharged. The boy's mother, Katrina Regis, lived with Andrew, her other children, and her boyfriend, Desmond Walters, a 19-year-old black man. On the day of the killing she was next door talking with a neighbor; Desmond was looking after Andrew when he died. He told police that the child choked on some popcorn and vomited. He responded by giving the young boy Tylenol and Kool-Aid, which Andrew also vomited. However, investigators soon determined the real cause of death, and Desmond Walters became the prime suspect. It later emerged that another youngster in the family feared Desmond, who allegedly disciplined the child excessively. It took another five months, however, to piece together enough information to charge Walters with murder. Apparently his cousin told investigators that Walters abused Andrew when Katrina Regis was not around. At the trial it came out that the burns were due to scalding water. Desmond Walters was found guilty of murder in 1996 and sentenced to 23 years in prison.

*Poverty, Inequality, and Unemployment*  In modern state societies, those who commit homicide are much more likely to have low incomes and little accumulated wealth.[23] They are also much more likely to be officially defined as poor. Modern definitions of poverty are "relational" insofar as they compare a person's or a family's financial standing to that of others. Whatever the effects of being poor, they likely work through people's perception and negotiation of their economic plight vis-à-vis the situation of others, rather than through the debilitating material effects of a lack of finite resources alone. Researchers have documented powerful connections between inequality and homicide rates.[24] Given that the vast majority of persons do not own substantial wealth, their financial standing typically depends upon their ability to earn money. Not surprisingly, many studies show that the higher the levels of unemployment, the higher the homicide rates.[25] For example, Shihadeh and Flynn find that for African Americans, higher rates of employment correlate with lower homicide rates.[26]

In a manner consistent with the broader literature on homicide in general, many of the 83 domestic child killings took place in households burdened by the blight of poverty, inequality, and the marginalization often felt through unemployment of underemployment. I have already mentioned how Edgar and Magdalena Benitez sought food stamps, how Frankie Amin was unemployed before he killed Kathy DeLeon, how Carla DeLeon had to appeal to the Honduran embassy for funds to bury her daughter, and how the Casis family lived in poverty. Without more extensive data on unofficial as well as official sources of income, it is very difficult to draw any firm conclusions about the relationship between differing levels of poverty, inequality, and unemployment and the child deaths. Put differently, without much more precise information on how individuals experience and negotiate poverty, inequality, and unemployment, it is difficult to confront the issue of why nearly all families in modern state societies who experience these deleterious effects of capitalism do not end up killing their children.

As I pointed out in Chapter 1, a number of authors have highlighted the relationships between child abuse and neglect and poverty, and between child homicides and poverty.[27] The Florida cases in which girls and boys were killed mirror these research findings, although the overall results from Florida are marred by missing data. In 34 of the 83 deaths (41 percent) the multiagency files did not contain sufficient information on the financial status of the caretakers or parents to determine whether they might qualify as being poor. Although I applied no hard-and-fast objective measure of poverty, if files mentioned that the caretakers or parents were unemployed, or if they received state aid, lived in public housing, qualified for food stamps, or worked in low-paid occupations, and, further, if the families reported being in financial distress, then I counted them as poor. Living in a run-down, dangerous neighborhood did not in itself qualify as living in poverty. Of the 49 deaths (59 percent of the total) where sufficient information was available to make an informed determination of whether the child's caretakers or parents lived in poverty, 36 (73.5 percent) of the families qualified as "poor." This left 13 cases (26.5 percent) where the families do not appear to have been touched by poverty.

The relevant investigations suggest, as noted above, that it is not so much the objective condition of poverty that affects behavior. Rather, it is the ways in which social actors perceive their economic standing vis-à-vis other persons, and negotiate their plight relative to other pressures, that provide insights into the relationship between poverty and child homicide. To elaborate upon this point, I turn now to another case history.

On February 1, 1994, while eating at her baby-sitter's house, Rebecca Merton, a black girl aged 2, choked, vomited, and eventually lost consciousness. The baby-sitter, Donna Dubb, placed her in the bathtub and washed the vomit from her clothes. Rebecca passed out in the tub. Donna administered CPR and the child was then rushed to the hospital, where she was pronounced dead at 11:32 A.M. The Dade County Medical Examiner's Office determined the cause of death to be abdominal trauma that had lacerated the young girl's liver. Earlier that morning Rebecca's mother, Clarisse Merton, dropped her and her older sister, Margaret, off at the baby-sitter's. Clarisse had known Donna Dubb for 10 years, a friendship dating back to their native Trinidad. It had apparently been a hectic morning for Clarisse. Her boyfriend, Wilson Pitt, stayed over at her apartment the night before. Clarisse was running late for work and was in a hurry to get the children to Donna's home. She was also very angry with Wilson and felt that, since he owned his own business, he could have taken the children to the baby-sitter. Clarisse, on the other hand, worked for a credit union in Miami and was expected to arrive on time. She later told investigators that she was under threat of dismissal for being late for work. When Clarisse arrived at Donna's house no one was home, forcing her to wait in the car with her two daughters. Rebecca began to cry, and Clarisse lifted the girl into her lap. Clarisse, too, began to cry, and later told investigators that she said, "I can't take this anymore. No matter what I do it always comes out wrong." She then began to pound her fists into her lap, where her daughter was still sitting. Clarisse said to investigators that she did not think she had hurt Rebecca, although she had observed a "sad look" that she had never seen before on the girl's face when she eventually took her into Donna Dubb's home. Clarisse did not tell Donna that she had pounded Rebecca in the car. The only instruction she gave her friend was that under no circumstances was she to bathe either of her children during the day. Donna commented to investigators that she found this statement strange, since she had bathed the sisters before when they got dirty. Within four hours Rebecca was dead.

After failing a polygraph test, Clarisse admitted to pounding her daughter. She was charged with first-degree murder and aggravated child abuse. Clarisse later pled guilty to manslaughter and was sentenced to 15 years' probation and to psychiatric treatment. The investigation into Rebecca's death revealed that although Clarisse held a job she was still experiencing great financial distress. She and her husband, Brian, who was an ordnance technician in the air force, had separated in September 1993. Since then Clarisse had lived as a single mother. In addition to her financial difficulties, she told investigators she was in the process of giving up smoking, was concerned that her car was damaged and that she did not have enough money to repair it, and was worried about being late for work. With her financial stress at the center of a constellation of concerns, she reported that on the day of the killing she felt that her life was just out of control.

Brian Merton remarked to police that he had a very poor marriage with Clarisse from 1989 to 1993. He resented that they no longer had sex and that she was "totally unmotivated to do anything most of the time." It was Brian who initiated the separation by asking Clarisse to move out. His mother complained to child abuse investigators that Clarisse "did nothing as a mother, that Brian came home from work and cooked, cleaned, shopped, while Clarisse watched TV and attended the University of Miami in an attempt to finish her degree in computer science." Brian voiced the same complaints to police and child protection workers. At one point he commented he had "three children [Clarisse and his two babies] to take care of." However, Brian also said that he could not envisage his wife ever abusing the children in any way, and he expressed surprise when police told him she had failed the polygraph exam. He remarked that Clarisse suffered from low self-esteem and observed that she had "cried throughout her second pregnancy."

This case raises important questions about the role of poverty in child homicides. Although Clarisse Merton reported being extremely anxious about her financial plight, it seems that her poverty was only one aspect of the situation. Clarisse's whole life seemed out of her control. This strain was accompanied by what seems to have been depression of long standing, although there is no evidence of treatment for it. From the information available in the multiagency files, there is no indication that she was a battered woman. There is also no evidence of prior child abuse directed by Clarisse or Brian at their two daughters. If one focuses solely on income, Clarisse Merton was relatively well-off financially compared to a number of the other perpetrators of child homicide. She had a white-collar job and a bachelor's degree. Even though there was no formal divorce agreement, the files indicate her estranged husband did pay child support. These facts highlight the importance of examining not just the material conditions in which child homicides occur, but of scrutinizing the meaning attached to them by the social actors involved. The death of Rebecca Merton points out that it is the socially situated meaning of poverty rather than its objective articulation that matters in cases of child deaths.

*Criminal Record of Perpetrators*   As I indicated in Chapter 2, criminal histories did not feature prominently in the biographies of men who committed multiple domestic homicides (see Table 2.5). However, I noted in Chapter 4 that 43 percent of the men who killed their intimate female partners had criminal records (see Table 4.3). Available multiagency files reveal that 22 of the perpetrators of child homicide (26.5 percent) had criminal histories. Nineteen of these 22 perpetrators were men. Two of the women who killed children had juvenile offenses only. The other female offender confessed to an earlier child homicide at the same time as she confessed to killing her own child. In Appendix 2, I document the known criminal records of the 22 persons who killed children. This paves the way for a discussion of two cases that illustrate the relationship between criminal histories and the commission of child homicide.

Steve Tilling, a 35-year-old black man, held Kirsti Knoffler, a 23-month-old black girl, under a scalding shower. Her screams were heard by her 5-year-old sister, who was downstairs at the time. Kirsti sustained third-degree burns over her back and buttocks. The outer skin layers were also missing from Kirsti's right shoulder area, right upper arm, and right forearm. Three or four days later, she was pronounced dead at a hospital.[28] The physician who attended her in the emergency room told detectives that the well-defined lines bordering the affected areas on Kirsti's skin indicated that the wounds had been caused by immersion in scalding liquid. The physician was also able to point out that because the young girl's wounds were localized she must have received them with "assistance." Another physician later concurred with this medical opinion and added that Kirsti "was probably in extreme pain from the time that she was burned until the time she died."

Steve Tilling had been living with Kirsti's mother, Gay Russell, a 23-year-old black woman, for a month. The two had been dating for 8 or 9 months. He had moved into her apartment and was able to "care" for her four children (aged 23 months to 5 years) while Gay worked evenings at an adult entertainment club. Gay said to police that she knew Steve had done some time in prison but did not know what for. When she came home from work to find Kirsti seriously burned, she told Steve they must take her daughter to the hospital. He cautioned Gay that if she did this, child protection workers would remove all her children from the home because of suspected abuse. Steve recommended they treat Kirsti themselves with ointments. Gay apparently agreed. However, Kirsti's condition worsened, and they both took her to the emergency room. There, she was pronounced dead, 3 or 4 days after the scalding.

Since the burns were inconsistent with Steve Tilling's statement that Kirsti's five-year-old sister, Felicity, had bathed the girl and inflicted the injuries, detectives suspected him from the outset. Tilling failed a polygraph test;[29] when confronted with the results he changed his story, stating that he might have inadvertently caused the burns. His criminal history was well known to police, and doubtless his earlier child abuse convictions stood out prominently as they interrogated him.

Tilling's criminal pedigree began with a number of minor offenses in the mid-1970s. In 1975 he was arrested for selling stolen clothing. Six months later he was arrested again for being a lookout while an accomplice removed a wheel from a car. In conducting an inventory search of Tilling's vehicle at the time of the arrest, police found marijuana. Within a year Tilling was stopped for a routine traffic infraction, having apparently reversed his car improperly at a junction. During the stop, officers noticed a plastic bag of marijuana beside the left front bucket seat. According to their report, Tilling twice attempted to hide the "baggie" from the plain view of officers. He ended up spending two weeks in jail for the marijuana possession. By 1979, he had been arrested for auto burglary and grand theft, offenses for which he received four years' probation. Within a year he was found guilty of possession of less than 20 grams of cannabis and fined $46.25 and costs. The first major offense to appear on Tilling's rap sheet was an attempted armed robbery that took place in 1981. With the assistance of an accomplice, he accosted a black man on the street with a sawed-off shotgun, pointed it toward the victim's head, and demanded his money. The man told Tilling and his accomplice to "get out of my face." At this point, Tilling struck him with the weapon. Although he was later arrested and charged with aggravated assault, the state's attorney's office declined to prosecute because the "victim was unavailable." This incident, an aggravated assault in the course of an attempted armed robbery, was the first sign of violence in Tilling's official criminal history.

There is little other recorded activity until March 1987, when Tilling was arrested for street fighting with another black man. Apparently 30 or so persons were standing around watching the fist fight when police arrived. Steve Tilling was arrested at the scene for "interfering with a police officer" who was apparently trying to calm things down. Four months later at age 30, Tilling was taken into custody for disorderly conduct. As in his arrest earlier that year for interfering with police, Tilling was reportedly hostile to law enforcement personnel. He and a friend were riding their bicycles on the sidewalk when, according to the police report, Tilling rode his bike into the path of a patrol car. The two then apparently rode through a red light. When stopped by the patrol officers, Tilling reportedly said, "What's your problem, man?" As the officer was writing Tilling the ticket for running the red light, Tilling, in the words of the report, became "hostile" and said, "[Y]ou are only hassling me because I'm black." He then waved his hands in the officer's face and shouted words to the effect, "I am six feet of solid beef that you can't handle!" A crowd gathered and Tilling was arrested and taken to jail.

According to the official record, in May 1992 Tilling consented to be searched on the street by a patrol officer. He told Tilling that he was looking for weapons and drugs. Tilling took off his waist pouch and handed it to the officer. He apparently asked if he could search the pouch, and Tilling, obviously no stranger to the criminal justice system, apparently consented. The patrol officer reported finding a clear baggie with several small, off-white rocks in the pouch. He then placed Tilling under arrest for possession of cocaine. Tilling apparently "spontaneously" told the patrolman that he was going to "geek it" (mix it with marijuana and smoke it). He then searched Tilling (incident to lawful arrest) and found five more baggies. Due to the amount of cocaine, the way the rocks were packaged, and Tilling's possession of $150 in cash, he was charged with intent to sell cocaine.

Child abuse first appears on Tilling's criminal record in 1992. It seems he was living with a woman who had a daughter who was less than 12 years of age. In a sworn statement to police she stated that Tilling would sexually abuse her while her mother was at work or asleep. The report notes that Tilling

> grabbed her arms and pulled her into the bathroom. He pulled her pants down, laid a towel on the floor and rubbed Vaseline between her legs and pushed her face down on the floor. He placed his penis between her legs and moved up and down. He tried to penetrate her vagina and anus without success. He returned to moving in and out between her legs until he ejaculated. He gave the victim a cloth to wipe herself off. He told her not to tell anyone and promised to give her money. Later that day he gave her $4.00. The victim disclosed Tilling has sexually abused her since she was age 9. Apparently he made the victim perform oral sex on him approximately three times. He regularly attempted vaginal and anal intercourse. He always ejaculated after. The victim said she felt pain every time he did this to her. Her skin would be raw.

Tilling was found guilty of felonious sexual battery on a child under 12. At the time he killed Kirsti, he was still on probation for this offense. It seems unlikely that his history of using criminal violence predisposed him toward the child sexual battery and the homicide. Most violent criminals do not sexually batter and kill children, and most cons despise child abusers. This observation, however, should not be taken to mean that committing prior criminal acts, particularly acts of violence, is irrelevant to the perpetration of child homicide. In the Tilling case one might also ask if his use of crack cocaine somehow intensified his anger and violent tendencies to the point where he was capable of brutally violating one child, and later torturing another with scalding water, causing her death. Again, many men use crack, but few abuse children the way Tilling did. Was his perception that police "hassled him," stopped him, searched him, and so on because he was black a source of sufficient rage to push an occasionally violent property offender and drug dealer in the direction of child abuse? As Chambliss's study of the Rapid Deployment Units in Washington, D.C., points out, many African-American men are hassled illegally or for dubious reasons by police.[30] The "hassled by law enforcement" factor may be a frame of reference, but it is likely not the central reason. Or was the likelihood that Tilling would engage in acts of child abuse sown in his own childhood? Perhaps he himself suffered abuse? The Tilling case and others like it raise these kinds of questions and many others.

There are similar questions in the case of Rocardo Ventura, a white Latino male aged 27, who killed his son, Richie Ventura, aged one month. Rocardo shook him to death while attempting to stop the infant from crying. Before this killing Rocardo had been sentenced to five and a half years in prison after having been found guilty of the aggravated abuse of two of his other children; he also had convictions for burglary (1986) and larceny (1987). In 1989, in response to police inquiries regarding injuries to his son Emilio, Rocardo said that the boy had cracked his skull when he accidentally fell off a bed. It later transpired that Emilio, who had been born prematurely, had fallen while Rocardo was tossing him in the air. He was convicted of cruelty toward a child and aggravated child abuse. Benita, Rocardo's former wife and the mother of Emilio and another son, Lee, is quoted in court documents as remarking that Rocardo "said he liked to see the baby crying, so he would hit him so the baby would cry." Emilio died in March 1990. Medical examiners concluded the cause of death was chronic lung problems stemming from his premature birth. Also in 1990, his son Lee, aged three months, was hospitalized with a broken leg. According to Rocardo, the child was soaped up and slipped through his hands while he was in the bath. Medical authorities disagreed, saying it would take much more force to break the thigh bone. In 1990 Rocardo was convicted of aggravated child abuse for hurting Lee and sentenced to probation. Court records indicate he was supposed to attend therapy and counseling groups, although he often failed to go. In July 1990, Rocardo's probation status was revoked because of his failure to meet its conditions and he was sentenced to five and a half years in prison for aggravated child abuse. However, because of prison overcrowding, he was released early, in July 1993. According to divorce court transcripts, his former wife, Benita, divorced Rocardo "because she could no longer trust him with the children."

Rocardo Ventura moved in with his new girlfriend, Francia Rosario, Richie's mother. On the day his son died, Rocardo had been feeding him when Richie stopped breathing. Rocardo shook the baby, allegedly to restart his breathing. Francia told investigators that Rocardo warned her to say that "she was feeding the child, because people would suspect him." He threatened her in front of his brother, Alaine, saying "they would be in trouble" if they did not support his story. Francia also mentioned that Rocardo had battered her in the past, so she went along with him for a while out of fear. She then said to investigators that it was not until doctors told her of Richie's injuries that she suspected that Rocardo had "done something wrong."

Rocardo's official criminal history is far less eclectic than Steve Tilling's. With only two prior convictions, one for burglary and one for larceny, he hardly seems a candidate for committing aggravated child abuse and child homicide. In a sense, Rocardo Ventura and Steve Tilling exemplify what appears to be the case in the biographies of most persons who kill children. Both men appear as angry, hostile, impatient, and prone to violent behavior. In their criminal endeavors, most perpetrators of child homicide are eclectic. It would be inappropriate to say that their killing of children is an activity central to their criminality. In this sense, those who kill children resemble other criminals who spread their talents around liberally.[31]

*Alcohol, Drugs, or Both*   In 13 of the 83 child deaths (15.7 percent), various intoxicants were deemed to be significant factors. Alternatively, one could argue that sobriety or something similar was a factor in roughly 85 percent of cases. My point is that alcohol and drug use is often portrayed as playing a causal or correlative role in domestic homicide without any real exploration of the nature of the links between the abuse of intoxicants and death. According to medical authorities, in four of the Florida cases of neonaticide, babies died in significant part owing to mothers' use of crack cocaine, either throughout the pregnancy, immediately before delivery, or both. These controversial medical determinations constitute the principal focus of my discussion. Four perpetrators were using alcohol but no drugs at the time the children died. (Two male perpetrators assaulted children while intoxicated, and two inebriated female caretakers fell asleep on babies, smothering them to death.) In five cases, persons who killed children were using both alcohol and drugs either during or before the fatal episode. Although probably an underestimation, three other cases revealed drug dealing (two cases) or chronic drug use (one case) as background factors not directly implicated in the fatality.

The Health and Rehabilitative Services report on the death of one-day-old Kevin Knacker in March 1994 revealed that he tested positive for "very high levels of cocaine at birth." This meant that his 30-year-old white mother, Merry Knacker, must have "ingested cocaine just prior to admittance to the hospital." Merry denied any drug use after her first trimester, although the report also notes that she had been arrested by police for cocaine possession in January 1994 and was on probation for a number of drug offenses at the time of Kevin's birth. She told investigators that she had only experimented with marijuana before coming to Florida. Since moving to the state she reported "getting in with the wrong crowd." Merry was in the process of divorcing her husband. She came to Florida with Kevin's father and was living with him at the time their son was born. The attending physician attributed the cause of death to two factors: the umbilical cord was wrapped two and a half times around Kevin's neck, and the newborn had high levels of cocaine in his body. The medical examiner's report added pneumonia to the list of causes of death, noting that "maternal cocaine toxicity" was one of the "other significant conditions." Putting the medical evidence together, the HRS report recommended classifying the death as "proposed confirmed for abuse/neglect on the part of the mother."

The circumstances were similar in the death of Lee Eade, a black male infant born after 32 weeks of gestation who tested positive for cocaine. Measuring 11 inches in length and weighing one pound and four ounces, Lee died of a number of different infections and of complications attributed to cocaine. Because of the long-standing drug problem of his mother, Gloria Eade, HRS workers were concerned about the safety of other young children in the home; they were removed to a paternal aunt via a shelter placement. Ric Eade, Lee's father, denied knowing that Gloria was still using cocaine, as did her aunt. The many family members in this case banded together and worked out a custody arrangement with the courts. They also made a firm commitment to oversee the care of the children while Gloria complied with all court orders. Notably, the presiding judge ordered Gloria Eade into residential drug treatment.

One detective I talked with about another neonaticide in the African-American community described what he saw as a tight support network for black women who use cocaine. That support network usually comes into play long before children's health might be compromised through maternal drug use. Put differently, the Eade case does not fit the rather stylized media portrayal of crack-cocaine-addicted black mothers.

Consistent with this observation about the matrifocal and matrilocal support network among black women, Elaine Roby's own mother was already caring for her daughter's three children when Elaine gave birth to Edwina Roby. The death of Edwina, born prematurely at 30 weeks, points up just how problematic it is to attribute fatalities among newborns exclusively to maternal crack cocaine use. Whereas Elaine Roby, a black woman aged 34, admitted using crack two or three days before giving birth, she was also an alcoholic who drank throughout her pregnancy. Although Edwina only weighed a pound and 12 ounces at birth, attending physicians concluded that it was "unknown whether the retarded intrauterine growth was due to the mother's drug use while pregnant." The attending physician also commented that if the baby did survive it would "likely have all sorts of problems, including cerebral palsy." He went on to say that "the child's facial features suggest . . . fetal alcohol syndrome." Although Elaine Roby's cocaine use was listed as one of the causes of death, a slew of other medical problems, not directly related in the report to the presence of that drug, also appear. An obstetrician I talked with in Florida about the role of prenatal cocaine use in child deaths confirmed my reading of the files, which finds that the "sole attribution" of death to maternal cocaine use is deeply problematic.

According to medical authorities, Casey Foner, a 6-day-old black boy born vaginally on April 4, 1994, after 37 weeks of gestation, died of complications due to his mother's use of crack cocaine. The medical examiner found that the "cause of death was due to exposure to drugs and hemorrhaging of the brain." The HRS investigation held that Casey's death was due to "abuse and neglect" on the part of his mother. The assessment concludes, "[T]he cause of death was due to the mother's use of cocaine." Sylvia Foner, aged 32, was a cocaine addict with a long history of crack use. Homeless, she had six other children, ranging in age from 4 to 15, all of whom had been placed with relatives. Sylvia also had two other infants who died just after being born, one in 1984, the other in 1991.

The HRS narrative on Casey Foner opens with a caution about the appropriateness of his mother taking him home after he was born. The abuse report begins at birth, when Casey tested positive for cocaine. The HRS file notes that Sylvia tested positive for cocaine on October 21, 1993, and was a known drug addict. In his first days of life, Casey himself appeared to be "OK" with "no cocaine addiction symptoms" except that he was "a little jittery." Sylvia expressed a strong desire to "to raise this infant because she failed in raising the other children." Since she had a serious drug problem, no place to live, and no plan for taking care of Casey, HRS workers removed her son from her and placed him in a shelter on April 7, 1994. He died three days later.

Although the medical examiner and the HRS investigators attributed the death largely to Sylvia's ingestion of cocaine, local law enforcement would not proceed criminally against her. She refused mental health counseling and drug treatment. However, the HRS file does note that Sylvia was introduced to Norplant as a form of contraception. Such introductions to Norplant constitute one of the controversial aspects of the so-called crack epidemic. Critics have argued that the focus by the news media and criminal justice personnel on crack cocaine use by pregnant black women constitutes yet another thinly veiled attack on the African-American community. At the same time, they assert, the more widespread use of other drugs by women in general during pregnancy is ignored. Dorothy Roberts argues:

> A growing number of women across the country have been indicted for criminal offenses after giving birth to babies who test positive for drugs. The majority of these women . . . are poor, and black. Most are addicted to crack cocaine. . . . Between 1985 and 1995, at least two hundred women in thirty states were charged with maternal drug use.[32]

The media construction of the pregnant, crack-using black woman "as an irresponsible and selfish woman who puts her love for crack above her love for her children" and "who sometimes traded sex for crack, in violation of every conceivable quality of a good mother,"[33] stigmatized these women and undermined black motherhood in general. Importantly, Roberts points out that crack cocaine use was said to "destroy the natural impulse to mother."[34] The assumption here, as Drew Humphries has observed, is that "motherhood was instinctual."[35]

Although Roberts argues that the selective prosecution of African-American women for drug use that impacts their newborn children is racist, others are less convinced. Randall Kennedy suggests that what seems to be the selective prosecution of black women may reflect the widespread perceptions among criminal justice professionals that using crack cocaine during pregnancy is more hazardous than using other drugs and that black women are more likely to use crack.[36] From the small number of Florida cases in my sample, it is not possible to level any charges of racism in the prosecution of crack-related deaths, especially since none of the women were actually prosecuted for using cocaine during their pregnancies.[37] However, one point that emerges from my case analyses does seem to get lost in the debate about differential prosecution. That point is the presence of vibrant, female-centered social networks in the African-American community. My research, preliminary as it is, suggests that if and when black women of childbearing years use crack cocaine, there is an informal support network among their relatives and friends that usually intervenes to protect black children.

*The Easy Availability of Weapons*  Although adults perpetrated most of the domestic child homicides, a small number were committed by juveniles with easy access to weapons. This fact is mirrored in the broader literature on child fatalities, which reveals that significant numbers of juveniles die each year at the hands of other juveniles who use weapons, especially firearms.[38] Just as such crimes often seem to arise out of street cultures and lifestyles permeated by the widespread acceptance and use of weapons,[39] certain domestic child homicides are similarly situated in a social milieu where ready access to weapons is the norm. Two cases illustrate the quick resort to weapons by persons linked through domestic relationships.

Nine-year-old Peter Border was shot dead by his 13-year-old stepbrother Piers King. The incident occurred in a neighbor's garage, where the stepbrothers were playing with two other boys. According to a psychologist's report on Piers King, he saw a shotgun in a closet and, out of curiosity, removed it. Apparently, Peter Border was irritating Piers and the other boys by shooting a BB gun, so his stepbrother decided to scare him. Piers grabbed the shotgun and asked Peter if he was frightened. Peter said no. Piers then lowered the muzzle, and his finger apparently accidentally triggered the gun. He shot his stepbrother in the head. Both boys had been socialized into the world of guns through their stepfather, who took them to a shooting range to fire BB guns.

Jeff Porter, a black male aged 15, killed his younger brother Stan Remish, a black male aged 10, with a pistol he casually and easily acquired on the street. As in Wright and Decker's research into armed robbers, one finds Jeff Porter's facility with weapons embedded in the routines of everyday life in a neighborhood where armed robbery was not uncommon and the attendant tools of the trade were always available. The two children lived in a poor area, in a house with burglar bars on all the windows. Their mother, Sharon Remish, had been separated from her first husband, James Porter (Jeff's father) for 11 years. Jeff stated that he obtained the gun used in the shooting from his friend Felix Nadire. Jeff had the pistol for about two weeks and kept it in a shoe box under his bed. He said he carried a gun because "everyone else has guns." On the night of the shooting he thought the safety catch was on. After Jeff shot his brother he went out into the street and discharged the rest of the bullets into the air "because he was angry." Nadire denied giving the gun to his friend. However, he said he was present when Jeff paid another black male $20 for the pistol. Nadire informed police that Jeff needed the gun to "make some money." At the time of the investigation Felix Nadire himself was on probation for armed robbery.

### Conclusion

Girls and boys made up 26 percent of all domestic-homicide victims in Florida in 1994. Of all those killed, they are the least likely to be recorded in official police files. Unlike most other research into domestic child homicide, this chapter explores the deaths of children killed in homicide-suicides and familicides, as well as those fatalities resulting from abuse, neglect, or both. Taking all these domestic deaths together, I identified three major groups of perpetrators. Biological fathers were responsible for just over a quarter of child deaths, and mother's boyfriends for just over a fifth. Men in general killed almost two-thirds of the children. Biological mothers were the chief culprits among female offenders. According to official documents, including court records, they killed as many children as did biological fathers. Among the 83 child victims, only 25 lived in homes where the parents or caretakers were married and living together. For whatever reasons, domestic child fatalities occur more often among those parents who are either cohabiting and unmarried, or single.

In concert with the extant research it is also clear that men and women kill children in different ways. Generally, child homicides committed by women are less violent, and more likely to stem from neglect and indifference. Notably, men committed at least 14 of the 17 violent killings caused by head injuries. Women were held responsible for the deaths of children attributed at least partially (and questionably) to drug use during pregnancy. Additionally, two women smothered children by rolling over on them while drunk.

Although boys and girls died in roughly equal numbers, it is clear that younger children are more susceptible to homicide. This age-related vulnerability is consistent with the findings of other researchers. It reflects both the physical helplessness of young children and the fact that they are less likely to be identified as "at risk" by service agencies because of their lack of contact with those agencies. Again in a manner consistent with the extant research, the Florida sample revealed that African-American children were disproportionately vulnerable to domestic homicide compared with their presence in the population. However, the reasons for this differential vulnerability by race are not clear, and I return to this important issue in Chapter 7.

As in other chapters, I used the detailed archival materials to identify the major correlates or situational antecedents to the child fatalities. From scrutinizing the files, financial hardship predictably appears in almost three-quarters of the cases (36 of 49) for which data are available. However, to argue that poverty is the root cause of the deaths is overly simplistic. At least a quarter of the men and women who killed children did not live in poverty; more important, the vast majority of poor persons do not end up killing their children. Rather, the effects of poverty are more likely to be found in how social actors negotiate their plight, and in how their economic hardships are mediated through the presence of family systems, other informal supports, and beliefs and values, including phenomena such as religious commitment.

Approximately half of the cases for which information is available showed a history of domestic violence between the parents or caretakers, and a similar proportion revealed a history of abuse directed at the child. There was considerable overlap between these two populations of cases. Notably, in 18 of the 30 cases where child deaths were preceded by a history of adult domestic violence, child abuse, neglect, or both accompanied that violence. In only 12 cases was there adult domestic violence without reports of child abuse. This finding, despite being somewhat anecdotal, suggests an important and hitherto unexplored link between adult domestic violence and child domestic homicide.

Such a potentially important link means that confronting domestic violence among adults may provide multiple points of proactive intervention against child deaths in the home.

Although roughly half the killings of children involved a history of child abuse, neglect, or both, only one-quarter of the 83 girls and boys who died were known to child protective agencies, or, less significantly, to other social service providers. Likewise, from the available data, just over a quarter of those who killed children were known to criminal justice agencies and had criminal histories. Finally, although the extant research literature alludes to a strong correlation between drug and alcohol abuse and child deaths, the available files did not point to a strong association, with a little over one-eighth of the deaths occurring while perpetrators were intoxicated in some way.

Last, it is very difficult to determine from the multiagency files what the precise intent of perpetrators was at the time they killed their children. It seems that in most cases, even after the most violent deaths, men and women stated they "lost control" or did not intend to kill. In many of these cases, it is likely that the physical fragility of children, combined with their isolation from state agencies and other outside observers, exacerbated their likelihood of dying during episodes of family violence. If this is the case, then perhaps one should not treat child fatalities as conceptually distinct from other forms of child abuse that produce sublethal injuries. As a corollary, one might also move away from a discourse on child fatalities that presents these tragedies in the language of what Bromley, Shupe, and Ventimiglia once called "atrocity tales."[40]

# 7. Making Sense
# of Domestic Homicide

Very few intimate human relationships, whether they involve lovers, parents and children, or other family members, end in homicide. Much more prevalent than domestic killings are those interpersonal assaults that produce life-threatening injury. More common still are the everyday physical, sexual, and emotional assaults that do not result in death or potentially fatal injuries but nevertheless evidence deep conflict in interpersonal relationships. As my analysis of the microdynamics of domestic homicide reveals, there is a clear relationship between everyday and life-threatening interpersonal violence on the one hand and domestic homicide on the other. My archival analysis, in concert with other research, demonstrates that the former usually precedes the latter. Other modes of social interaction also accompany the range of violations extending from ordinary interpersonal assault to domestic homicide. Among these modes, I have identified men's assumption of proprietary rights over women, obsessive-possessive behavior, the negotiated process of escaping conflictual relationships, the resort to potentially supportive state agencies, and the search for respect between family members and others.

These "interrelated antecedents" to intimate-partner homicide also constitute the sinews of patriarchal relations; as such, they present themselves in many intimate relationships, the majority of which do not erupt in homicidal violence.[1] Therefore, the interrelated antecedents are not "red flags" for domestic homicide. It is not my purpose here to develop a predictive formula to identify those cases likely to end in death. Nevertheless, the presence of various permutations and combinations of antecedents could still form the basis for proactive intervention in tumultuous domestic relationships. At a minimum, one could say that those domestic cases exhibiting a large number of the interrelated antecedents are probably much closer to a lethal outcome than are the majority of relationships troubled by intimate-partner violence, grinding emotional abuse, or both.

The links between intimacy and death are mediated by culture, social structure, and the various burdensome legacies of the past. Given that all cultures in the United States place a high value on the sanctity of human life, it is hardly surprising that the incidence of domestic homicide is low in all cultural groups.[2] However, the fact that domestic homicide is socially and culturally patterned warrants close attention. Two key interrelated findings emerge from my archival analysis. The first is the obvious gendering of all forms of domestic homicide. Clearly, men kill much more often than women, and they do so for different reasons. Second, all forms of domestic homicide, and particularly the Sex Ratio of Killing in intimate-partner homicide, vary by culture. Notwithstanding the relative rarity of domestic homicide, it is apparent that the crime in all its forms is much more common in African-American communities. In particular, black women are much more likely to kill their intimate male partners than are Caucasian or Latino women. As I have noted, such homicides involving Latino women are rare in Florida.

## The Gendered Nature of Domestic Homicide

I have used the term "gendered" to indicate not only that more men commit domestic homicide than women, but that men kill for different reasons. Men perpetrated 106 of the 132 intimate-partner homicides (80.3 percent),[3] 103 of the 141 family homicides (73 percent),[4] all 15 of the love triangle killings, and 39 of the 44 suicides (88.6 percent). Notably, no women killed intimate female partners, nor did any kill other women in a love triangle dispute over a man or a woman. Only two women killed other women in family disputes.

*Men as Perpetrators*   Men usually kill their intimate female partners after violently abusing them, often for long periods. Of the 102 male perpetrators of intimate-partner homicide, not one convincingly showed he acted in self-defense or that his resort to lethal violence was precipitated by either the proximal or distal violence of women. Rather, these men typically engaged in a regime of domestic terrorism to attempt to keep their female partners in a subordinate position. Usually this terrorism took the form of woman battering that long preceded the fatal episode. This battering appears to have been accompanied by an oppressive, soul-destroying emotional abuse that gradually eroded the identities of the women.

The attempts to render women more malleable to the wishes of men by erasing their identities is entirely consistent with the historical tradition of patriarchy. At various times, married women could not divorce, legally refuse their husbands sex, enjoy their own property rights, or vote. Indeed, under this legacy, men had a right to discipline their wives through the use of physical violence.[5] In a sociocultural and historical sense, old habits die hard. These patriarchal beliefs and practices are much more than mere cultural residues from the past.[6] Indeed, the Florida archival materials reveal acute forms of these beliefs, values, and norms deep in the ideological bone marrow of most of the men who killed—they saw their female partners as their property. Men's sense of proprietary rights was expressed through their obsessive-possessive behavior regarding the activities of those women. Many accused their partners, usually falsely, of infidelity. Others voiced these accusations to the point of appearing paranoid. Concerned that women were slipping out from under their grip, a number of men threatened to kill their partners if they left the relationship. Some husbands and boyfriends threatened women's lives if they had some contact with other men (however fleeting) or appeared to express even a modicum of interest in other persons of either sex. As men exerted ever tighter controls and demanded more from women, their wives and girlfriends often experienced a growing sense of entrapment, mixed with a combination of acute fear, shame, and humiliation. These women were not paralyzed, though. Often they countered the control initiatives of men with new maneuvers of their own. Given the difficulties of finding safe, affordable housing and adequate protections, however, many remained in their abusive relationships. Others devised strategies for leaving, and some finally left.

Whatever women did short of killing men, husbands and boyfriends did not give up their property rights without a fight. The multiagency case files for the multiple and single killings of intimate female partners reveal that in roughly two-thirds to three-quarters of cases the parties were either separated, estranged, or divorced at the time of the fatality. It is safe to assume from the case histories that many men who killed were making good on threats against the lives of their fleeing partners. Documentable male obsessive possessiveness was found in at least half of these deaths. In anywhere from a third to a half of such cases, the archival files reveal that women, their neighbors, or their friends had called police to the residence to deal with domestic violence. Given that some police departments did not log their calls to domestic disturbances, or else coded them as offenses such as drunk and disorderly behavior, it is likely that many more than a third to a half of the batterers had prior contact with police about their use of violence. Fully one-quarter of men had been the objects of court orders of protection before the killing. Combining these observations on earlier contact with the police and the courts, it is clear that a significant number of abusive husbands and boyfriends were not deterred from future violence by formal legal sanctions. These observations are consistent with the fact that a sizable proportion of men had criminal histories of violence.[7] A good number of male perpetrators, especially those who committed single acts of intimate-partner homicide, were socially marginalized by their minority status, by their unemployment or underemployment, or perhaps by not being married. As Lawrence Sherman once put it, men who have a "low stake in conformity" are more difficult to deter from future acts of domestic violence simply by arresting them.[8] Ironically, although these marginalized men realized fewer of the fruits of capitalist patriarchy, they did exercise their property rights over their female partners and at times killed love triangle antagonists. The same population of men figures prominently among those who fought, and sometimes died, to win respect in family feuds.

My analysis indicates that the 102 Florida men used violence against women for a long time before killing them. They did this either to establish control or to reassert control that they felt was ebbing away. In this sense my archival findings are consistent with the work of Jalna Hanmer, who observes that male violence against women, whether perpetrated by men known or unknown to them is "designed to control, dominate and express authority and power."[9] It is also clear from the archival materials that many of the women who were subjected to male violence, including lethal violence, lived in extremely compromised circumstances. Although they may have wished to leave their violent victimization behind, they had neither the resources, support, nor, in some cases, the wherewithal to do so. It is essential, therefore, that the analysis not stop at the level of interpersonal violence and the respective roles played by the parties in negotiating the attendant conflict and pain. Rather, the intimate-partner killing of women is a socially situated phenomenon that exhibits numerous continuities with the political, economic, and social standings of both men and women. In short, killing is but one way that many men keep many women in their place as socially subordinate subjects in a patriarchal order. Lethal violence is no doubt a crude and highly visible way of maintaining the structure of patriarchy. (As Steven Lukes once remarked, the most insidious use of power is that which goes unnoticed.)[10] In other words, killing women because men sense they are losing control, face, or both is problematic as a long-term strategy of social control. Killing women brings male domination into sharp focus and invites questions about the legitimacy of patriarchy, or at least its more coercive elements. In the final analysis, violence is the last resort of most enduring political regimes. Patterns of domination and subordination are normally reproduced through more insidious and seemingly benign social practices. The patriarchal order is no exception here; as Walby eloquently points out, violence is but one of the panoply of control initiatives. My point is that the numerous links I have identified between killing and intimacy must be viewed in the context of a much broader set of social practices that perpetuate everyday notions of intimacy itself.

Men also kill male competitors whom they perceive to be usurping their rights of ownership over women. As I have indicated, these killings often take place as a relationship is breaking up and the woman is moving on to a new lover. These examples are reminders that patriarchy is not just characterized by men's subordination of women. Rather, patriarchal relations involve a fierce competition between men for access to women. Indeed, the competitive ethics of patriarchy are continuous with and homologous to the competitive and alienating effects of industrial capitalism. Just as wage workers find themselves competing against each other, so too do men struggle between themselves to lay claim to the bodies of women. Indeed, it may be significant that intimate-partner killings were much more likely to be perpetrated by men who had enjoyed less success in accumulating the material trappings of a capitalist society.[11] Put differently, do "less successful" men use sublethal and lethal violence against women to compensate somehow for their perceived lack of economic success, social esteem, and (formal) political advantage in a capitalist democracy?

None of this should be taken to mean that poverty and unemployment are the basic reasons for intimate-partner killings. Rather, I suggest that batterers' assertion of power and control is often intensified by their perceptions that they have failed to gather the desired material and status trappings required by a dominant value system that celebrates individual achievement. If the respective sets of fundamental principles of patriarchy and capitalism do converge, it is around the issues of ownership and control. Consequently, one should not be surprised that those men at the margins of capitalist production are more likely to engage in coercive acts of control in their interpersonal relationships. Indeed, at the point of intersection of class and gender relations lies the socially constructed and situated impulse to covet. The perceived failure of men deeply wounded by their dearth of material and status trappings in the capitalist marketplace may, quite literally, bleed over into their interpersonal relationships.

Male perpetrators also commit most family homicides. Indeed, if the killing of children is excluded, all but two of them were perpetrated by men. Caucasian and African-American men committed equal numbers of family homicides, meaning the latter are heavily overrepresented compared with their presence in the population; this mirrors their disproportionate perpetration of homicide in general. Men who commit family homicide are usually acting to preserve their honor or social standing in the face of a perceived threat. In the Florida sample, this display of puffery as a defense of masculinity is typically steeped in economic marginality. These killings cannot be explained solely by culture; rather, one must recognize the intersection of culture and broader social structural phenomena to form the context behind many of them.

There are a number of cultural continuities between family killings and the struggle for respect between men on the street.[12] In most of these homicides, men refused to back down from a dispute with another male family member or relative. In the case of younger men, and younger black men in particular, Elijah Anderson traces the inclination to violence to the diminished life chances of the ghetto poor and to "the lack of jobs that pay a living wage, the stigma of race, the fallout from rampant drug use and drug trafficking, and the resulting alienation and lack of hope for the future."[13] The willingness to resort to violence—and the public recognition of that willingness—are essential elements in gaining the sense of respect that is so difficult to obtain through more socially approved methods. Unfortunately, having laid out the intimate links between economic and cultural factors, Anderson lapses into a culturalist explanation by observing that "the code of the streets is actually a cultural adaptation to a profound lack of faith in the police and the judicial system. The police are most often seen as representing the dominant white society and not caring to protect inner-city residents."[14] I would argue that the code of the streets is born from the intersection of economic and cultural phenomena. These are inextricably linked in a way that renders either/or explanations incomplete and rather misleading.

That family members other than those linked by the bonds of sexual intimacy or the parent-child relationship kill each other reminds one that the argument that the family is primarily a social site of harmony, nurturing, and love is at best incomplete and at worst deceptive. The etiological similarities and continuities between family homicides and street killings involving young, marginalized men are a reminder that hegemonic masculinities operate in both the private and public spheres. Indeed, the obvious resemblances between the two styles of homicide call into question the efficacy of distinguishing between public- and private-sphere violence. In fact, it is noteworthy that a number of family killings involving men occurred during disputes in which friends were present, often in the family home of one or more of the parties to the homicide.

In Chapter 5, I discussed the killing of Buster Newman by his brother Joe Newman, which stemmed from a dispute during a card game. Both men had extensive criminal histories, including involvement in the illegal drug trade, and both lived in a particularly poor neighborhood. I had a number of conversations with criminal justice professionals in Florida who described such killings as "meaningless" or as stemming from "trivial motives." These professionals would tell me "life tends to be cheaper" in the neighborhoods where such honor contests are more likely to take place. However, as criminologists of homicide note, these standoffs are anything but trivial to the parties involved.[15] When the status of the participants is devoid of the trappings of established family life, breadwinner standing, and other material signs of achievement, personal honor is often all they have. Given the code of the streets, defending their honor and their masculinity was, for the economically marginalized men in the Florida sample, likely a matter of survival.

If men kill their intimate female partners out of their proprietary rights in a patriarchal society, their love triangle antagonists out of competition, and other male family members or relatives out of a desire to protect their masculine honor, then why do men kill children? The cross-cultural studies of infanticide reveal greater tendencies for girls and boys to be killed if they are not the biological offspring of one or both involved parents; if infants are somehow malformed or unlikely to survive; and if the parents', particularly the mother's, life circumstances and material resources are not conducive to raising the child.[16]

Biological fathers and stepfathers (including mother's boyfriends) killed similar numbers of children in the Florida sample (24 and 23, respectively). Eight boys and girls died at the hands of biological fathers during the commission of multiple domestic homicides. Although these children were not known to child protection agencies before the killings, one cannot assume the fathers had not abused them. This means that perhaps 16 children were killed by biological fathers in what might be called "child abuse deaths." In concert with other investigators,[17] my research indicates that stepfathers committed child homicides in the course of abusive episodes to a slightly greater degree than biological fathers. Without data on the percentage of children in Florida living with stepfathers, it is impossible to arrive at any precise estimate of the risk of lethal child victimization from stepfathers as opposed to biological fathers. However, given that children more often live with biological fathers than stepfathers, the elevated risk from stepfathers is likely much higher.[18] As I pointed out in Chapter 6, stepfathers often killed boys and girls during periods of extreme rage in which they had become exasperated with them. It seems as if some stepfathers have a lower tolerance for children and less willingness to invest in relationships with them than do natural fathers. Given that stepfathers do not have the same history of bonding with the children from birth, this is understandable. In fact, the case studies clearly reveal that in a number of instances stepfathers saw a youngster as a hindrance to developing their relationships with the child's mother. It is biological mothers who are much more likely to have custody of their children in the event of a divorce or separation from the natural father.[19] Consequently, it is stepfathers, not stepmothers, who are likely to represent the bulk of the threat to children's lives from substitute parents. Daly and Wilson suggest that the mother is much less likely to forsake the child if he or she is older. Put differently, with older children from previous relationships, maternal bonds have formed and are presumably more difficult to break, or at least compromise. New male lovers will likely be less successful in trying to drive a wedge between mothers and their older children. Specifically, in cases where girls and boys are abused or killed by stepfathers, Daly and Wilson observe that "the natural mother is often implicated in—or at least turns a blind eye to—the violence and neglect. . . . [T]he baby is a resented impediment to the new relationship, and the mother has to make a choice."[20]

The Florida findings regarding woman battering and its links to child killing point out that fear is also an important reason that some mothers are unable to intervene in the killing of their own children by either biological fathers or stepfathers. The presence of woman battering greatly complicates the development of a new relationship between the male lover, the mother, and the child. This is not simply a matter of the stepfather killing the child because she or he compromises the establishment of a new intimate relationship with the mother. Rather, one must ask what kind of relationship the stepfather is trying to establish with the mother. If the would-be stepfather is attempting to set up a coercive regime of patriarchal control within the new family, then it is perhaps this context, rather than the mere selective advantage conferred by not wasting valuable time and resources on another man's offspring, that provides a more comprehensive frame of reference for making sense of at least some of the killings by stepfathers.

*Women as Perpetrators*   As I have noted, women did not kill female love triangle antagonists, did not kill lesbian partners, did not commit familicide, and, except in two instances, did not kill adult family members other than intimate partners. Those who did commit domestic homicide therefore fell into two major categories. First, 24 women killed their intimate male partners. Second, 30 women were deemed to be responsible for the deaths of their children. The two groups warrant close attention.

The Sex Ratio of Killing in the Florida intimate-partner homicide cases is 25.5. This means that, on average, for every four men who kill female intimates, one woman kills an intimate male partner. The archival findings clearly show that nearly all the male victims precipitated their own demise through the use of proximal and distal acts of violence. Although the precipitating violence, and especially its more enduring distal manifestations, did not always emerge from formal police archival sources such as homicide reports, interviews with various social actors close to the case usually uncovered it. Through case narratives I situated coercive male violence within an overall array of patriarchal control tactics. Regardless of race or ethnicity, the women who killed intimate male partners were profoundly trapped in their relationships. In contrast to the female intimates who were killed by men, entrapped women who killed men were far less likely to be separated or estranged from their abusive partners. They also appear to have been far less likely to have used the police, courts, and shelters as sources of support or as part of an overall resistive strategy. These results are entirely consistent with the central findings of the archival analysis that women, in various ways, were essentially defending themselves, their children, or both as a matter of last resort when they killed their intimate male partners.

Although the women who committed homicide had typically been violently victimized by men, often over long periods, I documented cases where women killed without apparently being under threat of proximal violence. For example, Erin Newcombe is currently serving a life term for killing her husband by shooting him dead while he was talking with someone on his mail route. I also introduced two cases where the archival materials present conflicting accounts of the possible existence and extent of precipitating male violence.

In these homicides committed by Marion Brown and Alison Murray, it is possible to read the evidence and reach the conclusion that these two women either "gave as good as they got," as one attorney I interviewed put it, or that they were the long-term aggressors in the relationship. Although I did not discuss the case at length, Kelly Krish killed her boyfriend without any apparent history of either proximal or distal precipitating violence.

Although criminal justice personnel have told me that they saw women as overall aggressors in two or three cases, advocates for battered women typically explain the female-perpetrated killings by using the language of self-defense. Given the available evidence, I would not rule out the possibility that one or more women in the Florida sample were the aggressors of sorts in their relationships and did kill in the absence of proximal and distal precipitating violence. However, one must look at this small number of cases in the context of patriarchal violence. Men are not systematically victimized by women in any way approaching the regime of violence they direct at women. Women's interpersonal violence is usually isolated, episodic, mostly defensive or preemptive, and not continuous with the more extensive network of coercive and consensual social controls that characterize patriarchal societies.[21] Even in the small number of cases where women can be construed as acting as aggressors, one would do well to examine their biographies. Amidst these life stories there is likely a history of male violence or abuse directed at them or at other female family members.

After having examined thousands of pages of archival materials documenting men's previous violence against women, I am amazed that more women do not kill their intimate male partners. This reaction is consistent with Meda Chesney-Lind's recent thoughts on women's criminal and violent behavior in general. She, too, sees women's violence as a socially situated response to the power relations of patriarchy.

> The work on women's entry into criminal behavior, taken altogether, illuminates the ways in which the injuries of girlhood produce problems that young women often solve on the streets of poor neighborhoods. . . . In addition, it is evident that violence is a part of life in these communities, that women have always been exposed to large amounts of violence, and that women are capable of responding in ways that can be categorized as "violent." Generally, it has served the interests of the powerful to ignore or minimize women's ability to engage in violence. . . . Given the amount

of violence women suffer at male hands, the remarkable story is that women are not more violent.[22]

Chesney-Lind's observations recall the work of bell hooks, who talks of the dangers inherent in seeing social spaces where anger can be expressed as being the preserve of men. Her comments are further reminders not to shy away from recognizing the volatile, aggressive, and potentially powerful meaning of women's anger. hooks eloquently expresses her fear of the social construction of difference, which

> makes it appear that there is some space of rage and anger that men inhabit, that is alien to us women. Even though we know that men's rage may take the form of murder (we certainly know that men murder women more than women murder men; that men commit most of the domestic violence in our lives), it's easy to slip into imagining that those are "male" spaces, rather than ask the question, "What do we do as *women* with our rage?"[23]

The possibility that women may kill men without proximal or distal precipitating violence does not negate the existence of a patriarchal order. Only if it is assumed that such a patriarchal order is rooted in sexual rather than gender differences do women's rare killings of male intimate partners that were not brought on by the victims undermine the notion that intimate-partner homicide arises out of patriarchal power-control imperatives. Put differently, a patriarchal order refers to the existence of a historically enduring social pattern of oppression. Not every single intimate relationship needs to exhibit these dynamics. Nor does every act of offensive violence between intimate partners have to emanate from men for the patriarchal pattern to be upheld.

Women were found responsible, although not necessarily criminally culpable, in 30 of the 83 child deaths. In at least 4 of these cases women were being battered by male partners before the killing. In 6 other cases girls and boys lost their lives to mothers during multiple domestic killings.[24] As noted in Chapter 3, these mothers were deeply depressed, in dire straits generally, and had apparently not abused the children prior to killing them.[25] In all but 1 of these 6 deaths the mother subsequently committed suicide. Even though the psychiatric literature may make reference to delusional altruism to describe their states of mind, it is more appropriate to try to make sense of these killings as the rational actions of loving mothers in a patriarchal society that has not provided for them or their children. In a sense, such homicides are the logical endpoint for some women in a society which socially prescribes that mothers be the ones ultimately responsible for the care and well-being of children.

In general, women who killed younger boys and girls seemed overwhelmed by the burdens of child care and the other difficulties in their lives. Few of them set out to deliberately kill children. One woman suffocated her child and attempted to blame the fatality on sudden infant death syndrome. It later turned out that she had killed another mother's child whom she was baby-sitting a year before killing her own child. Another woman knifed her nine-year-old son to death because he had been mean to his younger brother. These cases aside, most of the other female-perpetrated child homicides fall into the categories of excessive discipline, inappropriate care and handling, or neglect.

Chapter 6 addressed some of the interconnections between woman battering and the deaths of children. Doubtless these are even more substantial and complex than the archival material documents. Many child protection workers and police officers do not see intimate-partner violence as an important factor to include when writing up cases of child deaths, or indeed when investigating child abuse. It is necessary to learn more about these interconnections between intimate-partner violence and child deaths, because the power dynamics involved may offer rich insights into instances where men, and for seemingly different reasons women, take the lives of children. Recognizing parental or caretaker violence as a context for child killing might also provide multiple points of intervention into families that hitherto only dealt with agencies involved in child protection and criminal justice.

Only five women in the Florida sample took their own lives. In just one of these cases was there clear evidence of woman battering preceding the suicide. However, it would be a mistake to think that this single case is the only female suicide traceable to woman battering. Clearly, as I noted in earlier chapters, a large number of women who attempt or succeed in committing suicide do so because of their violent interpersonal victimization and the accompanying entrapment. In Chapter 3, I narrated the case of Beth Colthurst, a profoundly depressed battered woman of long standing who finally killed her abusive husband, Roger, before taking her own life. In general, neither male nor female suicides are classified as domestic homicides. This is a mistake, because often these deaths stem from the same dynamics as many of the killings I have discussed. The failure to include female suicides arising from battering among the ranks of domestic homicides leads to an underestimation of the destructiveness

## TABLE 7.1
Intraracial/intra-ethnic SROKs between sexual intimates

| Perpetrator | Victim | Married | Married SROK | Unmarried | Unmarried SROK | Total | Overall SROK |
|---|---|---|---|---|---|---|---|
| WM | WF | 24 | 25 | 19 | 15.8 | 43 | 20.9 |
| WF | WM | 6 | | 3 | | 9 | |
| BM | BF | 15 | 33.3 | 21 | 47.6 | 36 | 41.7 |
| BF | BM | 5 | | 10 | | 15 | |
| LM | LF | 9 | 11.1 | 8 | 12.5 | 17 | 11.8 |
| LF | LM | 1 | | 1 | | 2 | |
| M | F | 48 | 25 | 48 | 29.2 | 96 | 27.1 |
| F | M | 12 | | 14 | | 26 | |

Code: W = White; B = Black; L = Latino; M = Male; F = Female

of patriarchal relationships and, as a consequence, feeds into the notion that the threat of homicide from strangers is greater than it actually is.

## Intimate-Partner Homicide, History, and Culture: Some Reflections

Blacks are disproportionately overrepresented in intimate-partner homicides and family homicides compared with their presence in the population. The rates of intimate-partner homicide per 100,000 for African Americans, Latinos, and Caucasians are 2.67, 1.11, and 0.45, respectively.[26] Put differently, the black intimate-partner homicide rate is six times that of whites, and two and a half times that of Latinos. As Table 7.1 shows, the Sex Ratios of Killing vary considerably by race or ethnicity and by marital status. The SROK for blacks is very high compared with that of Caucasians and especially Latinos. In tandem with findings from other research, in the Florida sample 1.58 black women per 100,000 kill their intimate black male partners, compared with 0.15 white women and 0.23 Latino women who kill their male partners. The apparent cultural variation in overall rates of intimate-partner homicide and the SROKs warrants careful attention. I will address these issues separately, although clearly they are interrelated.

*The High Black Intimate-Partner Homicide Rate*   Families are one of the principal means through which persons learn their values, beliefs, norms, ideas, and behavior—in short, their culture. Consequently, it comes as no surprise that social scientists should seek explanations for socially patterned behavior such as violence and homicide amidst the rich tapestry of family life and broader cultural matrices. As noted, the Moynihan Report attributes much of the crime and violence in the African-American community to the "tangle of pathology" centered in the black family and, by implication, in broader black cultural mores. Moynihan argues that slavery broke up the black family and set in motion a series of historical events that resulted in the relatively large numbers of households headed by women in the black community. Such households were poorly equipped for socializing children. They were also at odds with mainstream white culture, where households headed by men were the order of the day. At one point, Moynihan remarks: "Ours is a society which presumes male leadership in private and public affairs. . . . The arrangements of society facilitate such leadership and reward it. A subculture, such as that of the Negro American, in which this is not the pattern is placed at a distinct disadvantage." [27] Borrowing from the language and logic of biology, Moynihan argues: "The very essence of the male animal, from the bantam rooster to the four-star general, is to strut. Indeed, in 19th century America, a particular type of exaggerated male boastfulness became almost a national style. Not for the Negro male. The 'sassy nigger' was lynched." [28] Although Moynihan emphasizes that urbanization, segregation, unemployment, and underemployment exacerbated the pathogenic character of the black female-headed family, the "matriarchal" character of many African-American families remains at the center of his explanatory rationale. [29]

For my purposes, the Moynihan Report not only attributes the failure of African Americans to thrive economically to the matriarchal family, but also argues that the failure to properly instill cultural norms led to more antisocial behavior in the black community. Specifically, the report identifies the tangle of pathology as the "principal source of aberrant, inadequate, or antisocial behavior that perpetuates the cycle of poverty and deprivation." [30] Put another way, the absence of black men creates poverty by reducing family income. This absence means that women must work for wages to support the family, or become dependent upon welfare. The absence of men in the family also means that black boys and younger black men do not benefit from the presence of a male role model. According to Moynihan, young black men have lower self-esteem, do less well in school and drop out more than their white peers, and suffer much higher rates of delinquency.[31] Alvin Poussaint argues that the subculture of violence in the black ghetto derives in part from self-hatred, especially among young black males.[32] The excessive violence results in the increased incarceration of younger black men, thus depleting the pool of those eligible to be marriage partners.

The arguments embedded in the Moynihan Report, and the subsequent attempts to explain differential rates of black violence by familial or cultural pathology, are not convincing for a number of reasons. My archival analysis, like numerous other studies, rejects the notion that it is the pathology of black families or black culture that produces more per capita intimate-partner homicide.

One simply cannot uncouple culture and society in the way that social science in the Moynihan genre assumes. Persons' values, beliefs, and, particularly, adherence to mainstream behavioral expectations embodied in social codes such as the law cannot be divorced from their broader social situation, especially their respective life chances.[33] As I noted in my discussion of the role of poverty in child deaths, it is relative poverty and how social actors negotiate it—rather than the dollar levels of their income, wealth, and so on—that seem to provide important insights into the possible role of poverty in domestic homicide. This does not mean that being objectively poor plays no direct role. Rather, it means that material conditions are mediated by human agency, particularly collective human agency, at both familial and cultural levels. It is the cultural meaning of poverty that is important, a fact that inextricably couples culture to society. Whatever the machinations of the statisticians in controlling for such social forces as objective poverty, unemployment, and class, their effects cannot be isolated from race and ethnicity in anything but the crudest of ways. When statisticians allegedly control for objective poverty, unemployment, and what they term social class, they resort to an abstracted empiricism that essentially robs social phenomena of their socially situated meaning. One can no more easily control for class and identify the effects of race on domestic homicide than one can exclude "external" influences on the black community and somehow talk of black culture in the abstract, as if it were an island in a sea of Caucasian mores. African Americans have always been uniquely disadvantaged in the American capitalist economy, variously used as cheap sources of labor, strikebreakers, and potential threats to white labor. The archival materials and my own fieldwork in Florida convince me that it is impossible to read a person's income from his or her tax returns, stated income in surveys, or other quantitative measures. Persons in disadvantaged positions may struggle to survive, but they do so creatively by exploiting all kinds of opportunities to make money, cut a deal, return a favor, and the like. To think these tactics are readily quantifiable reveals one of the several fault lines in abstracted empiricism: it is often out of touch with what people do.

The historical record, as I have already pointed out, contradicts the argument that slavery destroyed the fabric of the African-American family, paving the way historically for female-headed forms. As a number of researchers have shown, most black girls and boys were raised in two-parent families during slavery and after its abolition. The rise in black households headed by women is a recent historical phenomenon. Indeed, the vibrancy of black family life during and after slavery is a testament to cultural resistance rather than a manifestation of cultural pathology. I have already discussed the contributions of Herbert Gutman and bell hooks to this debate about the enduring historical character of the primarily nuclear black family. Other authors reach similar conclusions. For example, in his analysis of slave letters, autobiographies, plantation records, and other archival material, Blassingame points to the rich sense of community and family life among African Americans. Specifically, he observes that slavery was not "an all powerful, monolithic institution which stripped the slave of any meaningful distinctive culture, family life, religion or manhood."[34]

My archival analysis does not indicate that female-headed households, psychologically emasculated black men, or any combination thereof led to intimate-partner homicide. Many black families are indeed headed by women, but very few experience intimate-partner homicide. In fact, if the case studies show anything, it is that the presence of a controlling patriarch who sees his female partner as his property and backs up that perception with violence is the most significant correlate to domestic killing. The etiology of woman battering, male proprietary rights, and female entrapment emerge similarly in all racial groups and are wholly at odds with the notion of a black matriarchy.

In a related vein, the contention of Moynihan and others that the African-American family is somehow pathological relies upon an idealized understanding of the white middle-class family as harmonious and stable. Such a position is itself a form of patriarchal ideology masquerading as social science. To presume that the white middle-class family is successful and harmonious, and to tout it as the building block of a stable and cohesive social order, is to ignore the immense amounts of conflict, violence, subordination, and oppression within many families. Although black families experience higher rates of marital dissolution, and black women report higher levels of intimate violence, the differences between white and black families are ones of degree and not of kind, and are doubtless associated with the social disadvantage and diminished life chances of African Americans in general. Again, as the case studies of intimate-partner homicide revealed, intimate relationships that ended in death were riddled with consistent patterns of conflict, antagonism, entrapment, and despair that were confined by no racial or ethnic boundaries.

Another reason for not uncoupling culture and society is that police response to violence within the black community has likely shaped beliefs about what is and is not acceptable and sanctionable interpersonal behavior. The criminal justice system has never been rooted in black culture or the black community, and even today is not accountable to that community. Due to traditional police reluctance to intervene in the black community, Hawkins notes the existence of something approaching "vigilante justice" in which persons have learned to settle their own scores rather than rely on the whims of the police and the courts. If such a system of vigilante justice has evolved among some African Americans, Hawkins and others rightly trace the accompanying high homicide rates to the historic inaction and passivity of the criminal justice system. This long-standing pattern of police passivity toward violence among black persons likely served to drive up the intimate-partner homicide rate. Domestic disputants could not rely on law enforcement officers to intervene. Consequently, disputes escalated to the point of lethal violence. If the historic failure of emergency medical services to permeate the black community is added to this, one sees yet another reason that violent interpersonal assaults were more likely to result in death.

The notion that violence is normative among African Americans, or that black men in particular behave as "normal primitives," has important implications for my study of intimate-partner homicide. Without effective intervention and protection early on in conflictual domestic relationships, the parties may resort to settling their own scores. If interpersonal vigilantism is one reason that black intimates, and particularly black women, resort to violent forms of dispute resolution, then, as Hawkins puts it, such resort only reinforces the stereotypical belief that violence is normative among black persons. Yet this expression of violence cannot, by any stretch of the imagination, be seen as a cultural or subcultural product. Rather, one must look to the interface of dominant white culture and disadvantaged sectors of the black community, and the acquiescence of the former in the illegalities of the latter. Gunnar Myrdal locates the stereotypical beliefs about black disorderliness amidst broader American cultural mores:

> It is part of the Southern tradition to assume that Negroes are disorderly and lack elementary morals, and to show great indulgence toward Negro violence and disorderliness "when they are among themselves." They should, however, not act it out in the presence of whites, "not right out on the street." As long as only Negroes are concerned and no whites are disturbed, great leniency will be shown in most cases.[35]

Marginalized black subcultures have been created in part out of interaction with dominant social institutions such as the criminal justice system. From the earliest days of slave-based agricultural production, slave patrols policed African Americans on and off the plantations.[36] After the end of Reconstruction, huge numbers of younger black men were criminalized through the use of disorderly conduct codes, vagrancy statutes, and loitering ordinances. These and similar laws served, in part, to socially demarcate the territory available to black persons, and they helped create rigid patterns of racial segregation, especially in fast-expanding urban areas.[37] Blacks who migrated north in hope of bettering their social and economic lot found themselves segregated into neighborhoods either bordering or within traditional red-light districts. Once black citizens had been isolated in these areas, police largely failed to offer protection, instead monitoring them for inappropriate incursions into white social space or for cultural activities inconsistent with dominant white mores. Nearly all of the major urban disturbances of the twentieth century were triggered by the overzealous and brutal policing of African Americans.[38] The U.S. Supreme Court gradually became aware of the regular use of torture to extract confessions from black suspects. In *Brown v. Mississippi* (1936), the Court threw out the convictions of three black men who had confessed to a homicide after being tortured. One was hung from a tree by his neck; the other two were beaten on their bare backs with metal-studded belts by sheriff's deputies.[39] This legacy of hostility between the police and the black community is a deeply embedded one. It is culturally reinforced every time police use excessive force, harass a young black man on the street, or routinely employ racist epithets.[40]

During my fieldwork in Florida I talked with many social actors who are involved in responding to domestic violence. Most of them, including law enforcement officers, health professionals, judges, attorneys, and advocates for battered women, acknowledged that 20 years ago violence in the black community was either not policed at all, policed passively, or only policed when it spilled over or had other deleterious effects upon dominant white culture. In this sense, the monitoring of the black community had changed little in a century or more. However, this passivity, acquiescence, and indifference to violence so long as it involved only African Americans seems to have changed. Most informants argued that the housing projects in Florida are policed much more closely nowadays. They also argued that whereas two decades ago the delivery of medical services to the black community mirrored the delivery of police services, emergency medical service delivery today is as swift as it is in the white community. These observations on policing and the delivery of emergency medical services are at least superficially borne out by the log data from the homicide files. I could discern no differences between racial or ethnic communities' receipt of police or medical services.

If my observations and those of key informants in Florida are accurate, they are consistent with other studies which show that with the advent of community policing black neighborhoods have been policed and surveyed far more closely than ever before.[41] The motives for this change are often less than admirable, and they likely have a lot to do with perpetuating the criminal justice industry through the dubious arrest and subsequent incarceration of politically vulnerable young black men. In particular, one might note the massive arrest and incarceration of young African-American men for crack cocaine offenses. Nevertheless, one by-product of this more enthusiastic policing may be the well-documented reduction of domestic homicide among black men and women.[42] It is not my argument that with the advent of community policing the law enforcement agencies of the state suddenly became more attuned to and concerned with the plight of African Americans. Rather, through more intense policing, it is likely that the state has invented yet another way to punish young black males. Indeed, one notes that the massive increase in their incarceration corresponds with the rise of community policing initiatives and the decline of black intimate-partner killings.

The cultural sense that police have rather passively managed domestic violence in the black community is, as Hawkins suggests, an important factor contributing to the disproportionately high rates of black intimate-partner homicide. If one adds to this the long-standing perception, particularly on the part of African-American women, that there is little institutional support to assist them in fleeing violent men, one can see how an interpersonal vigilantism, rooted in male violence, may have come to flourish in the black community. Although for black women as a whole these perceptions of the delivery of state services may be changing, the archival data suggest that for a significant number of black women, entrapped to the point of using resistive lethal violence, traditional beliefs and perceptions of vulnerability die hard.

However, there are perhaps several ways that the new policing initiatives may have prevented some black partners from committing intimate homicide. First, the policing initiatives of the last 20 years have taken large numbers of African-American men out of families and off the streets, thus lessening their opportunities to engage in domestic violence. Conversely, it could be argued that when these often-incarcerated men return to their families, partners, and children, they are more experienced, angrier, and meaner than before and hence more, not less, likely to kill. Second, with increasing police intervention in domestic violence in the black community, the message about the potential consequences of intimate violence may have begun to circulate. Third, heightened police responsiveness to violence in black households may have augmented and intensified beliefs and values regarding the inappropriateness of this behavior. Fourth, growing police enthusiasm for responding to disorder involving black persons means officers arrive more quickly, thus nipping potentially lethal violence in the bud. Many criminal justice personnel made the point that the difference between aggravated assault and homicide can be the speed and effectiveness with which police and medical services are delivered in the first hour after an assault. It is likely that such enhanced responses, which are associated with developments in community policing, saved the lives of some black domestic disputants.

If the decrease in the black intimate-partner homicide rate over the last two decades is due in part to increased law enforcement presence and responsiveness, then it suggests that the much longer historical legacy of police passivity may have been profoundly important in sending a message that black life was more expendable than white life. Regardless of the degree to which the factors mentioned above contributed toward a reduction in domestic homicide, it is clear that in 1994 black women, and, to a much lesser extent, black men, are at least as willing as their white and Latino peers to summon the police during or after a domestic dispute. These observations in Florida are mirrored by the latest Bureau of Justice Statistics Report on intimate-partner violence and policing, which reveals not only that black women are more victimized by domestic violence than their white and Latino counterparts, but that black women are more likely to call the police.[43]

I have argued against seeing the black family and black culture as pathological and as the source of disproportionate rates of intimate-partner homicide. Rather, I contend that the legacy of oppression, discrimination, disadvantage, and social despair plays a major part in producing violent interpersonal relationships. One cannot disaggregate these historical burdens and contemporary sources of disenchantment from the commission of interpersonal violence. Many brutalized persons do not engage in violent, brutal acts themselves. Many children who witness violence between their parents do not become batterers themselves. Put simply, people negotiate their use of violence in interpersonal relationships, and many men do not have to use violence to realize the fruits of patriarchy. However, the idea that black life has been devalued strikes me as a real reason for expecting that intimate violence and homicide would be higher in the African-American community. Indeed, some social scientists have framed this long-standing differential police response to the black community as part of a much broader cultural and historically enduring contempt for black persons. Under this way of thinking, the fact that blacks have higher rates of domestic homicide, or indeed violent crime in general, comes as no surprise. Some writers have argued that the increased propensity for violence among black disputants stems from the legacy of racial oppression in the United States and from black cultural roots in Africa.[44] Others point to the way in which African Americans were socialized into violence through the brutalizing effects of slavery.[45] These perspectives are not necessarily mutually exclusive. Some researchers attach more importance to how white culture, and particularly the criminal justice apparatus, devalues blacks.[46] Darnell Hawkins points out that this cultural contempt for black men and women, and particularly the devaluation of black life, is so pervasive that it also permeates the black community. It is for this reason, among others, that black-on-black violence is so pronounced. Hawkins also argues that the historical legacy of devaluing black life has had specific effects in the arena of domestic violence. He argues that because black life is valued less than white life, the consequences for black men and women who commit acts of domestic violence, and indeed domestic homicide, have traditionally been less severe than for white persons who injure or kill their intimate partners.[47]

At the same time, African-American culture has been variously and inaccurately essentialized as criminogenic, a drain on welfare funds, drug infested, and, to use Moynihan's phrase, a "tangle of pathology." My point is that black culture, whatever it is or was, is inextricably tied up with broader social structural patterns and is laced with a plethora of dominant value prescriptions concerning religious beliefs, families, education, and community. Put differently, one cannot talk of culture as if it were an adjunct to social structure or some kind of epiphenomenon. Values, beliefs, and norms do not stand alone, detached from social patterns such as class relations. The art of social intercourse mediates and is itself shaped by patterns of employment, experiences of formal social control mechanisms, and the collective memories of the past. To ignore these intersections between culture, structure, and history is to do a grave disservice to the complex and multifaceted social phenomenon of domestic homicide. Likewise, to talk of subcultures as if they were bounded off from mainstream cultural formations, or immune to the machinations of the capitalist marketplace or patriarchal structures, is to deny the historical fluidity of social life itself. Bearing these comments in mind, I now proceed to explore the intersection of gender, culture, and history as a possible means of making sense of how the Sex Ratios of Killing vary among blacks, Latinos, and Caucasians.

*SROK*  Not only do rates of domestic homicide differ by culture, but the sex ratios of intimate-partner killing exhibit distinctive cultural variations as well. For blacks and whites the SROKs also differ by the marital status of the parties. As Table 7.1 reveals, the SROKs for blacks, whites, and Latinos are 41.7, 20.9, and 11.8, respectively. Among blacks there is a significant difference between the SROKs for married (33.3) and unmarried (47.6) partners. In contrast, the SROK for white married partners (25) is considerably higher than that for unmarried partners (15.8). For Latinos, the SROKs do not seem to differ for married and unmarried partners, with both being significantly lower than the figure for white and, especially, black couples.

Any attempt to explain variations in SROKs must, at a minimum, explore historically embedded patriarchal formations in different cultural settings. The anthropological evidence strongly suggests that where women have at least some political and economic clout vis-à-vis men they are likely to be better insulated from cruder and more coercive patriarchal controls.[48] The Florida findings are consistent with this anthropological research. The SROKs are highest in matrilocal and matrifocal familial systems (e.g., among blacks), where women have traditionally worked outside the home and have been more likely to be the sole or more-substantial economic provider. In those families, and for a variety of reasons, men are more likely to be physically absent from the home. The SROKs are lowest among families where women are less likely to work for wages outside the home and where men tend to be physically present to a greater degree (e.g., among Latinos). I will focus first upon the low numbers among Latinos before exploring the high numbers among African Americans.

Latino women in Florida come from diverse backgrounds and geographical locations, and they have distinct histories. All I can do here is to introduce some historical, cultural, and social structural phenomena that may help explain why only a small number of Latino women commit intimate-partner homicide.[49] Upon presenting the low Latino SROK to audiences in Florida, as well as to the numerous players I came into contact with during the course of my research, the reply was almost always the same: "Latino women are respectful of their male partners"; "Latino women are more subordinate than Caucasian and black women because of their culture, family structure, and the influence of Catholicism." At the same time, Latino women in particular are quick to point out that their compromised position as a group varies among Mexicans, Central and South American Latinos, Puerto Ricans, and Cubans. In what follows, I discuss those aspects of Cuban and Mexican-American social and cultural history that offer an entrée into making sense of the low Latino SROKs.

Migration from Cuba to the United States began in small numbers in the 1830s and accelerated after a protracted insurrection against Spanish colonists began in 1868. As Perez points out, prominent among the early migrants were cigar manufacturers; they set up traditional Cuban enclaves on the outskirts of Tampa in Ybor City and also in Key West. Many of these households were multigenerational, with men forming the center of patrilocal socialization patterns. Among these early immigrants who set up what were essentially company towns, Perez notes the cultural importance of the double standard with regard to the behavior of males and females: "The double standard of morality formed part of a strong patriarchal tradition that Cuban immigrants brought with them from the island's colonial society. It was a tradition that was reflected in, and protected by, the Spanish civil code, which was in effect in Cuba even after the end of Spanish colonial rule in 1898."[50]

The legally, but not factually, subordinate status of Cuban women was modified in 1940 by the addition of a constitutional clause that "reaffirmed a married woman's full civil status."[51] A number of other progressive changes in family law put Cuban women's status ahead of that of others in Latin America.[52] Indeed, Perez notes the higher rate of "marital conflict and divorce" among Cuban couples compared with other Latino groups in the contemporary United States. In her view,

> [i]t is likely that definitions of the male role have not totally adjusted to the realities of female employment so as to permit greater sharing of household tasks. Consequently, Cuban women have the double burden of employment and domestic responsibilities. This situation, of course, is not unique to Cubans. But it is likely that, compared with the norms in the dominant society, the male role has remained somewhat more traditional among Cubans, whereas the expectations of the performance of women in domestic tasks has remained fairly high.[53]

However, these changes, progressive as they may have been, came much later than comparable changes in U.S. laws extending formal civil rights to white American women with regard to owning businesses, enjoying custody of children, administering wills, and the like. Put differently, the lingering cultural effects of acute patriarchal controls are likely to be felt more intensely among Cuban women than among other American women of comparable social class.

Maxine Baca-Zinn suggests that "family is one of the strongest areas of life, more important for Mexicans than for Anglos. This pertains not only to the nuclear family but also to a wider circle of relatives . . . that includes aunts, uncles, grandparents, cousins, in-laws, and even compadres."[54] She argues that *compadrazgo* (a system of fictive kin, such as godparents and coparents) is another important component of family life, also less well developed in Anglo family systems. Mosqueda notes that *compadrazgo* is nominally rooted in Catholic religious ceremony and serves as a means of extending the boundaries of family to incorporate nonblood kin.[55] Historically, this system was one way of staving off the threat of poverty by widening the circle of social support around families. As Mosqueda points out through his interview work, compadres feel honored to be called upon to enter this circle and morally obliged to commit to it.

Baca-Zinn argues that although male domination is present in Mexican families it is not as acute as it was depicted to be in some of the early studies of them. Blea makes the same point, observing that the picture of the Mexican woman as "docile, passive, uncomplaining, all-suffering, all-forgiving and hard-working" is a well-documented stereotype, along with other notions that she is the "victim of a violent, unfaithful male."[56] She goes on to say that because Mexican-American women earn far less than Anglo women, they are forced into a relationship of greater interdependence with men. Here again one sees the simultaneous influence of cultural and social structural factors on patriarchal family forms. As Mexican migration proceeded, gender power relations were mediated by broader structural, especially economic, conditions. In particular, Blea notes the role of women's work outside the family as one mechanism that has sometimes empowered Mexican women vis-à-vis their husbands. However, this outside work cuts both ways. If Mexican women earn well, their wage work may be empowering. As Blea points out, though, Mexican-American women typically earn a lot less than their Anglo counterparts. Such low wages, in combination with responsibilities for housework and child care, may actually increase Mexican-American women's stress and their dependence upon men. Zavella's study of Chicano families in the Santa Clara Valley revealed women's employment as cannery workers was part-time and seasonal. Men saw women's wage labor as an extension of their household responsibilities. As such, it did not transform their relationship with men in the patriarchal family, but in the end only accentuated their dependence.[57]

Unlike Cuban-American families, those of Mexican Americans tend to be poorer and have much higher birthrates. Both factors compound the compromised position of women in Chicano families. Domestic violence is more prevalent in poorer families, and it is also the case that the burdens of child care are borne excessively, and at times exclusively, by women. Blea traces the subordination of women in modern Mexican families back to the Spanish Conquest. Other researchers stress how the traditional power of the Mexican woman and her links with her family of origin were eroded after the Mexican-American War of 1848. Griswold del Castillo observes that although Mexican women were valued primarily for their "domesticity," they suffered an erosion of their traditional property rights enjoyed under Spanish and Mexican civil codes. He notes a number of court rulings that served to "strengthen the property rights of the husband at the expense of his wife and children."[58] Of contemporary gender power issues, Blea remarks: "Even at birth Chicano females and males do not start out the same. Boy babies are still preferred."[59]

My thumbnail sketch of some features of Cuban-American and Mexican-American families points to the diversity among Latino groups. However, they share a cultural legacy dating back to the Spanish Conquest, a history mediated by migration patterns to the United States, and the experience of negotiating the rigors of a dominant Anglo culture. Although Latino family forms are heavily patriarchal, they are differentially impacted by economic conditions. With higher incomes and fewer children, Cuban-American women seem less vulnerable to male domination than do poorer Mexican-American women.[60] As Doris Wilkinson points out, however, regardless of differences stemming from poverty, migration patterns, occupational opportunities, immigrant status, family customs, and regional variation, families of Spanish descent in the United States seem committed to certain core "solidifying beliefs." Among them is a commitment to "the functional dominance of males, complemented by a positive and traditional role for women . . . the reinforcement of sex role distinctions through child-rearing practices . . . the repression of feminine attributes in males, and a precedent for the male as head of the household."[61] It is this "functional dominance" and the traditional cultural ascendancy of men, accompanied by a strong norm toward respecting them as heads of household, that provides the most likely key to understanding why very few Latino women kill men, compared with the number of Latino men who kill women. Male dominance is likely enhanced when kin networks are patrilocal and women are isolated from their own families. Dominance and entrapment appear to be particularly acute among some migrant farmworker families. However, the archival material revealed that these entrapped Latino women have not resorted to lethal violence as a resistive strategy, perhaps in part because of their lack of citizenship and fear of losing their children.

The archival analysis of the female-perpetrated killings reveals that African-American women, in contrast to their Caucasian and especially Latino counterparts, are much more likely to kill their intimate male partners. I have already alluded to the historic failure of police to intervene in violence in the black community. However, there is no way of knowing precisely how the willingness of black women in Florida in 1994 to summon the police was associated with their higher rates of intimate-partner homicide. The latest BJS study and my field observations suggest black women are at least as likely to call police and as likely to have their homes reached by emergency services as are white and Latino women. However, for a variety of reasons, acutely entrapped and isolated African-American battered women still appear reluctant to call the police. It is from among their ranks that the female-perpetrated killing of male intimates is most likely to come. Other field research suggests that black battered women, for various reasons, are less willing to use domestic-violence shelters and, as a result, may be more likely to become entrapped to the point that they must resort to lethal defensive violence. Moreover, black women report experiencing more intimate violence than either Caucasian or Latino women, and this may be another possible reason that they kill intimate partners more frequently. And finally, out of sociocultural necessity, black women may have internalized the legacy of "vigilante justice" to a greater degree than their Caucasian or Latino counterparts. Such a historical internalization may also have augmented their likelihood of striking back against men with resistive lethal violence.

A number of African-American women I talked with in Florida told me that black women were less willing than Caucasians or Latinos to put up with intimate-partner violence. Readers will recall the words of Alison Murray, the black woman who killed her husband after he approached her with a lighter in one hand and a can of charcoal lighter in the other. Alison saw white women as being "taught to be obedient." However, one must be careful not to feed stereotypes of black women as "Sapphires." This identity, as I noted through mention of the work of bell hooks in Chapter 5, "has been projected onto any black woman who overtly expresses bitterness, anger, and rage about her lot."[62] hooks warns that the expression of this rage by black women may be a means of covering up the historic hurt and vulnerability of persons oppressed not only by their gender and social class locations, but also by their ongoing negotiation of racism. Under this way of thinking, the disproportionate level of lethal interpersonal violence dealt out by African-American women is a reaction to their historic oppression, not just to their victimization at the hands of individual men. Beth Richie, echoing the work of Darnell Hawkins, makes a similar point in talking about the collective devastation and individual despair permeating sectors of the black community. "Unfortunately," she notes, "in some instances, the alienation and hopelessness have led to aggression and violence turned inward."[63]

In addition to being inconsistent with the informative and enlightening work of authors such as hooks, Hawkins, and Richie, talk of African-American women as evil, vicious persons who kill their intimate partners with alarming frequency flies in the face of my archival findings and field research. Black women who killed, like their Caucasian and Latino counterparts, were essentially backed into a corner with nowhere to go. Like white women, some had children to care for, nearly all had been brutalized by their intimate partners, and most had, for whatever reasons, not sought out or received support from criminal justice and other state agencies. Their partners were often obsessively possessive, and a good number of these violent men had threatened to kill them. These are the continuities in the cases where women kill men, and these continuities transcend racial lines. The only reasonable conclusion is that more black women than Caucasian and Latino women appear to be entrapped to the point that they have to kill their intimate partners.

What, then, should be made of the convincing anthropological evidence which shows that where women's labor is valued and where women have increased political clout relative to men, they are less likely to be violently victimized? For example, Levinson, in a cross-cultural analysis of family violence, found that "women's economic power or solidarity with other women is a powerful predictor of the absence of wife beating."[64] Although I have argued against the existence of a black matriarchy, it is evident from the available research that there appears to be a higher degree of networking among black women than among Caucasian or Latino women. As Carol Stack has argued, this networking is in part an adaptive response to the pressures of poverty.[65] Does this seemingly more extensive networking among at least some women in the black community somehow provide a means for understanding the high African-American SROKs? Is there something about this networking that empowers black women vis-à-vis black men to the point that higher numbers of them are able to kill their abusers? There is no archival evidence that such a matrifocal network, if it does exist, works in this way. Indeed, the archival material shows no examples among the 24 cases of women killing men where women somehow planned, somehow drew support from each other, or somehow conspired to kill abusers. One ought not confuse a seeming solidarity among the disadvantaged with an empowerment to commit homicide. On the contrary, the African-American women who killed seemed at least as isolated as their Latino or Caucasian counterparts. Nor did the black women appear any more economically independent of their intimate partners. Indeed, in most cases both black men and black women were poor. Unlike the situation with Caucasians and Latinos, black women have more job opportunities, earn higher wages, and have higher levels of formal education than do their male intimates. However, this does not mean that they occupy ascendant positions in their intimate relationships with black men or suffer less battering than other women.[66] Even though the number of cases is small and the archival information on personal income is limited, black women in Florida in 1994 did not kill black men within what appeared to be the context of a relationship in which they were economically privileged compared with those men. Nor ought it to be assumed that if black women do earn more than their intimate male partners they will actually control the distribution of income within the family.

## Concluding Remarks: Social Policy Initiatives

My archival analysis provides insights into the microdynamics of domestic homicide. Men perpetrate most domestic killings, including the majority of family homicides. When women commit family homicide, they almost always kill their children. In most cases these child deaths involve abuse, neglect, or both. The fact that women do kill their children points up the tenuousness of trying to explain all domestic homicides through the power or control maneuvers of men.

Men perpetrate most intimate-partner homicides. They kill their intimate female partners as part of a stylized patriarchal pattern of increasingly controlling interpersonal behavior that usually involves battering. These homicides are typically crimes of cumulation, steeped in a multitude of tensions, discord, and violence. Women kill men mostly in self-defense. They typically do not act out of envy, to gain insurance money, or to assert their power and control. Indeed, it is one of the great travesties of our time that women who commit these offenses end up serving long prison sentences.

The microdynamics of intimate-partner homicide tend to transcend race, ethnicity, social class, age, and neighborhood characteristics. However, one should not take this to mean that women in different cultural settings understand entrapment to be the same thing. Likewise, women differ in their reactions to entrapment. The pervasiveness of these microdynamics, and their presence as at least contextual factors in some instances of domestic child homicide, might provide a rationale for screening out potentially lethal domestic-violence cases. As I have stated, it was not my intent in writing this book to produce a predictive matrix in any scientific sense. However, given all of the intimate-partner assaults, roughly half of which come to the attention of the police, the situational antecedents I identify might be a way of beginning to appreciate those cases at higher risk of lethality. Situations where agencies know men have beaten women for years, where men have threatened to kill women and communicated those threats to others, where abusers are obsessively possessive of their female partners, where men remain undeterred by criminal justice or other agency interventions, and where men have histories of criminal violence warrant the very closest attention. This scrutiny ought to be further amplified in cases where the woman is attempting to escape. However, it is not my conclusion that the instances of domestic homicide differ qualitatively from other cases involving violent domestic discord. Many batterers are obsessively possessive, and most feel that they have been betrayed by their victims in one way or another. Rather, the archival material suggests there are differences of degree, frequency, and intensity that may help to identify some of the pre-lethal situations.

My archival analysis is essentially a social postmortem on the deaths of family members. Its veracity is therefore shaped by the archival materials and the numerous and varied leads I have developed and pursued from those materials. In this sense, I have had at my disposal the same bodies of information, and have had access to the same microcircuits of knowledge, that parties from multiple state agencies tap into. Key players in those agencies, especially ones closer to the street, such as homicide detectives, doubtless had many more sources than I could muster in a somewhat cursory analysis of the 319 domestic deaths. Put differently, criminal justice players, judges, and social service providers have remarkable access to the daily details of people's lives. This degree of access is a mixed blessing. On the one hand, civil libertarians warn of the loss of privacy. They complain, rightly in my opinion, of the insidious erosion of Fourth Amendment rights. However, in the arena of domestic violence it is the privacy of the family in the home, among other things, that enables violence to escalate to lethal levels. Nevertheless, orchestrating state agencies to intervene on behalf of family members borders on the politically impermissible for some. To drop the debate about domestic homicide at the door of legal and civil rights, however, risks individualizing the problems and missing the patterns that, as my archival analysis has shown, far transcend particular persons and their broken relationships. I suggest, then, that if orchestrated, humane state intervention in domestic violence is to proceed to check and further reduce the incidence of domestic homicide, such state incursions should be informed by the kinds of microdynamics I have tried to elucidate through the archival sources.

There is an assumption here that agency intervention can save lives. I have already argued that the heightened availability of police services in African-American neighborhoods is one reason for the drop in domestic homicide rates in those communities across the country. It is not my reading of the archival files that it was solely the power and control of men in the family that led to the killing. Rather, the patriarchal order is a social one, extending beyond the boundaries of family life, blurring distinctions between the public and private spheres. As such, this patriarchal order is also articulated and reproduced through certain styles of policing that do not take woman battering seriously, through judicial dispositions that blame women for their own victimization, and the like. It is because of the social ubiquity of patriarchy that focusing on service providers may bear rich fruit in reducing domestic homicide. On the other hand, the history of social control is the history of oppression and subjugation; ironically, it is also the history of resistance, unanticipated outcomes, and unintended effects. Recommending greater surveillance and intervention in the family by state agencies runs the risk of feeding into the ludicrous buildup of the enormous criminal justice apparatus that increasingly permeates social life. Instead of swelling the growing army of the incarcerated, it would be wiser social policy to back away from the tendency to criminalize behaviors such as drug offenses while upgrading the criminal justice response to violence in families.

Rather than focusing here on policy possibilities at the level of individual agencies, I close by highlighting an emerging statewide policy initiative in Florida. Funded through the U.S. Department of Justice, it is designed to better understand, intervene in, and perhaps prevent domestic killings. I refer to the attempt to set up domestic-violence fatality review teams. These teams, currently being established in four jurisdictions in the state,[67] bring players from multiple agencies together to review domestic-violence fatalities and to ask this question: What, as service providers in this community, could we have done differently to have prevented this death? Team members then collectively develop ideas about how best to change the policies and procedures within member agencies, how to better coordinate existing strategies, and how to create new ones. With the central purpose of prevention in mind, it is essential that the teams be composed of agency members who possess the political clout to effect policy and procedural changes. At a philosophical level, the idea is to ask the "how could we have prevented it" question without lapsing into blaming particular agencies or individuals for errors of judgment, malfeasance, and so on that may have contributed in some way to the homicide. At the same time, the review process remains cognizant of the need for accountability on the part of service agencies. By using an approach that does not assign blame and shame within an ethos of accountability, agency members are encouraged to share information and strategies. The approach involves multiple agencies and multiple disciplines. It recognizes that domestic violence and domestic homicide are social problems that involve many service providers, among them the police, courts and corrections, public health workers (broadly conceived), and advocates for battered women. Alongside these general suggestions about how domestic-violence fatality review teams might operate, it also must be recognized that state agencies differ by region, funding levels, commitment to issues, bureaucratic organization, and the nature of their individual employees. Consequently, any attempts to standardize the review process beyond introducing basic philosophical premises, addressing etiologic patterns, and the like may be counterproductive.

Police departments can be sued for their failure to handle domestic cases properly. Many other criminal justice professionals, including sheriffs and judges, are elected to office. Due to these concerns about liability and election, and for other reasons, some states have enacted laws to guarantee the confidentiality of the information shared at domestic-violence fatality reviews.[68] The idea behind such legislation is to safeguard team members and their respective agencies from legal liability, thus encouraging them to share information more openly. The possible downside to confidentiality guarantees is that they might create the sense that information is being hidden from the people, to whom these agencies are perceived to be ultimately responsible. This is a thorny policy issue. Those working in the field of child-fatality reviews in Florida have told me that confidentiality guarantees are an essential accompaniment to the open discussion of agency involvement in the deaths of girls and boys. At the time of writing, the State of Florida has not passed legislation either to set up fatality-review teams or to guarantee the confidentiality of death reviews. In a related vein, it remains to be seen whether reporters, primarily newspaper journalists, will be involved in deliberations about domestic fatalities. The power of the mass media is immense. In the case of domestic homicides, as I have written elsewhere,[69] news organizations tend to fail to situate the deaths of domestic disputants within the broader power relations of gender. For instance, in the case of homicide-suicides, research shows that a history of woman battering usually precedes the fatal episode. Yet, it is unusual to see press reports of these events address the gendering of perpetration and motives. There is a need for more news coverage that addresses the social context of domestic killings.

Looking at homicide photographs showing the blood-soaked corpses of adults and the charred remains of babies, reading suicide notes, talking with persons who knew the deceased, and poring over the transcripts of interviews with those who have taken life are strange research activities. One becomes somewhat inured to the pain through a series of emotional maneuvers. At times, the horror caught up with me, but not very often. On occasion, I even glimpsed the potential virtues of abstracted empiricism! As I became increasingly familiar with the cases and with some of the players, I realized yet another aspect of the relationship between death and intimacy. To paraphrase Nietzsche, as one scrutinizes the abyss, the abyss looks back with an alarming gaze. As we as a society try to make sense of domestic homicide, we cannot escape or deny our relationship with it and our involvement in it. All the more reason to prevent it.

# Appendix 1

Synopses of the Prior Criminal Histories (Including Assaults on Partners) of the Male Perpetrators of Single Intimate-Partner Homicides in Florida, 1994

| Offender's Pseudonym | Prior Woman Battering | Synopsis of Offender's Criminal History |
|---|---|---|
| 1. Walter Critchley, W, 43 | Confirmed | Domestic violence (1988). |
| 2. Forbes Reese, B, 47 | Confirmed | Aggravated assault on a stranger (stabbing) (date unknown). |
| 3. Pat Crenard, B, 40 | Confirmed | Robbery; narcotics trafficking; homicide (two weeks before he killed his intimate partner) (dates unknown). |
| 4. Jack Ruben, 39, unknown race or ethnicity | Confirmed | Robbery; attempted burglary; prior domestic-violence offenses (dates unknown). |
| 5. Chuck Bradshaw, B, 46 | Confirmed | Aggravated assault (domestic violence) (date unknown). |
| 6. Jiminez Aguila, L, 61 | Confirmed | Domestic violence (1993). |
| 7. Ron Gemmil, B, 26 | Confirmed | Numerous domestic-violence offenses, including aggravated battery (dates unknown). |
| 8. Rod Clements, W, 22 | Confirmed | Drug dealing (date unknown). |
| 9. Alfred Simpson, W, 23 | Confirmed | Habitual felony offender; includes aggravated assault with a deadly weapon, aggravated assault with a knife, aggravated battery, and burglary and theft (dates unknown). |
| 10. Carl Lee, B, 39 | Confirmed | Aggravated assault (domestic violence) (date unknown). |

*Code:* W = white; B = black; L = Latino

| Offender's Pseudonym | Prior Woman Battering | Synopsis of Offender's Criminal History |
|---|---|---|
| 11. Pete Marino, B, 52 | Confirmed | Auto theft (1959); homicide (1962, first degree with firearm); homicide (1966, first degree with firearm); aggravated assault (1971); resisting arrest with violence (1971); attempted homicide (1979); aggravated assault (1979); firing a weapon in an occupied building (1979 [all of the 1979 charges were dismissed on grounds of insanity]); loitering and prowling (1983); carrying a concealed weapon (1984); gambling (1984); homicide (1984, second degree, not clear if he was convicted or served time); homicide (1987); aggravated battery (1993); misdemeanor battery (1994); homicide (1994). |
| 12. Frank Juno, B, 34 | Confirmed | Aggravated battery (domestic-violence offense) (date unknown). |
| 13. Eric Farnsworth, B, 34 | Confirmed | Aggravated assault; forgery; possession of marijuana; drug dealing (dates unknown). |
| 14. Felix Rendon, L, 45 | Confirmed | A number of domestic assaults and other criminal offenses (dates unknown). |
| 15. John Hendrix, B, 23 | No noted history of battering | Possession of marijuana; vehicle theft; carrying a concealed weapon; burglary; resisting a police officer (dates unknown). |
| 16. Dennis Broderick, B, 35 | Confirmed | Grand larceny (several indictments); shoplifting; domestic battery (dates unknown). |
| 17. Dick Marley, B, 22 | Confirmed | Sexual assault and battery (1991); cocaine dealing (1992); attempted homicide with firearm (1992); contempt of court (1992); cocaine possession (1993); larceny (1993); cocaine possession (1994); aggravated battery on pregnant female (1994). |
| 18. Jay Gould, W, 32 | Confirmed | Aggravated assault (date unknown). |

| Offender's Pseudonym | Prior Woman Battering | Synopsis of Offender's Criminal History |
|---|---|---|
| 19. Edson Pele, L, 51 | Not confirmed | Armed robbery; possession of a weapon during commission of a felony; carrying a concealed weapon (dates unknown). |
| 20. Rex Ticked, B, 38 | Confirmed | Aggravated assault; trespassing; resisting arrest without violence; possession of marijuana; burglary; shooting into an occupied building; receiving stolen property; sale of cocaine; obstruction of a police officer; introducing a controlled substance into a county detention facility (dates unknown). |
| 21. Steve Matt, W, 36 | Confirmed | Domestic violence (1993). |
| 22. Mike Beamon, B, 38 | Confirmed | Domestic violence (1990). |
| 23. Ellis Gabriel, B, 42 | Confirmed | Burglary (1990); DUI (1990); battery (1990); disorderly conduct (1990). |
| 24. Ray Hickey, W, 48 | Confirmed | Domestic violence (1994); reckless driving (1970). |
| 25. Phillipe Guevara, L, 25 | Confirmed | Violation of probation on an earlier assault charge (1994). |
| 26. Jack Rufus, W, 25 | Confirmed | Vehicular theft (1987); larceny (1987); cocaine possession and sale (1988); burglary (1990, 1992); battery of a corrections officer (1993); burglary (1994); aggravated battery of a police officer (1994). |
| 27. Bill Hendry, B, 28 | Confirmed | Extensive criminal history, including breach of the peace and disorderly conduct (1985); aggravated assault with a deadly weapon (1988, 1992); possession of cocaine (1988); domestic violence (1992); kidnapping (1992); violation of probation (1993). |
| 28. George Dempsey, W, 39 | Confirmed | Prior convictions for domestic violence and kidnapping (1991). |
| 29. David Rockford, W, 34 | Confirmed | Criminal mischief (1994); burglary (1994). |

# Appendix 2

Synopses of the Prior Criminal Histories of the Perpetrators of Child Homicides in Florida, 1994

| Offender's Pseudonym | Synopsis of Offender's Criminal History[1] |
| --- | --- |
| 1. Phoebe Limbaugh, WF, 20 | Prior homicide admitted when apprehended for killing her own child (date unknown). |
| 2. Alex Boyd, WM, 33 | In 1989 he was placed on probation for aggravated assault after he pulled a gun and threatened a motorist during a traffic dispute. Also marijuana possession (1989). |
| 3. Gene Hughes, BM, 30 | Prior arrests on drugs and firearms charges (dates unknown). In August 1992 he was arrested for possession of crack cocaine and marijuana, carrying a concealed firearm, and possession of a police scanner. In June 1994 he was arrested for possession of crack, resisting an officer without violence, and violation of probation. |
| 4. Rufus Ricksted, WM, 29 | Domestic violence directed at a number of different female partners. One former intimate partner had an injunction against him when he committed the child homicide. Prior allegations of child abuse (dates unknown). |
| 5. Ross Hendrix, BM, 35 | Prior domestic-violence convictions and drug offenses (dates unknown). |
| 6. Peter Floss, BM, 30 | Habitual felony offender, including battery (1984), fraud (1985), assault and battery (1986), domestic violence (injunction granted, 1991), and homicide (1992). |
| 7. Terrance Barwell, WM, 30 | History of assault, drug convictions (dates unknown). At the time of the child homicide he was on parole from a prison in Texas. |

*Code:* W = white; B = black; L = Latino; M = male; F = female

| Offender's Pseudonym | Synopsis of Offender's Criminal History[1] |
| --- | --- |
| 8. Rocardo Ventura, WL M, 27 | Burglary (1986), larceny (1987), cruelty toward a child and aggravated child abuse (1989). In 1990 he received 5½ years for aggravated child abuse; he served only 2 years. Within 18 months of his release he had committed child homicide. |
| 9. Piers Kunkel, BM, 26 | Carrying a concealed weapon (1986, 1987), aggravated assault (1988), probation violation (1988). |
| 10. Cedrick Toole, BM, 30 | Previous felony convictions, although not clear what they were (dates unknown). |
| 11. Steve Tilling, BM, 35 | Larceny (1975), possession of marijuana (1975, 1980), auto burglary and grand theft (1979), interfering with a police officer (1987), disorderly conduct (1987), possession and sale of cocaine (1992), and felonious sexual battery on a child under 12 (1992). |
| 12. Russell Biggs, BM, 31 | Weapons offenses and possession of a destructive device (1987). |
| 13. Ron Wisehart, BM, 15 | Drug trafficking (date unknown). |
| 14. Gavin Murdock, WM, 22 | Burglary (1989); petit and grand larceny (1990). |
| 15. Michael Robis, BM, 34 | Aggravated assault (1992). |
| 16. Zane Zoomlus, WM, 20 | Assaulting his brother (1993), battering his stepfather (1993), disorderly conduct (1993), carrying a concealed weapon (1992), and domestic disturbance (1994). |
| 17. Randy Lightfoot, WM, age unknown | Domestic violence directed at previous partners and on one occasion at a former wife's new boyfriend (dates unknown). |
| 18. Billy Bremner, BM, 35 | Domestic violence (dates unknown). |
| 19. Sandra Marx, WF, 15 | Prior juvenile offenses (dates unknown). |
| 20. Bill Stebbings, WM, 36 | Domestic violence. Aggravated battery and attempted murder (1988). |
| 21. Reggie Arthur, BM, 24 | Possession of cocaine (unknown year) and retail theft (unknown year). |
| 22. Sharon Cahill, BF, 19 | Carrying a concealed firearm and trespassing on school grounds (1993). |

# Appendix 3

## Methodological Considerations

*Understanding Domestic Homicide* derives from a study of domestic-violence fatalities funded by the Florida Governor's Task Force on Domestic and Sexual Violence, convened under the late Governor Lawton Chiles and overseen by Robin Hassler, its executive director. As a consultant on the project, I worked (and continue to work) with a number of agencies, among them police departments, domestic-violence centers (shelters), the courts, the Florida Coalition against Domestic Violence, advocates for battered women, child protection agencies, the Florida Department of Law Enforcement (FDLE), medical examiners, physicians, and public health professionals. For most of the domestic fatalities in Florida in 1994, I collected newspaper reports, crime scene investigations, detectives' follow-up investigative reports, details of any prior protective orders (known in Florida as injunctions), any criminal histories of the perpetrators and victims, medical examiners' reports, statements from witnesses, and, in the case of child fatalities, summary data and prior abuse histories from child protective agencies.

In addition to using these documentary sources, I also rode with police officers who worked domestic cases (including some involving fatalities); interviewed detectives who investigated domestic deaths; and talked with members of the governor's task force, advocates from the Florida Coalition against Domestic Violence, and a number of other key informants. Among the last, defense attorneys and prosecutors were especially valuable; as the text shows, they talked with me off the record.

This work thus blends field interviews and observations with extensive case materials collected from numerous agencies. However, I did not directly interview surviving perpetrators or victims, or their families or friends. The general feeling among members of the task force was that such interviewing might doubly victimize or traumatize the persons involved. No doubt such talks would have provided additional insights into the domestic fatalities, even though many of those involved had been questioned by investigators and I had obtained (and used) the transcripts from these hundreds of interviews. In particular, I did not speak with women who are at various stages of appealing their convictions for killing their male intimate partners. The most important reason for my decision was that in some cases their attorneys felt such interviewing might compromise the appeals process. The governor's task force collectively felt that to question women still seeking clemency would be a violation of their rights. According to some task force members, such interviews also might have raised false hopes of release among incarcerated women. In only one case did I speak with a woman acquitted of murdering her husband.

My starting point for collecting information about domestic homicides was the Florida Department of Law Enforcement's official list of such deaths for 1994. It did not contain the names of perpetrators and those killed, but it did identify jurisdictions and dates of deaths, and gave the age and sex of victims and their killers. I then explored newspaper reports of events in the jurisdictions mentioned to fill in names and other important details. From a more general reading of the newspapers, I uncovered new domestic homicides that did not appear on the FDLE's master list. Having carefully identified the names of as many of the victims and perpetrators as possible, I obtained the corresponding homicide files from police departments. I made some of these requests in writing and others in person. I visited all the bigger police departments in Florida between 1995 and 1998, including Miami, Metro–Dade, Tampa, Orlando, and Hollywood, as well as the Hillsborough, Duval, Broward, and Orange County sheriffs' offices. During these visits I soon learned to ask to see the homicide logs; on reviewing them, I found cases of domestic homicide that had been classified within another category of offense, such as "robbery." Reviewing the logs provided a cross-check on police department coding procedures that sometimes did not catch homicides that the Florida statutes deemed to be domestic.

The FDLE proved very helpful. Staff members provided what information they had on the existence of prior injunctions or restraining orders in domestic-violence cases that ended in fatalities. Since Florida jurisdictions have no centralized way of collecting data on injunctions, it would have taken visits to each of the state's 67 counties to uncover copies of all injunctions on file for particular victims and perpetrators. Luckily, police investigation files often contained copies of prior restraining orders, and I was able to acquire the orders through police agencies. The FDLE also cross-checked criminal histories against the final list of names of perpetrators and victims in domestic homicides and provided me with those histories.

Piecing all of this information together into what I came to call my "multi-agency archival analysis" yielded case files of varying length on each domestic-homicide victim. The length of a file depended in part upon the reporting agency's level of documentation. It also depended upon who was killed. In the case of child deaths, the archival files I utilize from child protective agencies are summary in nature. However, if the child was killed during a homicide-suicide or familicide, the files were enhanced by detailed police reports. There might also be extensive media coverage that included interviews with social actors sometimes not questioned by the police; in general, the more sensational the case, the greater the media coverage. Even where children died from abuse, neglect, or both, if there was a police investigation and I was able to obtain police homicide files, then the child protective agency files were again substantially enhanced. The only files closed to me involved cases that were pending prosecution or appeal. The number of these cases was small, since most trials took place within two years of the domestic death. In such cases I was still able to gather considerable information from detectives, attorneys, or other sources under a promise of confidentiality.

The case files on the 319 domestic homicides that were committed in Florida in 1994 enabled me to examine three aspects of the deaths in considerable detail. First, the overlapping case file materials allowed me to develop a complex profile of what I call the "perpetrator-victim dyad." In particular, I gathered varying amounts of information on the relationship between the parties, their sex, age, race or ethnicity, education, employment, place of residence, and income.

Second, and most important for this book, I gathered detailed information on the microdynamics of the relationship in the time preceding the lethal episode. I did this to explore what David Luckenbill[1] observes to be the interactional exchanges between all parties to a homicide. However, my analysis transcends the situational interactions occurring just before the killing to focus also on the long-term etiology of domestic deaths. In particular, I map socially situated relationship dynamics, such as a prior history and possible intensification of domestic violence or of child abuse, neglect, or both; a separation or growing distance between the parties; obsessive possessiveness or morbid jealousy displayed by the perpetrator and negotiated by the victim; any earlier police, judicial, or social agency involvement with the parties, and the detailed nature of that contact; any threats to kill the eventual victim and the social locus of these threats, be they issued between the parties, to family, to friends, to neighbors, and so on; the role played by alcohol, drugs, or both; and, finally, the role of weaponry.

Using what I call "the language of everyday empiricism," I develop a crude taxonomy of situational antecedents as a window into domestic relationships that may be more likely to end in homicide.[2] Since the archival materials are rich in what Clifford Geertz calls "thick description" of local culture,[3] my narratives of relationship conflict are embedded within a detailed appreciation of familial, kinship, friendship, and neighborhood social networks, as well as a broader sense of racial, social class, and gender inequalities. In particular, I explore the connections between power struggles in intimate relationships, kinship systems (including those of African Americans, Latinos, Caucasians, and Asian Americans), and intimate-partner fatalities.[4]

Third, and last, I document the domestic homicide itself, considering the crime scene, weaponry, and other details. Ironically, it is the minutiae of the crime scene that attract considerable and often disproportionate media attention, frequently at the expense of a more detailed appreciation of the social structural and situational antecedents to the fatalities.

# Notes

## Chapter 1

1. Mills, 1959: 138–39.
2. Ibid.: 138.
3. Florida Statute (1994) s. 741.28.
4. Jones, 1980.
5. Wilt, Illman, and Brodyfield, 1997.
6. For example, see Radford and Russell, 1992.
7. Bureau of Justice Statistics, 1998 (hereinafter BJS, 1998). Black women are more likely than women of other races to report such victimizations to the police. Approximately one-fifth of victims reported that police made an arrest at the scene of the disturbance.
8. BJS (1998) notes that intimates include spouses, former spouses, common-law spouses, same-sex partners, boyfriends, and girlfriends. Murder includes non-negligent manslaughter.
9. Ibid.: 7.
10. Block and Christakos, 1995.
11. Mercy and Saltzman, 1989: 596.
12. Daly and Wilson, 1988: 209.
13. Block and Christakos, 1995.
14. Stark and Flitcraft, 1996: 121.
15. Dobash et al., 1992; Kellerman and Mercy, 1992; Wilson and Daly, 1992.
16. Block and Christakos, 1995: 501.
17. Mercy and Saltzman, 1989: 595.
18. Ibid., figure 3: 597.
19. Stark and Flitcraft, 1996. Muscat (1988) reaches a similar conclusion in the case of childhood homicides. Although blacks had a higher rate of childhood homicide, the effect fades when socioeconomic status is taken into account.
20. Centerwall, 1984, 1995; Loftin and Hill, 1974; Williams, 1984.
21. Centerwall, 1984.
22. Centerwall, 1995: 1758.

23. Stark and Flitcraft, 1996.

24. Stark, 1993: 489.

25. BJS, 1998: 19.

26. Ibid.: 20.

27. Mann, 1988.

28. Doerner (1983) reaches a similar conclusion about the role of delayed or ineffective medical service delivery in homicide.

29. Zimring and Hawkins, 1997: 79–82. See also Davis, 1976.

30. Davis, 1976.

31. Block and Christakos, 1995: 502–3.

32. Ibid., table 2: 514.

33. Block, 1987; Mercy and Saltzman, 1989; Wilson and Daly, 1992a; Zimring, Mukherjee, and Van Winkle, 1983.

34. Totals are 106 women and 61 men; Block and Christakos, 1995: 499.

35. Wilson and Daly, 1992a: 189. Mercy and Saltzman (1989) found that wives in general were at 1.3 times greater risk of spousal homicide than husbands, although this effect was profoundly influenced by race. Later figures show that women constituted 41 percent of the perpetrators of U.S. interspousal killings (Dawson and Langan, 1994: 1).

36. Wilson and Daly, 1992a: 190.

37. Ibid., table 1: 191. Wilson and Daly rule out the possibility that the availability of guns in the United States makes it easier for women to kill men. They also dismiss the hypothesis that the disproportionately high numbers of U.S. women who kill their spouses is due to women's liberation or the large-scale entry of women into the paid labor market.

38. Moore and Tennenbaum, 1994: 177.

39. Ibid.

40. Block and Christakos, 1995: 512.

41. Mann, 1987: 180.

42. Rosenbaum, 1990: 1038.

43. Ibid.

44. Wilson and Daly, 1992a. These authors also mention that in one sample of interspousal killings from Africa the SROK was 6. This low figure strongly suggests that the SROKs among blacks in the United States reflect their social and historical condition in the culture of the country.

45. I use the term "matrilocal" in connection with residence patterns to refer to those situations where a woman lives with her female relatives.

46. Wilson and Daly, 1992a: 208; see also table 1: 191.

47. Ibid.: 209.

48. hooks, 1984.

49. Ibid.: 78.

50. Ibid.: 81.

51. BJS, 1998; Richie, 1996.

52. BJS, 1998.

53. Wolfgang, 1958a.

54. Barnard et al., 1982.

55. Ibid.: 274.

56. Ibid.: 278. A number of other studies report that large numbers of women who commit intimate-partner homicide assert they acted in self-defense. For example, Mann (1988: 44) found that among her sample of 145 women who killed someone in a domestic encounter 58.9 percent gave self-defense as a motive.

57. Wilson and Daly, 1985.

58. Ibid.: 65.

59. Daly and Wilson, 1988: 186.

60. Daly and Wilson, 1990.

61. Polk, 1994: 54.

62. Ibid.: 55.

63. Ibid.: 57.

64. For exceptions see Daly and Wilson, 1988; Heide, 1995; Mones, 1991.

65. Heide, 1995.

66. Mones, 1991.

67. Citing their own research, and that of Corder et al. (1976) and Russell (1984), Daly and Wilson (1988) observe that most cases of children killing parents involve sons, or more rarely daughters, killing abusive men who had a history of beating their wives (the children's mothers).

68. Heide, 1995: 7.

69. Ewing, 1997: 117.

70. Ibid.: 118.

71. Martin and Besharov, 1991.

72. McClain et al., 1993.

73. Ewing, 1998: 95.

74. Goetting, 1995: 113. She studied the deaths of children under the age of six in Detroit between 1982 and 1986.

75. Hicks and Gaughan, 1995: 860, table 4; see also Krugman (1983–85: 69) for a similar finding.

76. Schloesser, Pierpont, and Poertner, 1992: 7.

77. Gellert et al., 1995.

78. Copeland, 1985, table 2: 22.

79. Fontana and Alfara, 1982; Ludwig and Warman, 1984.

80. Gellert et al., 1995: 880.

81. See Sabotta and Davis, 1992. Some studies show that boys are more susceptible

to child abuse homicide than girls. See, for example, Copeland (1985), who found males constituted 61.8 percent of 62 child abuse fatalities in Dade County, Florida, from 1956 to 1982. Other studies pointing to an overrepresentation of boys among child abuse homicide victims include Christoffel, Anzinger, and Amari (1983), Paulson and Rushforth (1986), and Krugman (1983–85).

82. Christoffel, Anzinger, and Merrill, 1989: 1405 and table 3.

83. Christoffel, Anzinger, and Amari, 1983; Copeland, 1985; Paulson and Rushforth, 1986; Abel, 1986; Martinez, 1986; Goetting, 1990; Dawson and Langan, 1994.

84. Goetting, 1990.

85. Abel, 1986: 710.

86. Sorenson, Richardson, and Peterson, 1993: 726.

87. Anderson et al., 1983: 81.

88. Kunz and Bahr, 1996: 353.

89. Ibid.

90. Muscat, 1988: 822.

91. Palmer and Humphrey, 1980. For a more recent analysis of homicide-suicide in North Carolina, see Morton, Runyan, Moracco, and Butts (1998).

92. Wolfgang, 1958b. According to West's (1967) study of homicide-suicide in England and Wales, women made up 40 percent of the perpetrators. In Allen's (1983) investigation, 71 percent of the homicide victims in homicide-suicide episodes were the wives or girlfriends of the perpetrators.

93. Marzuk, Tardiff, and Hirsch, 1992: 3180. Marzuk and his collaborators refer to the research of Allen (1983), Berman (1979), and Dorpat (1966) to support their argument.

94. Currens et al., 1991.

95. Currens et al., 1991: 653. Studies cited in support of a prior history of domestic violence include Rosenbaum (1990) and West (1967).

96. Stack, 1997.

97. Stack's investigation of homicide-suicide is the largest to date, with a sample of 265 cases. In the qualitative studies the sample sizes were typically low. For example, Selkin (1976) examined 13 cases, Palermo (1994) analyzed 5 and Berman (1979) explored 20.

98. Stack, 1997: 449.

99. West, 1967; Mowat, 1966; Rosenbaum, 1990; Buteau, Lesage, and Kiely, 1993.

100. Marzuk, Tardiff, and Hirsch, 1992: 3181; Easteal, 1993: 89.

101. Cavan, 1965: 249.

102. Cohen, 1995.

103. Ibid.: 747.

104. Ewing, 1997: 135.

105. Stark and Flitcraft, 1996.

106. Wilson and Daly, 1993.

107. Daly and Wilson, 1988: 295; Easteal, 1993.

108. Hart, 1988: 242.

109. Browne, 1987: 10.

110. West, 1967; Lester, 1992; Buteau, Lesage, and Kiely, 1993.

111. Klein, 1993; BJS, 1998.

112. Dobash et al., 1992: 81. These major differences between spousal murders committed by men and women have been noted in a number of studies, including those carried out in Western societies other than the United States. For detailed references see Wilson and Daly, 1992a: 206.

113. Stark and Flitcraft, 1996: 124. Kellermann et al. (1993) note that a prior history of assaultive behavior in the home may signal the possibility of lethal violence.

114. Stark and Flitcraft, 1996: 146.

115. Goetting, 1995: 73–74.

116. Jones, 1980, especially chapter 2; Goetting, 1995; Grant, 1995: 316; Maguigan, 1991.

117. Goetting, 1995: 31.

118. Polk and Ransom, 1991: 20.

119. Daly and Wilson, 1988.

120. Ibid.: 202.

121. Ibid.: 295. See also Showalter, Bonnie, and Roddy, 1980; and Chimbos, 1978, cited by Daly and Wilson, 1988: 201.

122. Daly and Wilson, 1988: 202–5.

123. Easteal, 1993: 109.

124. Mowat, 1966; Rosenbaum, 1990; West, 1967.

125. Stack, 1997: 439.

126. Allen, 1983; Barnard et al., 1982; Browne, 1987.

127. Wilson and Daly, 1993.

128. Daly and Wilson, 1988: 219.

129. Wilson and Daly, 1993: 10.

130. Easteal, 1993: 102–3.

131. BJS, 1998: 14.

132. Dobash and Dobash, 1979.

133. Browne, 1987: 10–11.

134. Ibid.: 10.

135. Stark and Flitcraft, 1996: 148.

136. Easteal, 1993: 76.

137. Fagan, Stewart, and Hansen, 1983.

138. Klein, 1993.

139. Block and Christakos, 1995: 508.

140. BJS, 1998: 26.

141. Ibid.

142. Block and Christakos, 1995: 508–9; Easteal, 1993: 79–83.

143. Easteal, 1993: 79, figure 5.3.

144. Block and Christakos, 1995: 509.

145. Easteal, 1993: 81.

146. Sabotta and Davis, 1992.

147. Wilczynski, 1997: 245.

148. Fontana and Alfaro, 1982; Showers et at., 1985. Citing the 1,215 documented cases of child deaths in the United States in 1995 due to abuse and neglect, Ewing (1997: 95) notes that 46 percent of the cases had been under investigation by child protection services before the fatality.

149. Wilczynski, 1997.

150. Bowker, Arbitell, and McFerron, 1988; Stark and Flitcraft, 1996.

151. Bowker, Arbitell, and McFerron, 1988: 165.

152. Ibid.: 166.

153. Stark and Flitcraft, 1996: 83.

154. Ibid.: 87.

155. Southall et al., 1997.

## Chapter 2

1. Seventeen children died in multiple domestic homicides. Sixty-six other girls and boys also perished in domestic killings, giving a total of 83 child homicides. See Chapter 6 for a discussion of the child fatalities not examined in Chapters 2 and 3, and for summary data on all domestic child homicides.

2. Ewing, 1997.

3. Stack, 1997.

4. Geertz, 1973, 1983.

5. West, 1967.

6. Note that Table 2.5 is based upon information derived from available archival data and from any follow-up interviews with such key informants as detectives, defense attorneys, and prosecutors. It is likely that domestic violence was present in more than 34 out of 47 relationships and that available data did not capture all of the pre-fatal violence. The same is likely true for the other themes, especially "prior police contact" and "threats to kill."

7. Mahan, 1996; Websdale and Chesney-Lind, 1998.

8. Berman, 1979; Selkin, 1976.

9. Lester, 1992; Buteau, Lesage, and Kiely, 1993.

10. Daly and Wilson, 1988: 215.

11. Mercy and Saltzman, 1989: 596.

12. Wang, 1996. She defines "Asian American" broadly to include "all persons of Asian ancestry living in the United States" (1996: 152, n3). This incorporates peoples from East Asia (including China, Japan, and Korea), Southeast Asia (including Burma, Cambodia, Laos, Thailand, and Vietnam), South Asia (India), and the Philippines.

13. Ibid.: 171.

14. Ibid.: 175–76. See also Laurie Mengel's analysis of the Japanese women who migrated to Hawai'i from 1885 to 1908. Stereotypes abound about these women. Mengel observes, "Although she represents a minority of the women who emigrated from Japan to Hawai'i between 1885 and 1924, the 'picture bride' has become the stereo-typical representation of all Japanese female immigrants—passive, dutiful and subservient" (1997: 19).

15. hooks, 1996: 218.

16. Wilson and Daly, 1992b: 89, citing the case of *People v. Wood,* 391 N. E. ed 206.

17. Hart, 1988: 242.

18. Easteal reports that among her sample of perpetrators of homicide-suicide she found no relationship between type of employment and suicide. She also found that unemployed offenders did not have a higher rate of committing suicide after perpetrating homicide (1993: 101).

19. Wolfgang summarized this attitude as, "If I can't have you, no one else can" (1958b: 213).

20. See Buteau, Lesage, and Kiely, 1993; Rosenbaum, 1990.

21. Killing or injuring a pet is one of the risk criteria for lethal violence identified by Straus (1991).

22. West, 1967.

23. See also Cavan (1965), who argues that women perpetrators of homicide-suicide who killed their children did so out of a sense of altruism.

24. BJS, 1998.

25. Buteau, Lesage, and Kiely, 1993. Other studies of homicide-suicide find a lower frequency of separation in such deaths. For example, Morton and her colleagues' (1998) analysis of 99 female victims of homicide-suicide in North Carolina found separation in only 41 percent of cases. However, for these researchers separation is the most common precursor, eclipsing a history of domestic violence, which they were able to identify in only 29 percent of cases.

26. For a recent summary of intimate violence in gay and lesbian relationships, see Renzetti (1997).

27. In the other homosexual multiple killing, the perpetrator, a married man, killed his gay lover of eight years, who was known to be HIV positive. The perpetrator in this case had a serious problem with crack cocaine. As in the Juantorena–Castro and Cervantes case, there was no sign of a lovers' triangle or morbid jealousy.

28. Pleck, 1987.

29. West, 1967.

30. Cavan, 1965; Wolfgang, 1958b.

31. Ibid.

32. Cavan, 1965: 261.

33. Rosenbaum (1990) examined 12 cases of homicide-suicide and 24 of domestic homicide.

34. Seventy-five percent; eight men, one woman. Rosenbaum, 1990: 1038.

35. Polk and Ransom, 1991.

36. Rosenbaum, 1990: 1038.

37. Ibid.: 1039.

38. Marzuk, Tardiff, and Hirsch, 1992: 3181.

39. See also Easteal (1993: 90–91, 107), who notes a similar phenomenon among men who are suddenly placed in the role of taking care of elderly women and become severely depressed before killing them. She points out that "there were no homicides committed by older women in similar situations" (91).

40. Cavan defines suicide pacts as "the suicide of two or more persons at or near the same time in accordance with a previous agreement" (1965: 249). Of 391 cases of suicide in Chicago in 1923, she found only one that involved a suicide pact.

41. Cupitt, 1997.

42. Cited in Ewing, 1997: 143.

43. Ibid.

44. *Tampa Tribune,* August 2, 1994, Metro 3.

45. Heide, 1995.

46. Mones, 1991.


**Chapter 3**

1. Chesney-Lind, 1997: 96.

2. See also Rosen, 1982.

3. hooks, 1984: 18. Specifically, she notes: "The nakedness of the African female served as a constant reminder of her sexual vulnerability. Rape was a common method of torture slavers used to subdue recalcitrant black women. The threat of rape or their physical brutalization inspired terror in the psyches of displaced African females."

4. Chesney-Lind, 1997: 97.

5. Stark and Flitcraft, 1995: 55.

6. Ibid.: 46.

7. Ibid.

8. Stark and Flitcraft examined the medical records of women who came to the emergency service at Yale–New Haven Hospital as attempted suicides over one year.

They identified 176 such women who had attempted suicide at least once during the study year (see ibid.: 48).

9. Ibid.: 53.

10. Ibid.: 57.

11. Barry, 1981; Edwards, 1984; Mahan, 1996; Websdale and Chesney-Lind, 1998.

12. Daly and Wilson, 1988: 216.

13. Cavan, 1965: 256.

14. West, 1967.

15. Ibid.: 94.

16. Telephone conversation, September 16, 1997.

## Chapter 4

1. The word "single" denotes the death of one person, as opposed to multiple victims, in a domestic homicide.

2. See also Polk and Ransom, 1991: 23.

3. Stark and Flitcraft, 1996: 146.

4. Daly and Wilson, 1988: 295.

5. It is not true that the majority of Mariel Boatlift men had criminal records. See Mark Hamm (1995), who points out that only a very small number of Marielitos had criminal histories.

6. This was not Trish's only contact with an agency that serves battered women. In February 1994 she spent a couple of days at a domestic-violence shelter just before she was killed.

7. Wallace, 1986.

8. See Websdale, 1988: 14.

9. Browne, 1987: 10; Stark and Flitcraft, 1996: 148.

10. It seems likely that Gemmil suffered from paranoid schizophrenia, although this is difficult to confirm.

11. The Baker Act lays down the requirements for incarcerating a person on grounds of mental incapacity.

12. Keilitz, Hannaford, and Efkeman (1998) reached this conclusion in their six-month follow-up interviews with 177 women who had received civil protection orders through courts in Wilmington, Delaware, Denver, Colorado, and the District of Columbia Superior Court. Even women who had temporary protection orders reported benefits. Indeed, of these women many did not follow through and obtain a permanent order. The most common reason given for not obtaining a permanent order was that their abusers had stopped bothering them. However, Harrell and Smith (1998) found that 29 percent of women with temporary protection orders experienced severe violence at the hands of those men subject to the order. They also report that severe violence, other physical victimization, and threats of property damage were as common

among women with permanent protection orders as those without. Nevertheless, permanent orders did apparently significantly reduce psychological abuse. Klein (1998) cautions that civil protection orders do not adequately protect women from additional abuse and recommends using such orders only in conjunction with other strategies such as vigorous prosecution and significant sanctioning of batterers. Rigakos's research in British Columbia, Canada, suggests that one of the reasons for the ineffectiveness of protection orders is that the occupational subculture of policing leads to blaming female victims for domestic violence and fosters images of women as manipulative. Other research points to the way battered women sometimes feel empowered by obtaining a protection order, since the order gives them a modicum of control in their relationship that they did not have (see Ford, 1991; Fischer and Rose, 1995). For a general discussion of the efficacy of restraining orders see Buzawa and Buzawa, 1996.

13. Smart and Smart, 1978.

14. Regoli and Hewitt, 1996: 69.

15. Impulse control disorder is explained in the *Diagnostic and Statistical Manual* (American Psychiatric Association) under section 312.34. It is also possible that Chuck was suffering from paraphelia (see DSM-4, section 302.9).

16. Telephone interview with the officer, November 26, 1997.

17. Klein, 1993.

18. See Samuel Walker (1989) for a discussion of these issues.

19. Evidence presented in Chapter 2 shows that only 2 of the 47 male perpetrators of multiple killings had histories involving crimes other than domestic violence.

20. Cindy West, "Man Charged with Killing Girlfriend," *Pensacola News Journal,* March 9, 1994, 1C, 3C.

21. Gagne, 1996.

22. On the morning of the homicide police officers found welts and red spots on Steve Kray's arms, shoulders, and front and back torso.

23. Ewing (1997: 118) notes specifically in a number of cases involving adult sibling killings that "conflicts over space and/or control seem to have been major issues." Ewing also notes the presence of stressors such as unemployment, divorce, substance abuse, and illness.

## Chapter 5

1. The concept of "victim precipitation" was introduced by Hans Von Hentig (1941) and later developed by Marvin E. Wolfgang (1956, 1958a). See Rasche, 1993.

2. Wolfgang, 1958a.

3. Luckenbill, 1977.

4. As Tables 5.3 and 5.4 show, there was a prior history of domestic violence in 21 of 24 of these cases of intimate killing by women. In 3 other cases I am either unable to reach a conclusion as to the existence of prior domestic violence because of insufficient

information (2 cases) or the best evidence suggests that no such violence occurred (1 case). In the latter instance a woman injected her boyfriend with what turned out to be a lethal dose of cocaine. Although under Florida law this constituted a domestic homicide (second-degree murder), the state did not prosecute her. She died a year later of a self-administered overdose of pentazocine. The archival material showed no domestic violence in this case. I talked at length with a key informant who knew the woman from her school days, and she too reported an absence of prior domestic violence.

5. Browne, 1987: 135.

6. Joanna Bronte's appeal was denied, and the Florida Supreme Court will not hear her case. Consequently, her only hope of release is the Florida Battered Women's Clemency Project. As of December 30, 1997, her case is just being taken on by an attorney working with the clemency project.

7. Joanna's defense attorney told me that "she had a child and eight years was an unacceptable plea." Telephone conversation, December 30, 1997.

8. hooks, 1984, 1996.

9. hooks, 1984: 16. See also Fox-Genovese, 1988.

10. hooks, 1984: 35.

11. Moynihan, 1965.

12. hooks, 1984: 85. The name comes from a character on the radio (and later television) show *Amos 'n' Andy*. Broadcast nationally from 1928 to 1960, it purported to offer a comic "inside look" at the lives of a fictional group of African Americans. The program was created and produced by whites.

13. Rosen, 1982.

14. hooks, 1984: 86.

15. Maurice Tamman, "Brick to the Head Ends Lovers' Quarrel and Man's Life, Police Say," *Florida Today*, December 14, 1994, 1B, 2B.

16. Inciardi, Lockwood, and Pottieger, 1993; Bourgois and Dunlap, 1993; Bourgois, 1995.

17. Bourgois and Dunlap, 1993: 98.

18. Fullilove, Lown, and Fullilove, 1992.

19. Ibid.: 276.

20. Ibid. Also see Inciardi, Lockwood, and Pottieger, 1993.

21. Bourgois, 1995: 279–80.

22. The trial is tentatively scheduled to begin in January 1999. Charlotte Rentry is charged with second-degree murder. One key informant revealed (personal conversation, November 20, 1998) that the state had offered Charlotte a plea bargain. As part of the bargain she would accept a manslaughter plea instead of being prosecuted for second-degree murder. My source told me that the agreement involved some kind of community control for two years, followed by five years of probation. He alluded to

the fact that Charlotte is believed to have stabbed another boyfriend about two years after she killed Fred Kemble. Apparently the new boyfriend initially reported to police that Charlotte stabbed him but later recanted, saying that he had fallen on a broken bottle. When I asked for details about the suspected stabbing, my informant replied that he had none. He mentioned that prosecutors disagree about this case and are not sure whether Charlotte acted in self-defense the night she killed Kemble. At her upcoming trial it appears that a forensic psychologist, Lenore Walker, will argue that Charlotte suffered from battered-woman syndrome. According to my source, prosecutors feel that because Charlotte had hidden the knife in anticipation of Fred's return, she likely did not suffer from battered-woman syndrome. Another person close to the case told me that the sitting judge did not want the case to come to trial and was putting pressure on the prosecutor to plea-bargain it away.

23. One could also contend that Charlotte herself contributed to the argument before the killing through her handling of her own feelings of envy. However, this factor seems much less important than the overall concern Charlotte had for how Fred handled her violently.

24. Bowker, 1997.

25. According to Bert's statements to coworkers, Erin was addicted to these tranquilizers, which she obtained through prescription.

26. Quoted from the homicide file summary of the psychological report, not from the psychological report itself.

27. BJS, 1998.

28. Telephone interview, January 15, 1998.

29. Telephone interview, April 2, 1998.

30. Telephone interview, April 2, 1998.

31. Telephone interview, April 10, 1998.

32. Telephone interview, April 15, 1998.

33. Dobash et al., 1992.

34. Stark and Flitcraft, 1996.

35. Daly and Wilson, 1990.

36. Daly and Wilson, 1990: 81. By "competition," they refer to "any conflict of interests in which one party's possession or use of a mutually desired resource precludes the other party's possession or use of the same" (1990: 83).

37. Wolfgang, 1958a: Bourgois, 1995; Anderson, 1994.

38. See Bourgois, 1995; Anderson, 1994.

## Chapter 6

1. For an analysis of the links between child abuse and domestic violence, see Stark and Flitcraft, 1996: chapter 3; Bowker, Arbitell, and McFerron, 1988.

2. Schloesser, Pierpont, and Poertner, 1992.

3. Daly and Wilson, 1981, 1985, 1987.

4. Schloesser, Pierpont, and Poertner, 1992: 6.

5. Hicks and Gaughan, 1995: 855. These authors cite the work of Abel, 1986; Christoffel, Zieserl, and Chiaramonte, 1985; deSilva and Oates, 1993; Hodge and Ludwig, 1985; Jason and Andereck, 1983; Krugman, 1983–85; Paulson and Rushforth, 1986; Showers et al., 1985; and Somander and Rammer, 1991.

6. Schloesser, Pierpont, and Poertner, 1992.

7. Krugman, 1983–85.

8. Centerwall, 1984, 1995.

9. Perhaps surprisingly, twice as many children died between the ages of two and three as died between one and two. This finding may be an artifact of the small number of cases (17 aged two to three, compared with 9 aged one to two), or it may reflect the differential vulnerability of two- and three-year-olds to homicide.

10. See Hollander, 1986; Jason et al., 1982; Sabotta and Davis, 1992; and Wilczynski, 1997. Other studies found a lower proportion of child homicides preceded by child abuse. Copeland (1985) found that only 4.1 percent of 152 child homicides involving boys and girls under 13 years of age were antedated by child abuse. Abel (1986) identified only 8 out of 62 victims of child homicide as having discernible signs of battering at the time of autopsy. In their study of murder in families, Dawson and Langan (1994: 5) note that 79 percent of child homicide victims younger than 12 had suffered prior abuse.

11. Wilczynski, 1997.

12. Orloff and Rodriguez, 1997.

13. Ibid.: 148.

14. Ibid. See also Klein and Orloff, 1993.

15. Detective Linda Burton, who heads up the Child Death Review Team of Hillsborough County, Florida, reports that at least two-thirds of the children killed in homicides there between 1994 and 1998 had mothers or other female caretakers who had been beaten by their intimate male partners. Conversation, March 11, 1998.

16. Daly and Wilson, 1988: 49.

17. Such convergences are well documented in the research into the social portrayal of crime (see Hall et al., 1978).

18. *St. Petersburg Times,* March 5, 1995, 13A.

19. *Miami Herald,* June 8, 1995, 3C.

20. These details were conveyed to me in a conversation with a key informant on March 3, 1998.

21. John Lantigua, "Mother Recounts Horror of Miami Mass Slaying," *Miami Herald,* February 2, 1994, 2B.

22. The child protective services agency operating in 1994 in Florida was known as the Department of Health and Rehabilitative Services (HRS); it is now called the Department of Children and Families (DCF).

23. Wolfgang, 1958a: 37. Numerous studies support this finding, including Wolfgang and Ferracuti's (1967) review of research conducted in Denmark, England, Finland, Italy, Mexico, South Africa, Sri Lanka, and the United States. See also Goetting, 1995; Polk, 1994; and Silverman and Kennedy, 1993.

24. Messner and Golden, 1992.

25. Cooney, 1997: 384. These findings mirror research showing a positive relationship between unemployment and crime (see Chiricos, 1987, for a review of 63 studies, 75 percent of which found a positive correlation). Importantly, Carlson and Michalowski (1997), in finding a positive correlation between structural (chronic, longer-term, more deeply rooted) unemployment and crime, emphasize that joblessness is not just an economic phenomenon, but is rather a lived "social experience" that is historically contingent.

26. Shihadeh and Flynn, 1996.

27. For the role of poverty in child abuse and neglect, see Gelles (1992); for its role in child homicide, see Christoffel, Anzinger, and Merrill (1989), Goetting (1995), Jason and Andereck (1983), and Muscat (1988).

28. Showers and Garrison's (1988) analysis of 139 boys and girls assessed for abuse by burns revealed that these types of injuries were much more likely to be inflicted on children younger than three. They also found, contrary to earlier studies, that girls were just as likely as boys to be burned abusively.

29. I do not mean to imply that polygraph findings reflect truth. Indeed, I concur with a large body of critics who find the tests unreliable. However, the effects of such examinations on some of the suspects in the Florida sample were profound in "encouraging" them to confess.

30. Chambliss, 1994.

31. Petersilia, Greenwood, and Lavin, 1977.

32. Roberts, 1997: 153.

33. Ibid.: 156.

34. Ibid.

35. Humphries, 1993: 36.

36. Kennedy, 1997.

37. Humphries (1998) argues that ABC, CBS, and NBC evening news programs broadcast between 1983 and 1994 constructed different images of "crack mothers." White, middle-class women were portrayed as psychologically addicted, guilt ridden, and good candidates for treatment. Poor black women, by contrast, were represented as "mindlessly addicted" and as mothers who knowingly exposed their fetuses to crack.

38. Ewing, 1997: 154–55; BJS, 1994, 1995.

39. See, for example, Richard Wright and Scott Decker's (1997) analysis of armed robbers. The authors situate these criminals' use of firearms amid the routines of everyday life and the broader social environment.

40. Bromley, Shupe, and Ventimiglia, 1979.

## Chapter 7

1. According to the BJS (1998: v) there were roughly 990,000 intimate-partner assaults in 1996, compared with a little over 1,800 intimate-partner homicides. Put differently, the homicides constitute only 0.18 percent of the assaults.

2. There are many norms designed to preserve life. Laws against homicide, public health strictures regarding hygiene, highway safety regulations, and health and safety regulations in the workplace are but a few examples. Indeed, as Foucault (1991) once put it, we live in a society fascinated by "security" and deeply underpinned by a commitment to it.

3. This produces an overall SROK of 25.5. This figure is slightly lower than that given in Table 7.1, which shows the intraracial/intra-ethnic SROKs. Thirty-five men killed intimate partners during multiple domestic homicides (Chapter 2) and 67 during the single killings of women (Chapter 4). This means that a total of 102 men killed intimate female partners. Two men killed intimate male partners among the single killings of men (Chapter 5). Two women killed intimate male partners in the course of multiple domestic killings (Chapter 3) and 24 killed male intimates among the single killings of men (Chapter 5).

4. Men committed 19 family homicides among the multiple killings (Chapter 2); 11 among the single killings of women (Chapter 4); 19 among the single killings of men (Chapter 5); and they killed 54 children (Chapter 6). Women committed 5 family homicides in the course of multiple domestic homicides (Chapter 3); 2 among the single killings of women (Chapter 4); 1 among the single killings of men (Chapter 5); and they killed 30 children (Chapter 6).

5. See Pleck, 1987; Gordon, 1988; Websdale, 1992.

6. See Walby, 1990.

7. This was especially the case for those men who committed single acts of intimate-partner homicide. See Tables 2.5 and 4.3.

8. Sherman (1992: 362), making use of a term coined by Toby (1957). In Sherman's work on the desirability of arrest as a tool for deterring recidivism by batterers, he identifies black, unemployed, and unmarried men as having lower stakes in conformity and therefore less likely to be deterred by such formal legal interventions. For important reinterpretations of Sherman's work see Zorza (1994) and Garner, Fagan, and Maxwell (1995).

9. Hanmer, 1996: 8.

10. Lukes, 1974.

11. This may also be the reason there is much more domestic violence among lower-status socioeconomic groups. See BJS, 1998.

12. Archival materials revealed that only 2 of the 20 family killings involved competition over a woman, or woman battering.

13. Anderson, 1994: 81.

14. Ibid.: 82.

15. See Wolfgang, 1958a: 189; Polk, 1994: chapter 4.

16. See Daly and Wilson, 1988: chapter 3.

17. Daly and Wilson, 1988.

18. Daly and Wilson (1988: 89) report that "[a]n American child living with one or more substitute parents in 1976 was therefore approximately 100 times as likely to be fatally abused as a child living with natural parents only."

19. Ibid.: chapter 3.

20. Ibid.: 91.

21. Indeed, feminist perspectives on male violence are supported by official government studies showing that women experience the majority of intimate-partner violence. See BJS, 1998.

22. Chesney-Lind, 1997: 142.

23. hooks, 1996: 211.

24. In one case a mother killed her daughter's friend and seriously injured her daughter in an attempted familicide.

25. Daly and Wilson (1988: 79) also note the role of maternal depression in both infanticide and the killing of older children. They distinguish between the two as follows: "Infanticide is primarily the recourse of young women who want to live but cannot cope with the present baby, whereas mothers who kill older children are frequently in a quite different state of depression."

26. These rates are based on a Florida population of 14 million, 83.1 percent of which is white, 13.6 black, and 12.0 percent Latino.

27. Moynihan, 1965: 75.

28. Ibid.: 62.

29. Moynihan's position echoes previous research by writers such as E. Franklin Frazier (1939), who was one of the first to document what he saw as the way slavery destroyed the black family and psychologically and emotionally emasculated black men.

30. Moynihan, 1965: 47.

31. Black Power advocates have made similar points. See Ransford and Miller, 1983.

32. Poussaint, 1972.

33. Raymond Williams (1958) makes this point in one of the earlier texts in what has become known as cultural studies.

34. Cited in Taylor, 1998: 22. Genovese's (1974) research also points to the durability of the nuclear family in the black community until the years after World War II. See also Murray, 1984: chapter 9.

35. Myrdal, 1944, vol. 2: 55.

36. Wintersmith, 1974. Although the system of slavery itself served to control blacks, the slave codes allowed the land- and slave-owning aristocracy in the South to use poor whites to police blacks.

37. See Gerber, 1976. Also see Massey and Denton (1993: 17), who note that during Reconstruction many American cities, including New Orleans, Charleston, Chicago, Detroit, Cleveland, and Philadelphia, exhibited considerable integration between blacks and whites.

38. See Hawkins and Thomas, 1991.

39. *Brown v. Mississippi,* 297 U.S. 278 (1936).

40. See, for example, the case of a black drug dealer, Larry Davis, who was unanimously acquitted by a jury of black and Hispanic householders in The Bronx on charges that he attempted to kill a police officer. The jury accepted Davis's plea that he opened fire on the police because he feared that they had not come to arrest him peacefully. As Andrew Hacker comments, "We should presume that the police want to bring their suspects in alive; that they are professionals, trained to use their weapons only as a last resort. This may be the view of most whites. It is not commonly shared by black Americans" (1992: 190).

41. See for example Chambliss, 1994.

42. BJS, 1998.

43. Ibid. See also Richie, 1996: chapter 4; she argues that African-American women she interviewed were more brutalized than white women.

44. Brearley, 1932.

45. Silberman, 1978.

46. See Hawkins, 1987: 192. The devaluing of African Americans by the criminal justice system also appears in the sentencing research. For example, in *McCleskey v. Kemp* (1987) the Supreme Court heard evidence that murderers who killed a white victim had a four times greater chance of receiving the death penalty than killers of black victims. See *McCleskey v. Kemp,* 107 S.Ct. 1756 (1987).

47. Hawkins (1987: 194 and footnote 3) cites the research of Johnson (1941). See also Hawkins's coverage of the work of Bernstein, Kelly, and Doyle (1977), who also found judges sentenced black felons less severely than whites because they felt the offenses of blacks were seen to be less serious by the black community. Lundsgaarde (1977) argues that the devalued status of black victims also means that black domestic murderers receive lighter sentences than whites.

48. See Levinson, 1989; Messerschmidt, 1986.

49. As noted, Latino perpetrators of domestic homicide come from a wide range

of homelands, including Mexico, Honduras, Puerto Rico, Cuba, and the Dominican Republic.

50. Perez, 1998: 109.

51. Ibid.: 111.

52. Ibid.

53. Ibid.: 119.

54. Baca-Zinn, 1998: 85.

55. Mosqueda, 1986.

56. Blea, 1992: 125.

57. Zavella, 1987.

58. Griswold del Castillo, 1979: 69.

59. Blea, 1992: 127.

60. According to the U.S. Bureau of the Census (1991), the median family income was $23,240 for Chicanos, $18,008 for Puerto Ricans, $31,439 for Cubans, and $23,445 for families from Central and South America.

61. Wilkinson, 1993: 35.

62. hooks, 1984: 86.

63. Richie, 1996: 162.

64. Levinson, 1989: 84.

65. Stack, 1975.

66. In *Tally's Corner,* Eliot Liebow observes the life of black people in inner city Washington, D.C. Regarding domestic violence, he notes how the economically compromised black man sometimes resorts to the only kind of ascendency possible within his family. Liebow comments, "Sometimes he strikes out at her or the children with his fists, perhaps to lay hollow claim to being man of the house in the one way left open to him, or perhaps simply to inflict pain on this woman who bears witness to his failure as a husband and father and therefore as a man" (1967: 212–13).

67. Metro–Dade, Hillsborough Country, Palm Beach Country, and Putnam–Volusia Counties.

68. Pursuant to California Penal Code ss.11163.3–11163.5. See Bowman, 1997.

69. See Websdale, 1996; Websdale and Alvarez, 1998.

## Appendix 2

1. Of the 22 perpetrators of child homicide who had criminal records, 19 were male and only 3 were female. Of these men, 11 were black, 8 were white, and 1 was Latino.

## Appendix 3

1. Luckenbill, 1977.

2. It is not my intent in this book to enter the game of predicting which domestic

relationships are more likely to end in homicide. Rather, the spirit of my archival inquiry is to identify prominent relationship themes that might enhance our collective awareness about deeply troubled domestic life. I leave the prediction work to statistical model builders who, unlike myself, are more convinced of the efficacy of treating relationship characteristics as scientific variables.

3. Geertz, 1973, 1983.

4. According to the U.S. Census Bureau (1990), blacks make up 13.6 percent of Florida's population, whites 83.1 percent, Hispanics 12.0 percent, and Asian/Pacific Islanders 1.2 percent. (Note that I use the term "Latino" throughout the book, though I recognize that some people prefer the term "Hispanic." For the purposes of this book the term Latino refers to that diverse population sharing ancestral ties to Spain or Latin America.

# References

Abel, Ernest L. 1986. "Childhood Homicide in Erie County, New York." *Pediatrics* 77:709–13.

Allen, N. H. 1983. "Homicide Followed by Suicide: Los Angeles, 1970–1979." *Suicide and Life-Threatening Behavior* 13(3):155–65.

Anderson, Elijah. 1994. "The Codes of the Streets." *Atlantic Monthly,* May, 81–94.

Anderson, Rosalie, Robert Ambrosino, Deborah Valentine, and Michael Lauderdale. 1983. "Child Deaths Attributed to Abuse and Neglect: An Empirical Study." *Children and Youth Services Review* 5:75–89.

Baca-Zinn, Maxine. 1998. "Adaptation and Continuity in Mexican-Origin Families." In Ronald Taylor, ed., *Minority Families in the United States: A Multicultural Perspective,* 77–94. 2d ed. Upper Saddle River, N.J.: Prentice-Hall.

Barnard, George W., Hernan Vera, Maria I. Vera, and Gustave Newman. 1982. "Till Death Do Us Part: A Study of Spouse Murder." *Bulletin of the AAPL* 10 (4):271–80.

Barry, Kathleen. 1981. *Female Sexual Slavery.* Engelwood Cliffs, N.J.: Prentice-Hall.

Berman, Alan L. 1979. "Dyadic Death: Murder-Suicide." *Suicide and Life-Threatening Behavior* 9 (1):15–22.

Bernstein, Ilene Nagel, William R. Kelly, and Patricia A. Doyle. 1977. "Societal Reaction to Deviants: The Case of Criminal Defendants." *American Sociological Review* 42 (October): 743–55.

Blea, Irene I. 1992. *La Chicana and the Intersection of Race, Class, and Gender.* New York: Praeger.

Block, Carolyn R. 1987. "Lethal Violence at Home: Race/Ethnic Differences in Domestic Homicide in Chicago, 1965–1981." Paper presented at the American Society of Criminology annual meeting.

Block, Carolyn R., and Antigone Christakos. 1995. "Intimate Partner Homicide in Chicago over 29 Years." *Crime and Delinquency* 41 (October): 496–526.

Bourgois, Philippe. 1995. *In Search of Respect: Selling Crack in El Barrio.* New York: Cambridge University Press.

Bourgois, Philippe, and Eloise Dunlap. 1993. In Mitchell Ratner, ed., *The Crack Pipe as Pimp*, 97–132. New York: Lexington Books.

Bowker, Lee H. 1997. "A Criminological Perspective: Redefining 'Battered Women' for Use in Legal Procedings." *Domestic Violence Report* 2 (2):17–18, 29.

Bowker, Lee H., M. Arbitell, and J. R. McFerron. 1988. "On the Relationship between Wife Beating and Child Abuse." In Kersti Yllo and Michele Bograd, eds., *Feminist Perspectives on Wife Abuse*, 158–74. Newbury Park, Calif.: Sage.

Bowman, Alana. 1997. "Establishing Domestic Violence Review Teams." *Domestic Violence Report*, August–September, 83, 93–94.

Brearley, H. C. 1932. *Homicide in the United States*. Chapel Hill: University of North Carolina Press.

Bromley, David G., Anson D. Shupe, and J. C. Ventimiglia. 1979. "Atrocity Tales: The Unification Church and the Social Construction of Evil." *Journal of Communication* 29 (3):42–53.

Browne, Angela. 1987. *When Battered Women Kill*. New York: Free Press.

Bureau of Justice Statistics, U.S. Department of Justice. 1994. *Violence between Intimates*. NCJ-149259 (November).

———. 1995. *Spouse Murder Defendants in Large Urban Counties*. NCJ-156831 (September).

———. 1998. *Violence by Intimates: Analysis of Data on Crimes by Current or Former Spouses, Boyfriends, and Girlfriends*. NCJ-167237 (March).

Buteau, Jacques, Alain Lesage, and Margaret Kiely. 1993. "Homicide Followed by Suicide: A Quebec Case Series, 1988–1990." *Canadian Journal of Psychiatry* 38:552–56.

Buzawa, Eve, and Karl Buzawa (editors). 1996. *Do Arrests and Restraining Orders Work?* Thousand Oaks, Calif.: Sage.

Carlson, Susan M., and Raymond Michalowski. 1997. "Crime, Unemployment, and Social Structures of Accumulation: An Inquiry into Historical Contingency." *Justice Quarterly* 14 (2):209–41.

Cavan, Ruth S. 1965. *Suicide*. 1928. Reprint, New York: Russell and Russell.

Centerwall, Brandon S. 1984. "Race, Socioeconomic Status, and Domestic Homicide, Atlanta, 1971–1972." *American Journal of Public Health* 74:813–15.

———. 1995. "Race, Socioeconomic Status, and Domestic Homicide." JAMA 273 (22):1755–58.

Chambliss, William. 1994. "Policing the Ghetto Underclass: The Politics of Law and Law Enforcement." *Social Problems* 41 (2):177–94.

Chesney-Lind, Meda. 1997. *The Female Offender*. Thousand Oaks, Calif.: Sage.

Chimbos, Peter D. 1978. *Marital Violence: A Study of Interspousal Homicide*. San Francisco: R and E Research Associates.

Chiricos, T. G. 1987. "Rates of Crime and Unemployment: An Analysis of Aggregate Research Evidence." *Social Problems* 34:187–212.

Christoffel, Kathrine K., Nora K. Anzinger, and Mary Amari. 1983. "Homicide in Childhood: Distinguishable Patterns of Risk Related to Developmental Levels of Victims." *American Journal of Forensic Medicine and Pathology* 4 (2): 129–37.

Christoffel, Kathrine K., Nora K. Anzinger, and David A. Merrill. 1989. "Age-Related Patterns of Violent Death, Cook County, Illinois, 1977 through 1982." *American Journal of Diseases of Children* 143:1403–9.

Christoffel, Kathrine K., E. Zieserl, and J. Chiaramonte. 1985. "Should Child Abuse and Neglect Be Considered When a Child Dies Unexpectedly?" *AJDC* 139: 876–80.

Cohen, Daniel A. 1995. "Homicidal Compulsion and the Conditions of Freedom: The Social and Psychological Origins of Familicide in America's Early Republic." *Journal of Social History.* Summer: 725–64.

Cooney, Mark. 1997. "The Decline of Elite Homicide." *Criminology* 35 (3):381–407.

Copeland, Arthur R. 1985. "Homicide in Childhood: The Metro–Dade County Experience from 1956 to 1982." *American Journal of Forensic Medicine and Pathology* 6 (1):21–24.

Corder, B. F., B. C. Ball, T. M. Haizlip, R. Rollins, and R. Beaumont. 1976. "Adolescent Parricide: A Comparison with Other Adolescent Murder." *American Journal of Psychiatry* 133:957–61.

Cupitt, Margaret. 1997. "Identifying and Addressing the Issues of Elder Abuse." *Journal of Elder Abuse and Neglect* 8 (4):21–30.

Currens, Sherry, et al. 1991. "Homicide Followed by Suicide—Kentucky, 1985–1990." *CDC Morbidity and Mortality Weekly Report,* (September 27) 40 (38):652–59.

Daly, Martin, and Margo Wilson. 1981. "Abuse and Neglect of Children in Evolutionary Perspective." In R. D. Alexander and D. W. Tinkle, eds., *Natural Selection and Social Behavior.* New York: Chiron.

———. 1985. "Child Abuse and Other Risks of Not Living with Both Parents." *Ethology and Sociobiology* 6:197–210.

———. 1987. "Children as Homicide Victims." In Richard J. Gelles and J. B. Lancaster, eds., *Child Abuse and Neglect: Biosocial Dimensions,* 201–14. Hawthorne, N.Y.: Aldine de Gruyter.

———. 1988. *Homicide.* Hawthorne, N.Y.: Aldine de Gruyter.

———. 1990. "Killing the Competition: Female/Female and Male/Male Homicide." *Human Nature* 1 (1):81–107.

Davis, John A. 1976. "Blacks, Crime, and American Culture." *Annals of the American Academy of Political and Social Science* 423 (January):89–98.

Davis, K., and W. E. Moore. 1945. "Some Principles of Stratification." *American Sociological Review* 10 (2):242–49.

Dawson, J. M., and P. A. Langan. 1994. *Murder in Families.* U.S. Department of Justice, Bureau of Justice Statistics Special Report. Washington: U.S. Government Printing Office.

deSilva, S., and R. K. Oates. 1993. "Child Homicide: The Extremes of Child Abuse." *Medical Journal of Australia* 158:300–301.

Dobash, R. Emerson, and Russell Dobash. 1979. *Violence against Wives.* New York: Free Press.

Dobash, R. Emerson, Russell Dobash, Marso Wilson, and Martin Daly. 1992. "The Myth of Sexual Symmetry in Marital Violence." *Social Problems* 39 (1):71–91.

Doerner, W. G. 1983. "Why Does Johnny Reb Die When Shot? The Impact of Medical Resources upon Lethality." *Sociological Inquiry* 53 (1):1–15.

Donzelot, Jacques. 1979. *The Policing of Families: Welfare versus the State.* London: Hutchinson.

Dorpat, T. L. 1966. "Suicide in Murderers." *Psychiatry Digest* 27 (June): 51–54.

Easteal, Patricia W. 1993. *Killing the Beloved: Homicide between Adult Sexual Intimates.* Canberra: Australian Institute of Criminology.

———. 1994. "Homicides-Suicides between Adult Sexual Intimates: An Australian Study." *Suicide and Life-Threatening Behavior* 24 (2):140–61.

Edwards, Susan. 1984. *Women on Trial.* Manchester: Manchester University Press.

Ewing, Charles Patrick. 1997. *Fatal Families: The Dynamics of Intrafamilial Homicide.* Thousand Oaks, Calif.: Sage.

Fagan, J., D. Stewart, and K. Jansen. 1983. "Violent Men or Violent Husbands? Background Factors and Situational Correlates." In D. Finkelhor, R. J. Gelles, G. T. Hotaling, and M. A. Strans, eds., *The Dark Side of Families: Current Family Violence Research,* 49–67. Beverly Hills, Calif.: Sage.

Fischer, Karla, and Mary Rose, 1995. "When 'Enough Is Enough': Battered Women's Decision Making Around Court Orders of Protection." *Crime and Delinquency* 41 (4):414–29.

Fontana, V. J., and J. D. Alfaro. 1982. *High-Risk Factors Associated with Child Maltreatment Facilities.* Report to the Mayor from New York City's Task Force on Child Abuse and Neglect. New York.

Ford, David. 1991. "Prosecution as a Victim Power Resource: A Note on Empowering Women in Violent Conjugal Relationships." *Law and Society Review* 25 (2):313–34.

Foucault, Michel. 1991. "Governmentality." In Graham Burchell, Colin Gordon, and Peter Miller, eds., *The Foucault Effect: Studies in Governmentality,* 87–104. Chicago: University of Chicago Press.

Fox-Genovese, Elizabeth. 1988. *Within the Plantation Household: Black and White Women of the Old South.* Chapel Hill: University of North Carolina Press.

Frazier, E. Franklin. 1939. *The Negro Family in the United States.* Chicago: University of Chicago Press.

Fullilove, Mindy, Anne Lown, and Robert Fullilove, 1992. "Crack Hos and Skeezers: Traumatic Experiences of Women Crack Users." *Journal of Sex Research* 29 (2):275–87.

Gagne, P. 1996. "Identity, Strategy, and Feminist Politics: Clemency for Battered Women Who Kill." *Social Problems* 43 (1):77–93.

Garner, Joel, Jeffrey Fagan, and C. Maxwell. 1995. "Published Findings from the Spouse Assault Replication Program: A Critical Review." *Journal of Quantitative Criminology* 11 (1):3–28.

Geertz, Clifford. 1973. *The Interpretation of Cultures: Selected Essays.* New York: Basic Books.

———. 1983. *Local Knowledge: Further Essays in Interpretive Anthropology.* New York: Basic Books.

Gellert, George A., Roberta M. Maxwell, Michael J. Durfee, and Gerald A. Wagner. 1995. "Fatalities Assessed by the Orange County Child Death Review Team, 1989 to 1991." *Child Abuse and Neglect* 19 (7):875–83.

Gelles, Richard J. 1992. "Poverty and Violence toward Children." *American Behavioral Scientist* 35 (3):258–74.

Genovese, Eugene. 1974. *Roll, Jordan, Roll: The World the Slaves Made.* New York: Pantheon.

Gerber, David A. 1976. *Black Ohio and the Color Line.* Urbana: University of Illinois Press.

Goetting, Ann. 1990. "Child Victims of Homicide: A Portrait of Their Killers and the Circumstances of Their Deaths." *Violence and Victims* 5 (4): 287–96.

———. 1995. *Homicide in Families and Other Special Populations.* New York: Springer Publishing.

Gordon, Linda. 1988. *Heroes of Their Own Lives: The Politics and History of Family Violence, Boston 1880–1960.* New York: Penguin.

Grant, Christine A. 1995. "Women Who Kill: The Impact of Abuse." *Issues in Mental Health Nursing* 16:315–26.

Griswold del Castillo, Richard. 1979. *The Los Angeles Barrio: 1850–1890.* Berkeley and Los Angeles: University of California Press.

Guttmacher, M. S. 1955. "Criminal Responsibility in Certain Homicide Cases Involving Family Members." In P. H. Hoch and J. Zubin, eds., *Psychiatry and the Law,* 73–96. New York: Grune and Stratton.

Gutman, Herbert. 1976. *The Black Family in Slavery and Freedom, 1750–1925.* New York: Pantheon.

Hacker, Andrew. 1992. *Two Nations: Black and White, Separate, Hostile, and Unequal.* New York: Random House.

Hall, Stuart, Chas Critcher, Tony Jefferson, John Clarke, and Brian Roberts. 1978. *Policing the Crisis: Mugging, the State, and Law and Order.* London: Macmillan.

Hamm, Mark. 1995. *The Abandoned Ones: The Imprisonment and Uprising of the Mariel Boat People.* Boston: Northeastern University Press.

Hanmer, Jalna. 1996. "Women and Violence: Commonalities and Diversities." In Barbara Fawcett, Brid Featherstone, Jeff Hearn, and Christine Toft, eds., *Violence and Gender Relations: Theories and Interventions,* 7–21. Thousand Oaks, Calif.: Sage.

Harrell, Adele, and Barbara Smith. 1998. "Effects of Restraining Orders on Domestic Violence Victims." In *Legal Interventions in Family Violence: Research Findings and Policy Implications,* 49–51. Washington: U.S. Department of Justice, NCJ-171666 (July).

Hart, Barbara. 1988. "Beyond the Duty to Warn: A Therapist's Duty to Protect Battered Women and Children." In Kersti Yllo and Michele Bograd, eds., *Feminist Perspectives on Wife Abuse,* 234–48. Newbury Park, Calif.: Sage.

Hawkins, Darnell. 1987. "Devalued Lives and Racial Stereotypes: Ideological Barriers to the Prevention of Family Violence among Blacks." In R. L. Hampton, ed., *Violence in the Black Family,* 189–205. Lexington, Mass.: Lexington Books.

Hawkins, Homer, and Richard Thomas. 1991. "White Policing of Black Populations: A History of Race and Social Control in America." In Ellis Cashmore and Eugene McLaughlin, eds., *Out of Order? Policing Black People,* 65–86. London: Routledge.

Heide, Kathleen. 1995. *Why Kids Kill Parents: Child Abuse and Adolescent Homicide.* Thousand Oaks, Calif.: Sage.

Hicks, Ralph A., and Daniel C. Gaughan. 1995. "Understanding Fatal Child Abuse." *Child Abuse and Neglect* 19 (7):855–63.

Hodge, D., and S. Ludwig. 1985. "Child Homicide: Emergency Department Recognition." *Pediatric Emergency Care* 1:3–6.

Hollander, Nina. 1986. "Physical Abuse as a Predictor of Child Homicide." *Texas Medicine* 82 (June): 21–23.

hooks, bell. 1984. *Feminist Theory: From Margin to Center.* Boston: South End Press.

———. 1996. *Outlaw Culture: Resisting Representations.* London: Routledge.

Humphries, Drew. 1993. "Crack Mothers, Drug Wars, and the Politics of Resentment." In K. D. Tunnel, ed., *Political Crime in Contemporary America: A Critical Approach,* 31–48. New York: Garland.

————. 1998. "Crack Mothers at 6: Prime-Time News, Crack/Cocaine, and Women." *Violence against Women* 4 (1):45–61.

Inciardi, James, Dorothy Lockwood, and Anne Pottieger. 1993. *Women and Crack Cocaine.* New York: Macmillan.

Jason, Janine, and N. D. Andereck. 1983. "Fatal Child Abuse in Georgia: The Epidemiology of Severe Physical Child Abuse." *Child Abuse and Neglect.* 7:1–9.

Jason, J., S. L. Williams, A. Burton, and R. Rochat. 1982. "Epidemiologic Differences between Sexual and Physical Child Abuse." *JAMA* 274 (24):3344–48.

Johnson, Guy B. 1941. "The Negro and Crime." *Annals of the American Academy of Political Science* 217:93–104.

Jones, Ann. 1980. *Women Who Kill.* New York: Holt, Rinehart and Winston.

Keilitz, Susan, Paula Hanaford, and Hillery S. Efkeman. 1998. "The Effectiveness of Civil Protection Orders. In *Legal Interventions in Family Violence: Research Findings and Policy Implications,* 47–49. Washington, D.C.: U.S. Department of Justice, NCJ-171666 (July).

Kellermann, Arthur, and James Mercy. 1992. "Men, Women, and Murder: Gender-Specific Differences in Rates of Fatal Violence and Victimization." *Journal of Trauma* 33:595–99.

Kellermann, A., F. Rivara, N. Rushforth, J. Banton, D. Reay, J. Franciso, A. Locci, J. Prodzinski, B. Hackman, and G. Somes, 1993. "Gun Ownership as a Risk Factor for Homicide in the Home." *New England Journal of Medicine* 329 (15):1084–91.

Kennedy, Randall. 1997. *Race, Crime and the Law.* New York: Pantheon.

Kleck, Gary, and David J. Bordua. 1983. "The Factual Foundations for Certain Key Assumptions of Gun Control." *Law and Policy Quarterly* 5:271–98.

Klein, Andrew R. 1993. *Spousal/Partner Assault: A Protocol for the Sentencing and Supervision of Offenders.* Swampscott, Mass.: Production Specialties.

————. 1998. "Re-abuse in a Population of Court Restrained Male Batterers: Why Restraining Orders Don't Work." In *Legal Intervention in Family Violence: Research Findings and Policy Implications,* 52–53. Washington, D.C.: U.S. Department of Justice, NCJ-171666 (July).

Klein, C. F., and L. E. Orloff. 1993. "Providing Legal Protection for Battered Women: An Analysis of State Statutes and Case Law." *Hofstra Law Review* 21 (4):1022.

Krugman, Richard D. 1983–85. "Fatal Child Abuse: An Analysis of 20 Cases." *Pediatrician* 12:68–72.

Kunz, Jenifer, and Stephen J. Bahr. 1996. "A Profile of Parental Homicide against Children." *Journal of Family Violence* 11 (4):347–62.

Lester, David. 1992. *Why People Kill Themselves.* Springfield, Ill.: Charles C. Thomas.

Levinson, David. 1989. *Family Violence in Cross-Cultural Perspective.* Newbury Park, Calif.: Sage.

Liebow, Eliot. 1967. *Tally's Corner: A Study of Negro Streetcorner Men.* Boston: Little, Brown.

Loftin, Colin, and Robert H. Hill. 1974. "Regional Subculture and Homicide: An Examination of the Gastil-Hackney Thesis." *American Sociological Review* 29:714–24.

Luckenbill, David F. 1977. "Criminal Homicide as a Situated Transaction." *Social Problems* 25 (2):176–86.

Ludwig, Stephen, and Matt Warman. 1984. "Shaken-Baby Syndrome: A Review of 20 Cases." *Annals of Emergency Medicine* 13 (2):104–7.

Lukes, Steven. 1974. *Power: A Radical View.* London: Macmillan.

Lundsgaarde, Henry P. 1977. *Murder in Space City: A Cultural Analysis of Houston Homicide Patterns.* New York: Oxford University Press.

Maguigan, Holly. 1991. "Battered Women and Self-Defense: Myths and Misconceptions in Current Reform Proposals." *University of Pennsylvania Law Review* 140 (December):379–487.

Mahan, Sue. 1996. *Crack, Cocaine, Crime, and Women.* Thousand Oaks, Calif.: Sage.

Mann, Coramae R. 1987. "Black Women Who Kill." In Robert L. Hampton, ed., *Violence in the Black Family: Correlates and Consequences,* 157–86. Lexington, Mass.: Lexington Books.

————. 1988. "Getting Even? Women Who Kill in Domestic Encounters." *Justice Quarterly* 5 (1):133–51.

Martin, Susan, and Doug Besharov. 1991. *The Police and Child Abuse.* Washington: National Institute of Justice.

Martinez, L. 1986. *Illinois Child Fatalities: A Three-Year Statistical Profile.* Springfield: Illinois Department of Children and Family Services.

Marzuk, Peter M., Kenneth Tardiff, and Charles S. Hirsch. 1992. "The Epidemiology of Murder-Suicide." *JAMA* 267 (23):3179–83.

Massey, Douglas S., and Nancy A. Denton. 1993. *American Apartheid: Segregation and the Making of the Underclass.* Cambridge: Harvard University Press.

McAdoo, Harriette P., ed. 1993. *Family Ethnicity: Strength in Diversity.* Newbury Park, Calif.: Sage.

McClain, P. W., J. J. Sachs, R. G. Froehlke, and B. G. Ewigman. 1993. "Estimates of Fatal Child Abuse and Neglect, United States, 1979 through 1988." *Pediatrics* 91:338–43.

Mengel, Laurie. 1997. "Issei Women and Divorce in Hawai'i, 1885–1908." *Social Process in Hawai'i* 38:16–39.

Mercy, James A., and Linda E. Saltzman. 1989. "Fatal Violence among Spouses in the United States, 1976–85." *AJPH* 79 (5):595–99.

Messerschmidt, James. 1986. *Capitalism, Patriarchy, and Crime: Toward a Socialist Feminist Criminology.* Totowa, N.J: Rowman and Littlefield.

———. 1993. *Masculinities and Crime: Critique and Reconceptualization of Theory.* Totowa, N.J.: Rowman and Littlefield.

Messner, Steven F., and Reid M. Golden. 1992. "Racial Inequality and Racially Disaggregated Homicide Rates: An Assessment of Alternative Theoretical Explanations." *Criminology* 30:421–45.

Mills, C. Wright. 1959. *The Sociological Imagination.* New York: Oxford University Press.

Mones, Paul. 1991. *When a Child Kills: Abused Children Who Kill Their Parents.* New York: Pocket Books.

Moore, Angela M., and Abraham N. Tennenbaum. 1994. "Why Is There an Exceptional Sex Ratio of Spousal Homicides in the United States? A Replication and Extension of Wilson and Daly." *Journal of Contemporary Criminal Justice* 10 (3):164–83.

Morton, Emma, Carol W. Runyan, Kathryn Moracco, and John Butts. 1998. "Partner Homicide-Suicide Involving Female Homicide Victims: A Population-Based Study in North Carolina, 1988–92." *Violence and Victims* 13 (2):91–106.

Mosqueda, Lawrence J. 1986. *Chicanos, Catholicism, and Political Ideology.* New York: University Press of America.

Mowat, Ronald M. 1966. *Morbid Jealousy and Murder: A Psychiatric Study of Morbidly Jealous Murderers at Broadmoor.* London: Tavistock.

Moynihan, Daniel P. 1965. *The Negro Family: The Case for National Action.* Washington: U.S. Government Printing Office.

Murray, Charles. 1984. *Losing Ground: American Social Policy, 1950–1980.* New York: Basic Books.

Muscat, Joshua E. 1988. "Characteristics of Childhood Homicide in Ohio, 1974–84." *AJPH* 78 (7):822–24.

Myrdal, Gunnar. 1944. *An American Dilemma,* vol. 2, *The Negro Social Structure* New York: Harper and Brothers.

Orloff, Leslye, and Rachel Rodriguez. 1997. "Barriers to Domestic Violence Relief and Full Faith and Credit for Immigrant and Migrant Battered Women." In Byron Johnson and Neil Websdale, eds., *Full Faith and Credit: A Passport to Safety,* 147–65. Reno, Nev.: National Council of Juvenile and Family Court Judges.

Palermo, George. 1994. "Murder-Suicide: An Extended Suicide." *International Journal of Offender Therapy and Comparative Criminology* 31:205–16.

Palmer, Stuart, and John A. Humphrey. 1980. "Offender-Victim Relationships in Criminal Homicide Followed by Offender's Suicide, North Carolina, 1972–1977." *Suicide and Life-Threatening Behavior* 10 (2):106–18.

Paulson, Jerome A., and Norman B. Rushforth. 1986. "Violent Death in Children in a Metropolitan County: Changing Patterns of Homicide, 1958 to 1982." *Pediatrics* 78 (6):1013–20.

Perez, Lisandro. 1998. "Cuban-American Families." In Ronald Taylor, ed., *Minority Families in the United States: A Multicultural Perspective,* 108–24. 2nd ed. Upper Saddle River, N.J.: Prentice-Hall.

Petersilia, Joan, Peter W. Greenwood, and Marvin, L. Lavin, 1977. *Criminal Careers of Habitual Felons.* Santa Monica, Calif.: Rand Corporation.

Pleck, Elizabeth. 1987. *Domestic Tyranny: The Making of American Social Policy against Family Violence from Colonial Times to the Present.* New York and London: Oxford University Press.

Polk, Kenneth. 1994. *When Men Kill.* Cambridge: Cambridge University Press.

Polk, Kenneth, and David Ransom. 1991. "The Role of Gender in Intimate Homicide." *Australian and New Zealand Journal of Criminology* 24 (March):15–24.

Poussaint, Alvin. 1972. *Why Blacks Kill Blacks.* New York: Emerson Hall.

Radford, Jill, and Diana E. H. Russell, eds. 1992. *Femicide: The Politics of Woman Killing.* Boston, Mass.: Twayne Publishers.

Ransford, H. Edward, and Jon Miller. 1983. "Race, Sex, and Feminist Outlooks." *American Sociological Review* 48:46–59.

Rasche, Christine E. 1993. "Victim Precipitation and Social Policy: Clemency for Battered Women Who Kill." In *Questions and Answers in Lethal and Non-Lethal Violence.* NIJ Research Report 147480.

Regoli, Robert, and John Hewitt. 1996. *Criminal Justice.* Englewood Cliffs, N.J.: Prentice-Hall.

Renzetti, Claire M. 1997. "Violence in Lesbian and Gay Relationships." In L. L. O'Toole and J. R. Schiftman, eds., *Gender Violence: Interdisciplinary Perspectives,* 285–93. New York: New York University Press.

Richie, Beth. 1996. *Compelled to Crime.* New York: Routledge.

Rigakos, George S. 1995. "Constructing the Symbolic Complainant: Police Subculture and the Nonenforcement of Protection Orders for Battered Women." *Violence and Victims* 10 (3):227–47.

Roberts, Dorothy. 1997. *Killing the Black Body.* New York: Pantheon.

Rosen, Ruth. 1982. *The Lost Sisterhood.* Baltimore: Johns Hopkins University Press.

Rosenbaum, Milton. 1990. "The Role of Depression in Couples Involved in Murder-Suicide and Homicide." *American Journal of Psychiatry* 147 (8):1036–39.

Russell, Diana E. H. 1984. "A Study of Juvenile Murderers of Family Members." *International Journal of Offender Therapy and Comparative Criminology* 28:177–92.

Sabotta, Eugene E., and Robert L. Davis. 1992. "Fatality after Report to a Child Abuse Registry in Washington State, 1973–1986." *Child Abuse and Neglect* 16:627–35.

Schloesser, Patricia, John Pierpont, and John Poertner. 1992. "Active Surveillance of Child Abuse Fatalities." *Child Abuse and Neglect* 16:3–10.

Selkin, James. 1976. "Rescue Fantasies in Homicide-Suicide." *Suicide and Life-Threatening Behavior* 6 (2):79–85.

Sherman, Lawrence W., Janell D. Schmidt, and Dennis P. Rogan. 1992. *Policing Domestic Violence: Experiments and Dilemmas.* New York: Free Press.

Shihadeh, Edward S., and Nicole Flynn. 1996. "Segregation and Crime: The Effects of Black Social Isolation on the Rates of Black Urban Violence." *Social Forces* 74:1325–52.

Showalter, Robert C., Richard J. Bonnie, and Virginia Roddy. 1980. "The Spousal-Homicide Syndrome." *International Journal of Law and Psychiatry* 3:117–41.

Showers, J., J. Apolo, J. Thomas, and S. Beavers. 1985. "Fatal Child Abuse: A Two-Decade Review." *Pediatric Emergency Care* 1(2):66–70.

Showers, J., and K. Garrison. 1988. "Burn Abuse: A Four-Year Study." *Journal of Trauma* 28:1581–83.

Silberman, Charles E. 1978. *Criminal Violence–Criminal Justice: Criminals, Police, Courts, and Prisons in America.* New York: Random House.

Silverman, R. A., and L. H. Kennedy. 1993. *Deadly Deeds: Murder in Canada.* Scarborough, Ont.: Nelson Canada.

Smart, Carol, and Barry Smart, eds. 1978. *Women, Sexuality, and Social Control.* London: Routledge and Kegan Paul.

Somander, L. K. H., and L. M. Rammer. 1991. "Intra- and Extrafamilial Child Homicide in Sweden, 1971–1980." *Child Abuse and Neglect* 15:45–55.

Sorenson, Susan B., Barbara A. Richardson, and Julie G. Peterson. 1993. "Race/Ethnicity Patterns in the Homicide of Children in Los Angeles, 1980 through 1989." *American Journal of Public Health* 83 (5):725–27.

Southall, David P., Michael C. B. Plunkets, Martin W. Banks, Adrian F. Falkov, and Martin P. Samuels. 1997. "Covert Video Recordings of Life-Threatening Child Abuse: Lessons from Child Protection." *Pediatrics* 100 (5):735–60.

Stack, Carol. 1975. *All Our Kin: Strategies for Survival in a Black Community.* New York: Harper and Row.

Stack, Steven. 1997. "Homicide Followed by Suicide: An Analysis of Chicago Data." *Criminology* 35 (3):435–53.

Stark, Evan. 1993. "The Myth of Black Violence." *Social Work* 38 (4):485–90.

Stark, Evan, and Anne Flitcraft. 1995. "Killing the Beast Within: Woman Battering and Female Suicidality." *International Journal of Health Services* 25 (1):43–64.

———. 1996. *Women at Risk: Domestic Violence and Women's Health.* London: Sage.

Straus, Murray A. 1991. "Severity and Chronicity of Domestic Assault: Measurement Implications for Criminal Justice Intervention." Paper presented at the American Society of Criminology annual conference, San Francisco.

Taylor, Ronald, ed. 1998. *Minority Families in the United States: A Multicultural Perspective.* 2d ed. Upper Saddle River, N.J.: Prentice-Hall.

Toby, Jackson. 1957. "Social Disorganization and Stake in Conformity: Complementary Factors in the Predatory Behavior of Hoodlums." *Journal of Criminal Law, Criminology, and Police Science* 48:12–17.

United States Bureau of the Census. 1991. *The Hispanic Population of the United States: March 1990.* Current Population Reports, Series P-20, N. 499.

Von Hentig, Hans. 1941. "Remarks on the Interaction of Perpetrator and Victim." *Journal of Criminal Law, Criminology, and Police Science* 31:303–9.

Walby, Sylvia. 1990. *Theorizing Patriarchy.* Oxford: Basil Blackwell.

Walker, Lenore. 1984. *The Battered-Woman Syndrome.* New York: Springer.

Walker, Samuel. 1989. *Sense and Nonsense about Crime.* 2d ed. Pacific Grove, Calif.: Brooks Cole.

Wallace, A. 1986. *Homicide: The Social Reality.* Sydney: NSW Bureau of Crime Statistics and Research.

Wang, Karin. 1996. "Battered Asian-American Women: Community Responses from the Battered Women's Movement and the Asian-American Community." *Asian Law Journal* 3:151–85.

Websdale, Neil. 1992. "Female Suffrage, Male Violence, and Law Enforcement." *Social Justice* 19 (3):82–106.

———. 1996. "Predators: The Social Construction of 'Stranger-Danger' in Washington State as a Form of Patriarchal Ideology." *Women and Criminal Justice* 7 (2):43–68.

———. 1998. *Rural Woman Battering and the Justice System: An Ethnography.* Thousand Oaks, Calif.: Sage.

Websdale, Neil, and A. Alex Alvarez. 1998. "Forensic Journalism as Patriarchal Ideology: The Media Construction of Domestic Homicide-Suicide Events." In Donna Hale and Frankie Bailey, eds., *Popular Culture, Crime, and Justice,* 123–41. Belmont, Calif.: Wadsworth.

Websdale, Neil, and Meda Chesney-Lind. 1998. "Doing Violence to Women: Research Synthesis on the Victimization of Women." In Lee Bowker, ed., *Masculinities and Violence,* 55–81. Thousand Oaks, Calif.: Sage.

West, D. J. 1967. *Murder Followed by Suicide.* Cambridge: Harvard University Press.

Wilczynski, Ania. 1997. "Prior Agency Contact and Physical Abuse in Cases of Child Homicide." *British Journal of Social Work* 27:241–53.

Wilkinson, Doris. 1993. "Family Ethnicity in America." In Harriette P. McAdoo, ed., *Family Ethnicity: Strength in Diversity,* 15–59. Newbury Park, Calif.: Sage.

Williams, Kirk R. 1984. "Economic Sources of Homicide: Reestimating the Effects of Poverty and Inequality." *American Sociological Review* 49:283–89.

Williams, Raymond. 1958. *Culture and Society: 1780–1950.* Harmondsworth: Penguin.

Wilson, Margo I., and Martin Daly. 1985. "Competitiveness Risk Taking, and Violence: The Young Male Syndrome." *Ethology and Sociobiology* 6:59–73.

———. 1992a. "Who Kills Whom in Spouse Killings? On the Exceptional Sex Ratio of Spousal Homicides in the United States." *Criminology* 30 (2):189–215.

———. 1992b. "Till Death Us Do Part." In Jill Radford and Diana E. H. Russell, eds., *Femicide: The Politics of Woman Killing*, 83–93. Boston, Mass.: Twayne Publishers.

———. 1993. "Spousal Homicide Risk and Estrangement." *Violence and Victims* 8 (1):3–16.

Wilson, William Julius. 1987. *The Truly Disadvantaged: The Inner City, the Underclass, and Public Policy.* Chicago: University of Chicago Press.

Wilt, Susan A., Susan M. Illman, and Maia Brodyfield. 1997. *Female Homicide Victims in New York City, 1990–1994.* New York: New York Department of Health Injury Prevention Program.

Wintersmith, Robert F. 1974. *Police and the Black Community.* Lexington, Mass.: Lexington Books.

Wolfgang, Marvin E. 1956. "Husband and Wife Homicides." *Journal of Social Therapy* 2:263–71.

———. 1958a. *Patterns of Criminal Homicide.* Philadelphia: University of Pennsylvania Press.

———. 1958b. "An Analysis of Homicide-Suicide." *Journal of Clinical and Experimental Psychopathology and Quarterly Review of Psychiatry and Neurology* 19 (3):208–18.

Wolfgang, Marvin E., and Franco Ferracuti. 1967. *The Subculture of Violence: Towards an Integrated Theory in Criminology.* Beverly Hills, Calif.: Sage.

Wright, Richard, and Scott Decker. 1997. *Armed Robbers in Action: Stickups and Street Culture.* Boston: Northeastern University Press.

Zavella, Patricia. 1987. *Women's Work and Chicano Families.* Ithaca: Cornell University Press.

Zimring, Franklin E., and Gordon Hawkins. 1997. *Crime Is Not the Problem: Lethal Violence in America.* New York: Oxford University Press.

Zimring, Franklin E., Satyanshu K. Mukherjee, and Barrik Van Winkle. 1983. "Intimate Homicide: A Study of Intersexual Homicide in Chicago." *University of Chicago Law Review* 50:910–30.

Zorza, Joan. 1994. "Must We Stop Arresting Batterers? Analysis and Policy Implications of New Police Domestic Violence Studies." *New England Law Review* 28 (4):929–90.

.

# Index

Abel, Ernest L., 15
abstracted empiricism, 1–2
abuse: arrests and, 261n.8; child homicide victims and, 173–79, 180; multiple homicides (female) and, 69; parricide and, 12–13; prior, and child homicide, 174 table 6.5; single killings of women and, 81–84; substitute parents and, 262n.18; suicide, homicide, women and, 66–69; woman battering and, 34–39. *See also* woman battering
adult domestic violence: child homicide and, 24–25
African Americans: child homicide rates and, 14–15; devaluing of, in sentencing research, 263nn.46, 47; economic disadvantages of, 218–19; emergency medical attention and, 222; intimate-partner homicides, high rate of, 217–25; legacy of oppression, discrimination and, 224; matriarchal culture of, 9–10, 219; overrepresentation among group as perpetrators, 6, 120, 165; police responsiveness to, 7, 220, 221, 223; slavery, impact of on, 217–18, 262n.29; spousal homicide in U.S. vs. Africa, 248n.44; stereotypical beliefs about, 221; tangle of pathology and, 217; violence and, 220–21

African-American women: assertiveness of, 151–52; "Aunt Jemima" stereotype, 132; oppression of, 130–31; perceptions of entrapment of, 153–54; police aid and, 229–30; rape, slavery, and, 254n.3; reporting victimization to police and, 247n.7; "Sapphire" stereotype, 132; slave-based system, impact on, 131; stereotypes of, 10
agency contacts, intervention, 233–35; child homicide and, 24, 186–88; intimate-partner homicide and, 22
alcohol, drug abuse: child homicide and, 196–200; intimate-partner homicide and, 23; intimate-partner homicides (male perpetrators), 101–5; multiple homicides (men), 55–56
altruism, perceived, 73, 74–75
Anderson, Elijah, 209
Anderson, Rosalie, 15
Anzinger, Nora K., 14–15
Arbitell, M., 24
Asian Americans, 37–39; defined, 253n.12; stereotypes about, 253n.14
"Aunt Jemima" stereotype, 132

Baca-Zinn, Maxine, 227–28
Barnard, George W., 11
battered-husband syndrome, 114–15